Rating the Audience

Rating the Audience

The Business of Media

Mark Balnaves, Tom O'Regan and Ben Goldsmith

BLOOMSBURY ACADEMIC

First published in 2011 by:

Bloomsbury Academic
An imprint of Bloomsbury Publishing Plc
50 Bedford Square, London WC1B 3DP, UK
and
175 Fifth Avenue, New York, NY 10010, USA

CIP records for this book are available from the British Library and the Library of Congress.

ISBN 978-1-84966-341-0 (paperback)
ISBN 978-1-84966-342-7 (hardback)
ISBN 978-1-84966-461-5 (ebook)

This book is produced using paper that is made from wood grown in managed, sustainable forests. It is natural, renewable and recyclable. The logging and manufacturing processes conform to the environmental regulations of the country of origin.

Every effort has been made to trace all copyright holders, but if any have been inadvertently overlooked, the publishers would be pleased to make the necessary arrangements at the first opportunity.

Printed and bound in Great Britain by the MPG Books Group, Bodmin, Cornwall.

www.bloomsburyacademic.com

Contents

Figures

Tables

Preface

Afew years ago, the Arbitron company introduced the Portable People Meter (PPM) to measure radio listening in the United States. The resulting controversy, which was resolved in April 2010 through voluntary negotiations mediated by a senior member of the US Congress, neatly encapsulates many of the issues raised by Mark Balnaves and Tom O'Regan in *Rating the Audience*.

When Arbitron substituted the PPM for diaries in several major US markets, measured listening to minority-oriented radio stations, in particular those catering to the African American and Hispanic communities, dropped significantly in many cases, compared to the earlier diary ratings. Minority station owners, trade associations representing them and a public interest group advocating for them joined together to form the Portable People Meter Coalition (PPMC) to protest. These stakeholders were concerned that undercounting the minority audience would reduce its value to advertisers, thus threatening the viability of minority-oriented radio programming.

Those claiming the PPM ratings were inaccurate pointed to methodological issues regarding the PPM samples. They suggested that the samples underrepresented the minority population, including the younger demographic. They pointed to the relatively low share of mobile-phone-only households in the samples, in contrast to the above-average incidence of such households in the minority community. This was attributed in part to Arbitron's failure to employ street address-based procedures for choosing the sample. Moreover, in part because the PPM is more expensive to implement than the diary, PPM samples are smaller than diary samples. This could affect the precision of ratings estimates for subsamples of the radio audience. Arbitron argued that the PPM provides more accurate and detailed listening information.

The debate also involved the Media Rating Council (MRC), a private entity that evaluates audience research services and provides accreditation (although accreditation is not a legal prerequisite for operation of a ratings service). MRC is made up of users of audience research, including media outlets and advertising agencies. The Federal Communications Commission (FCC) also became involved, issuing a Notice of Inquiry (NOI) in May 2009. An NOI contains no regulatory proposals; rather, it seeks to gather information. The FCC related issuance of the NOI to its usage of Arbitron radio market definitions for enforcement and evaluation of its radio station ownership rules. The FCC sought comment on various aspects of the PPM situation, including the agency's legal authority to act. In the event, before any FCC action was proposed, Arbitron and PPMC came to an agreement. This included changes in the sample selection procedure designed to increase sample sizes and to increase representation of mobile-phone-only households in the PPM samples, plus other measures.

The US PPM episode reminds us that the nature of what the authors refer to as the 'audience rating convention' remains important and contested as audience delivery and measurement technology evolves. *Rating the Audience* provides a useful and entertaining look at the history of audience measurement, primarily in Australia, the United Kingdom and the United States. It includes discussions of the major stakeholders in determining the 'audience rating convention', the challenges posed to this convention by new technologies for delivering and measuring exposure to content, and changing attitudes of audience members with regard to privacy and willingness to participate in survey research. The analysis reminds us of the crucial role of audience measurement both for informing advertiser spending decisions and for guiding content production in the 'two-sided market' wherein broadcasters assemble audiences by providing attractive programming and then sell advertisers access to those audiences.

Rating the Audience includes illuminating interviews with many of the principal architects of audience research and reproductions of various historical artefacts. In the latter category is a 1970s letter that the McNair Anderson company sent to households it was trying to recruit for its Australian radio audience measurement panel. The letter described the purpose of the survey as follows:

The object of this survey is to obtain basic facts to enable those concerned to keep abreast of rapidly changing conditions and to guide them in their programme planning to give continually improved programmes and service to listeners.

So who are 'those concerned', and is it really the case that their only or primary purpose is to 'give continually improved programmes and service to listeners'? The authors stress the 'syndicated' nature of much audience research, i.e. that it is supported by a variety of clients. If we follow the money, we find, of course, that prominent among 'those concerned' are the radio stations and the advertisers. The latter may well have some concern for the quality of programmes, but it is best to view that concern as instrumental. Ultimately, what they want to do is increase their profits by selling more product. Advertising is an input to that process. So is programming, to the extent that it 'creates' the audience for advertisements.

Broadcasters themselves are also not insensitive to profits. They may be good citizens, eager to advance the public good, they may operate under licence conditions that require public service programming and desire in good faith to meet those conditions, but commercial broadcasters also want to make money. It may well be the case that the menu of broadcast programming that best meets audience preferences (hard, if not impossible, to determine precisely in practice) is different from the menu of broadcast programming that would maximize broadcaster profits (the difference between advertising revenues and broadcaster costs including, prominently, programming costs).

It is amusing and a bit ironic that McNair Anderson chose not to mention advertiser interests in obtaining ratings information, since these interests are so self-evident. And it is fair to say that the authors of *Rating the Audience* spend most of their time analysing the role of ratings in commercial transactions. As argued above, business firms advertise in order to increase their sales and profits, and they need some information about the impact of advertising on sales and profits in order to decide how much to spend on advertising and across which media and programmes to deploy it.

In drawing the distinction between collecting ratings information on the one hand and 'audience research' on the other, the authors remind us that a measure of audience size, even with some associated demographics, is just one input into figuring out what the advertiser really wants to know. Ratings only measure exposure to the advertising message. Ideally one would want to know something about the audience's engagement with the advertisement. Does an advertisement or advertising campaign prompt audience members to DO something – gather more information or actually make a purchase? And how does the nature of the advertisement itself affect engagement and action? Survey research and research on consumer buying patterns can help to answer these questions, but the decision-makers and their advisors clearly operate in an environment of some uncertainty. And speaking of uncertainty, how can we really be sure that the basic ratings data, based on sampling of the audience, are accurate? And if they are not completely accurate, are they still usable?

The authors address these questions by examining audience measurements from the viewpoint of various stakeholders – ratings providers, media providers (including stations and networks), advertisers and media planners, and those they refer to as 'ratings intellectuals' or 'media critics'. They discuss the evolution of audience measurement techniques – from telephone recall to telephone coincidental to diary to meter to peoplemeter to Portable People Meter to the installation of software on audience members' computers to measure online activity. Along the way they analyse a host of important issues. They examine sampling techniques, auditing of ratings results, how stakeholder consensus is reached regarding adoption of new measurement technologies, and the relationship between audience measurement and market research. And they address changing public attitudes toward participation in audience measurement activities and market research. Balnaves and O'Regan pay particular attention to the tension between audience members' desire for privacy and the desire of advertisers for the increasing amount of demographic and behavioural information about the audience that advances in technology are making it potentially possible to gather.

The authors also address the importance of the ratings to the audience. Free-to-air programming is what economists refer to as a public good, that is to say it is non-excludable (the television station cannot prevent individuals from consuming the programming) and non-rival in consumption (Balnaves' viewing of *American Idol* does not reduce the amount of programming available to O'Regan). Since it is not possible to charge audience members a fee for free-to-air programming, providers do not benefit from the information about consumer valuation of a product or service that the price system usually provides. The primary piece of information about consumer valuation of free-to-air programming is the size and demographic composition of the audience, as measured by ratings.

So production of programming which appeals to a particular subset of the audience is dependent upon reasonably accurate measurement of the media usage behaviour of that audience segment. If it is accurately measured, then advertisers wishing to reach that market segment would have a basis for purchasing exposures in programming that appeals to that segment. On the other hand, if a demographic, for instance Hispanic Americans, is undercounted in the ratings, one consequence may be a menu of programming that does not cater for the tastes, needs and interests of that group. As one assesses the evolution and performance of the audience rating system, it is important to keep in mind this interest of the audience stakeholders in the process.

The timely look back provided by *Rating the Audience* offers a useful framework for understanding today's audience ratings process. And it provides the tools for grappling with how technical change in audience delivery and measurement will challenge the convention in the years to come.

Jonathan D. Levy*

---

*Jonathan D. Levy is the Deputy Chief Economist of the US Federal Communications Commission. The opinions expressed herein are those of the writer and do not necessarily represent the views of the FCC or any other member of its staff.

Acknowledgements

The authors are very grateful for the cooperation and time of interviewees. Interviewees for this book have been involved in the foundation and operation of audience ratings in the United States, Australia and the United Kingdom or in their critique. They were generous with time and with help in documentation relevant to the development and operation of audience ratings.

United States

Helen Crossley is daughter of pioneer pollster Archibald M. Crossley and at the age of nine worked with her father counting radio listeners. She became an expert in public opinion polling in her own right and had a long association with the United States Information Agency (USIA), working with Leo P. Crespi to coordinate research surveys in Europe, Asia and Latin America. The surveys measured foreign public attitudes to US policy. Helen is a founding member of the American Association for Public Opinion Research (AAPOR) and the World Association for Public Opinion Research (WAPOR).

Gale Metzger is the retired co-founder and President of Statistical Research, Inc. (SRI). SRI created and provided a number of major media and consumer research services, including: the audience ratings for national network radio (RADAR: Radio's All Dimension Audience Research 1972–2001); studies and audits of television measurement systems, including the development – in collaboration with major networks and advertisers – of a complete ratings service for the digital era (SMART: Systems for Measuring and Reporting Television); ongoing services to understand how consumers use media – including TV, radio and the internet – in everyday life (MultiMedia Mentor); many sponsored studies related to media usage and advertising, including reactions to programming and products and ad campaigns. The Market Research Council inducted Gale into its Hall of Fame and the National Association of Broadcasters gave him the Hugh Malcolm Beville award in recognition of his distinguished professional career in broadcast audience research.

Peter V. Miller, Associate Professor at Northwestern University, Illinois, is editor of the scholarly journal, *Public Opinion Quarterly*. He teaches and conducts research on public opinion and research methods. He focuses on issues of validity in social science research, including public opinion polls, government surveys and audience measurements, and on the role of survey research in public policy.

James G. Webster is Professor of Media Technology & Society at Northwestern University, Illinois. His research interests include audience measurement, the behaviour of media audiences and media industries. He has been a member of the Editorial Board of the *Journal of Broadcasting & Electronic Media* since 1985.

Australia

Don Neely started with Anderson in 1959 as a sales representative, later sales manager and then Managing Director; Ken Sievers was appointed Managing Director of Anderson in 1961. Following restructuring on 1 July 1966, the McNair research business was in the hands of the 'three Ians', Ian McNair as Managing Director, Ian Muir as Media Research Director and Ian Pilz as Consumer Research Director. In December 1973 McNair merged with Anderson to begin McNair Anderson with Ian Muir as Managing Director, Don Neely as Media Research Director, Ian Pilz as Consumer Research Director, Roger Layton as Consultant, Jim Grant as General Manager and Max Eve as Secretary.

The authors are also grateful to Gwen Nelson, to Ken Chesterfield for help on the origins of frequency and reach, and to Des Foster for the role of ratings in radio management.

Ian Garland has helped the authors on numerous occasions to better understand developments in the subscriber/pay-TV market. He is the founding employee and managing director of Multiview Analytics. The company was established in 2009 to develop research and analytical services for the benefit of the subscription TV industry (STV) and to serve the broader media and marketing community. He was previously Managing Director of ACNielsen Media Australia from 1997 until 2001.

Professor Duane Varan, head of the Interactive Television Research Institute (ITRI) at Murdoch University in Perth, has been very generous with his time to provide explanations on his work and key issues emerging with changing models and metrics.

United Kingdom

Tony Twyman had a major role setting up Radio Joint Audience Research (RAJAR) as well as being Technical Director of Broadcasters' Audience Research Board (BARB). He has been a Director of Television Audience Measurement (TAM), the holder of the first UK television audience research contract.

Nielsen

Mark Neely and Nielsen assisted with checking statistics as well as general editing. The authors could not have provided the insights in this book without Mark's help and access to historical archives within the company. Historical and contemporary examples of analysis have been reproduced, with permission.

Permission to Reproduce

The authors drew on material from *Mobilising the Audience*, a University of Queensland Press 2002 text, in order to exemplify points about the rise of databases. The authors also thank all those who provided permission to reproduce pictures.

Finally, the authors wish to thank their respective families for their love and support. Warm thanks also to Emily Salz and Lee Ann Tutton, Bloomsbury Academic, for their support and counsel, and Howard Watson for his forensic copy-editing.

1 Why the Ratings Are Important

A huge apparatus is called into play.
Leo Bogart (Bogart 2000a: 301)

In this chapter the authors show why the measurement of audiences has become critical in modern society. Audience ratings are the currency by which decisions are made on whether an audience does, in fact, exist and the subsequent media buying and selling that happens as a result. Ratings, though, are also more than this. Like public opinion polls, they have become an established and socially accepted way of representing individuals and groups in markets or in political decisions. In order to gain this acceptance, modern ratings involves a large range of organizations, private and public, that have to agree on the methodologies and knowledge involved. This agreement is the basis of the ratings convention. As the number of media channels has grown, so has the capacity of audience ratings to represent everything, as the standard, come under pressure.

Introduction

Knowledge of audience preferences and behaviour is critical to the operation of contemporary media organizations. Systems of audience measurement, known colloquially as 'ratings', influence the timing, placement and markets for media content and advertising. Audience measurement companies emerged in the 1930s to fill this need. Over the years, these companies' abilities to describe and predict audience behaviour have varied, along with the techniques and technologies developed to measure audiences. While the technology, panels and survey frequency of ratings instruments have become more sophisticated over time, ratings *conventions* are still beset with the problem of the differential between the actual and the measured audience. Indeed, in the contemporary period, characterized by media fragmentation, niche channels and dispersed audiences, questions have been raised over the adequacy and appropriateness of ratings systems and instruments in measuring audience behaviour, with significant economic cost as a result (Napoli 2003). Investigation into the conventions that govern the relationship between measurement and markets has become more urgent. *Rating the Audience* provides the first historical study of the overall trajectory of the audience ratings technologies and conventions, the companies providing these ratings and the media organizations using them. The study provides a detailed analysis of the emergence, development and transformation of audience ratings in order to promote better public and media industry understanding of the nature, character, productivity, limits and challenges facing ratings conventions.

The aims of our study are to: (i) establish and interrogate the nature, character and evolution of the audience-ratings conventions used to address the complicated trade-offs between the need for accuracy and the acceptance of 'imperfections' (issues often confused in the public mind with the rigging or fixing of ratings by broadcasters); (ii) establish and interrogate the nature, character and evolution of methodologies and technologies used in audience ratings, such as diaries, interviews and peoplemeters; (iii) analyse the consequences of the audience-ratings conventions, in their different forms, for the operations of media audience markets and media content markets, over time; (iv) analyse the consequences of the decline in exposure-based pricing, typically cost-per-thousand (CPM), and alternative pricing structures; (v) analyse the balance between social control and manipulation in audience-ratings conventions and ethical and transparent conduct; and (vi) document the decline in audience participation in audience data collection.

Research on audience exposure technologies has typically been conducted for particular and local purposes, and largely without reference to existing and prior historical research. Audience measurement research is characteristically fragmented both institutionally and methodologically. Records on the development and application of audience research methodologies are also fragmented. Much of the knowledge about both the history and the rationale for selection and use of audience measurement methodologies and technologies is only available through interviews with those who made the selections and archives of media research companies. This book is based in large part on interviews conducted by the authors with historical and contemporary figures from around the world who have contributed to the development of audience ratings.

Audience ratings systems provide an economic foundation for advertiser-supported media. Consequently the audience measurement process affects the structure and behaviour of media companies and regulators alike. When the techniques and technologies of the ratings change, these changes can, as Napoli observes, have 'a significant effect on the economics of media industries (because these changes can affect advertiser behaviour), the relative economic health of various segments of the media industry, and the nature of the content that media organisations provide' (Napoli 2003: 65). The authors' own preliminary research into the ratings convention in Australia (Balnaves and O'Regan 2002; Balnaves and O'Regan 2008) confirms this estimation. These changes are driven by the desire on the part of all participants to the convention to minimize the inevitable gap between the measured audience and the actual audience for a service or programmes. With the advent of a more diverse and fragmented media environment and new methods for segmenting audiences, this gap has become even more evident, leading to challenges to the validity of ratings as currency for buying and selling media. Napoli suggests that changes in technologies and audiences are leading to a decline in the quality and value of the 'audience product' – data on who is watching (Napoli 2003). The provision of reliable third-party syndicated and customized audience measurement systems for the production of ratings, however, remains essential to good media management nationally and internationally. As industrialized countries move into a more fragmented and differentiated multichannel broadcasting environment these issues will become more important.

Napoli's recent analysis has identified the empirical trend for audience and content markets, which historically have been connected, to separate (Napoli 2003: 181). The audience market and ratings have traditionally informed programmers and advertisers on what content to provide and where to target advertising. With the emergence of cable, satellite and internet delivery systems, direct audience payment for content has become more common, with a series of implications for advertiser-supported media (Napoli 2003: 180). In the new media environment, it is technologically possible to gather more information about audiences than ever before, but media and audience fragmentation have made it more expensive for media producers and distributors to find audiences, to discover their viewing or listening preferences and to deliver content across a range of different media.

In order to understand the current situation and its difficulties it is worthwhile thinking about audience ratings development as falling into three major periods:

- 'The Old Regime', 1930–50. This was a period in which few media channels existed. Despite their desire to target narrow demographic groups, advertisers and programmers relied in this era on simple audience size as an indicator of audience value. Extensive audience segmentation was not technologically or economically feasible. This was the era of paper diaries and interviews, and the first audience segmentations (A,B,C,D) were focused on the family environment.

- 'The Transitional Regime'. The period 1950–90 was a time of increased fragmentation of the media system, more television channels, more radio channels, and increased sophistication of audience measurement systems. There were a number of challenges to the ratings conventions leading to a move towards a single convention in a media form. The introduction of peoplemeters continued the 'technologizing' of audience ratings that had begun with Arthur (Art) C. Nielsen's Audimeter, which began to be rolled out in 1942 in the United States but did not achieve national coverage until 1949 (Beville 1988: 20). With an increased number of media channels came demand for and development of increasingly sophisticated technologies of measurement (together with an erosion of the concept of a 'mass audience') (Turow 1997). Advertiser valuations of different audience segments now affected media content decisions. This 'transitional regime' is important to the study, because while the sophistication of the measurement technologies increased significantly, the emerging changes in the media technologies, such as the Internet, are also having effects on the nature of audiences and their accessibility to advertisers.

- 'The Contemporary Moment'. The period 1990 to the present involves increased sophistication in measurement technologies, including the rise of database analysis of audience exposure data on users' desktops. There is, at the same time, a decline in the quality of the audience market; a decline in television ratings panel participation, indicating growing reluctance to participate in audience ratings research and 'conduit multiplication' with network viewing dropping from 95 per cent to 40 per cent in the United States and elsewhere. The consequent 'audience fragmentation' makes it harder for advertisers to reach a critical mass audience. There is more 'ad avoidance', a trend that started with 'time shifting' equipment like VCRs. And there is 'ambience' in media, where television is shifting more to the background (like radio), with people doing more and more tasks (e.g. surfing the net) while watching television, and growing 'out of home' (OOH) viewing, which creates problems for the traditional home-based forms of measurement. In the United States the cable TV (know as subscription TV or pay-TV in Australia) industry benefited, initially, with the shift of audiences to 'pay for content' rather than 'advertising-supported' services. But the need to understand audience preferences on content remains and the decline in the quality of audience as a market is now affecting pay-TV (Turow 1997; Napoli 2003).

Significant effort in modern advertising is directed towards maximizing exposure – to ensure that a broadcast audience, for example, is exposed to an optimum number of messages in a media planning schedule. 'Interactivity' as it is emerging, however, has a dramatic effect on traditional assumptions about frequency and reach (how many times the message is repeated and how extensively it is received). Interactivity potentially shifts choice back to the audience allowing a 'bypassing' of attempts to repeat messages.

There has been significant cultural and media studies analysis and theorization about discursive practices associated with audience research and the idea of the audience itself (Ang 1991; Hartley 1992a; Hartley 2005; Nightingale 2003). Some of this has touched on the role of ratings, especially its limitations. There has been little or no analytical study, however, on the historical development of ideas about media exposure and engagement or the discourses surrounding those ideas. The idea or concept of exposure is at the heart of modern audience measurement for audience ratings. In the economics of media and advertising measurement of exposure is the key factor in making decisions on buying and selling media space. *Rating the Audience* examines in detail the history of the methodologies and conventions that have emerged to govern how measurement of exposure has played out in the marketplace.

Over forty years ago, for example, an Advertising Research Foundation (ARF) committee headed by Dr Seymour Banks, director of media research at Leo Burnett in the United States, created a model for evaluating media that has become the standard model for the media industry. That model was divided into six stages: distribution of the media advertising vehicle; audience exposure to the vehicle; audience exposure to a specific advertisement in the vehicle; audience members' perception of the advertisement; communication of the advertising message to the audience; and, eventual decision regarding whether to purchase the advertised item. There have been attempts by the ARF to update this model (Phelps 1989) and focus on 'engagement', rather than 'exposure', but as the debates about ratings measurement in Australia and elsewhere show, exposure is still perceived as key to making decisions about buying and selling but at the same time is not as viable for a modern metrics. Understanding the trajectories of measurement, therefore, is the key to understanding the future of the ratings 'currency'.

There has been an historical demand that ratings be public, transparent and, preferably, derived from an independent third party. But persuading the full range of media players from the competing media companies through to advertisers that a particular technology for collecting and analysing audience data is suitable is no small achievement (Miller 1994; Balnaves and O'Regan 2002: 33). *Rating the Audience* is both an analysis of the evolution of the concept of 'exposure' in methodologies for collecting ratings, from diary methods to ratings panels, and an historical and cultural account of the media players involved.

In countries like Australia ratings research itself has historically been a public issue. Bob Rogers in his talk-back radio programme on 4 February 1970 said that he had never met anyone who had completed a ratings survey and invited people with survey books to call in. Later he announced that several people had rung and they had admitted keeping their records in a 'slap-happy method'. One woman had turned her diary over to her nine-year-old daughter. Sydney TV stations TCN-9 and TEN-10 claimed that people had rung them saying they had heard prizes were being offered to holders of survey diaries. In the ensuing furore, the stations demanded that the whole four-week survey, the first of the year, be abandoned (Jones and Bednall 1980: 11). Public representatives also sometimes intervene to review audience research technology. For example, in 1963 a US Congressional committee investigated broadcast ratings and the issue of measurement. The hearings suggested that the illusion of exact accuracy was necessary to the ratings industry in order to heighten the confidence of their clients in the validity of the data they sell. 'This myth was sustained by the practice of reporting audience ratings down to the decimal point, even when the sampling tolerances ranged over several percentage points.' Audience research in the future, the US Senate hearings concluded, must face the task of distinguishing among different kinds of communications experience which are now represented under the heading of total-audience figures (Kover 1967: 50–54).

Arguments about the role of measurement, and the limitations of measurement in audience research, were well established in the marketing research literature by the 1960s and well before the contemporary debates about 'ethnography' and 'active audiences'. Bogart (Bogart 1966) and Kover (Kover 1967), for example, provided detailed critiques about audience conceptions and measurement that would fit easily into contemporary cultural studies journals. Industry reacted to these research critiques and public reviews, and qualitative research emerged as a complement to statistical ratings research.

The authors, in writing *Rating the Audience*, sought documentation from company archives such as Nielsen's archive of ratings books, through to personal archives, such as those of Tony Twyman and Gale Metzger. There is also significant documentation from international government hearings and research that have investigated issues in ratings methodologies, such as a controversy in the 1980s in the United States over sampling methodologies. Historical figures involved in developing methodologies, technologies and conventions were interviewed to help clarify many of the decisions to change conventions and methodologies.

The Single Number

We can get a sense of the importance of authoritative audience measurement by looking at how a new market entrant in the 1940s used it. In 1942 Joseph Creamer was the promotion and research director of WOR (World of Radio), owner and operator of an FM radio station in New York, W71NY. His company urgently needed to show advertisers and clients that W71NY's 60,000 FM set owners were a valuable audience. W71NY had won the first FM commercial contract with an advertiser in 1941. Creamer knew though that if radio ratings were showing

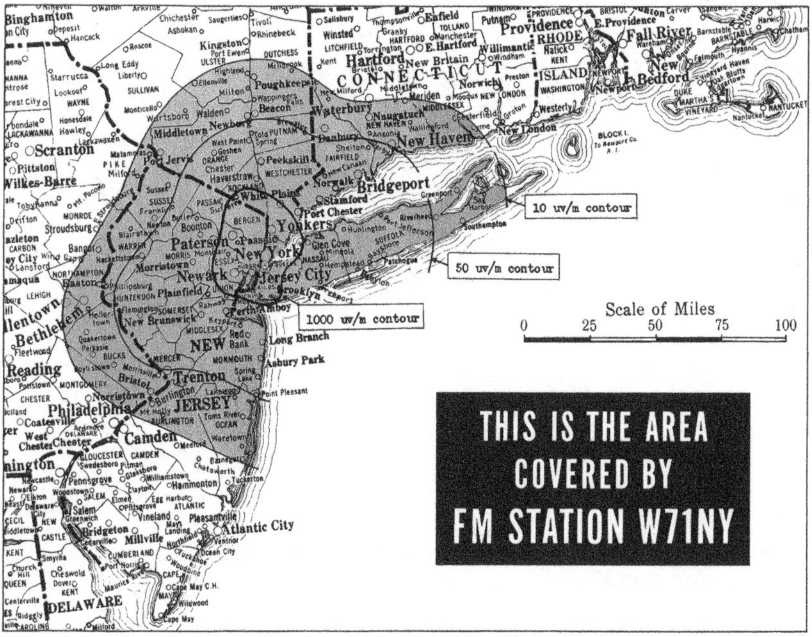

Figure 1.1 W71NY FM station coverage
Source: Nielsen Historical Archive

that FM listeners represented only a single demographic of classical music listeners, then that stereotype would affect advertiser perceptions. W71NY, as you can see above, was in 1942 broadcasting to a major metropolitan audience in the United States.

Creamer's answer was to undertake commissioned research by A.C. Nielsen, a broadcast ratings provider, to demonstrate to advertising clients like 'Miss Deane' (see next page) that a diverse audience for the radio station did in fact exist.

Creamer's letter and WOR's commissioned study on FM audiences are wonderful examples of the demands made upon those involved in the media industry to demonstrate the existence of their audiences. Creamer concludes in his report that 'listener families were scientifically distributed among ALL income groups: i.e. A, B, C, and D. That results are, in other words, representative of ALL kinds of people in ALL kinds of homes' (1942: 3). A,B,C,D were the social class classifications used in radio ratings. What the radio ratings produced for subscribers like WOR were *single numbers* that showed the size and the nature of the audience, in simple terms, for individual stations and programmes.

The basic system that Creamer would have seen for calculating share and rating has not changed. Share is the percentage of the total viewing or listening audience

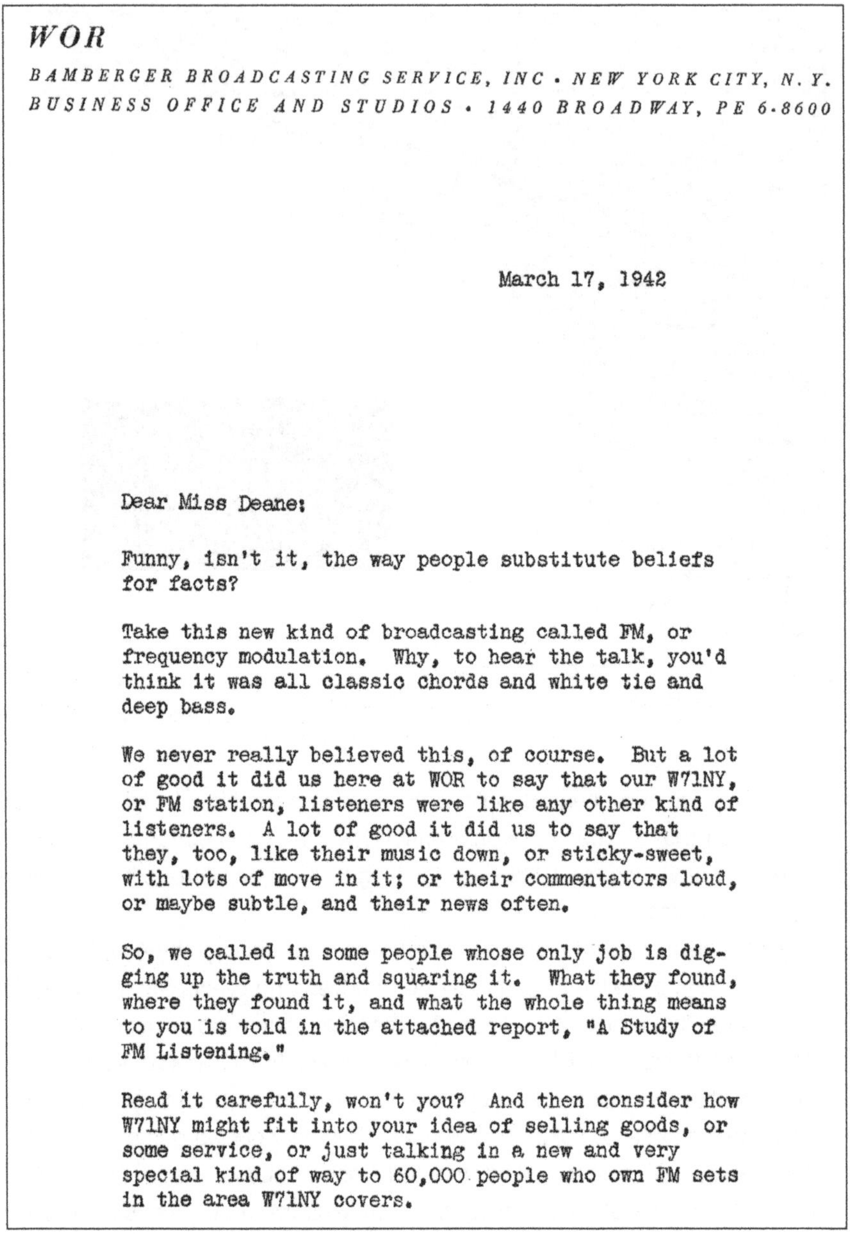

WOR

BAMBERGER BROADCASTING SERVICE, INC · NEW YORK CITY, N. Y.
BUSINESS OFFICE AND STUDIOS · 1440 BROADWAY, PE 6·8600

March 17, 1942

Dear Miss Deane:

Funny, isn't it, the way people substitute beliefs
for facts?

Take this new kind of broadcasting called FM, or
frequency modulation. Why, to hear the talk, you'd
think it was all classic chords and white tie and
deep bass.

We never really believed this, of course. But a lot
of good it did us here at WOR to say that our W71NY,
or FM station, listeners were like any other kind of
listeners. A lot of good it did us to say that
they, too, like their music down, or sticky-sweet,
with lots of move in it; or their commentators loud,
or maybe subtle, and their news often.

So, we called in some people whose only job is dig-
ging up the truth and squaring it. What they found,
where they found it, and what the whole thing means
to you is told in the attached report, "A Study of
FM Listening."

Read it carefully, won't you? And then consider how
W71NY might fit into your idea of selling goods, or
some service, or just talking in a new and very
special kind of way to 60,000 people who own FM sets
in the area W71NY covers.

Figure 1.2 Creamer's Letter to Clients
Source: Nielsen Historical Archive

for a particular programme. The rating is the percentage of all people or households
in a city, nation or a particular demographic tuned into a specific channel.

The breakdown of A,B,C,D for Creamer in 1942 is outlined in Table 1.1.

Table 1.1 Breakdown of audiences by social classification (US$)

Group	Income	% of Total
A	$5,000+	6.7
B	$3,000–4,999	13.3
C	$2,000–2,999	26.7
D	Under $2,000	53.3

Most radio programmes in Creamer's day were directed towards C as it had a high level of listening. WOR did not want FM to be perceived as only an A or B medium. What Creamer understood was that audience measurement, well established by the 1940s, not only analysed radio markets: they altered them. They were an active force transforming the broadcasting environment and not just a camera passively recording it. The distinction between 'engine' and 'camera' was made by Donald MacKenzie (MacKenzie 2006) in his analysis of financial markets where statistical measures and calculations were used to standardize a range of market transactions in the finance industry. This distinction is helpful as audience ratings are not only important because of the numbers they produce but also due to the whole set of agreements and activities that operate around them. Ratings were used as *currency* – as the basis for determining whether an audience in fact existed, prices in advertising, success or failure of programmes and, not least, in planning for the future.

The often stated idea that the buying and selling of audiences shapes media programming is of course a part of the phenomenon of ratings. At the time of the primacy of the free-to-air television networks in the United States, Erik Barnouw traced some of this history in *The Sponsor: Notes on a Modern Potentate* (Barnouw 1978). Barnouw showed that sponsors' demands for particular demographics helped shape the programming of both radio and television, but most particularly the latter. He shows how, as the TV ratings companies refined their total audience counts into age, sex and income demographics, sponsors began to offer networks investments worth millions of dollars to make shows aimed at women aged 18–49 and so on. The aim was to create programmes that would appeal to their target audience, and therefore increase the prospect of the advertising messages reaching their intended consumers. The sponsor linked his computer to the Nielsen rating computers in Florida and found that *Gunsmoke* had high ratings but bad demographics – its audience was too old and rural – so he shot down *Gunsmoke* in a blaze of bans.

Sponsorship also revolutionized the payment of actors. They could earn big money from appearing in commercials, some of which cost more than the programmes into which they were inserted, as Michael Arlen showed in his book about the production of just one of them, *Thirty Seconds* (Arlen 1980). By 1972, members of the Screen Actors Guild earned US$62 million from acting in commercials, US$38 million from acting in television films, and US$22 million from acting in feature films. Soup in a can, so to speak, became three times more valuable than film in a can. Sponsorship also revolutionized television drama as particular sponsors sought particular desired demographics with consequent shifts in programme type and orientation.

Ads themselves were designed to arrest attention long enough for an otherwise overlooked message to be delivered (Twitchell 1996). Twitchell claims that much TV drama was advertising friendly in another way: predominantly 'middle-class stories' revolving around 'consumable objects' and 'told in discrete twelve-minute segments', with the dramatic arc 'the result of the demands of the advertisers' (Twitchell 1996: 178). But all this started to change when the advent of pay-TV in the 1970s in the United States and afterwards elsewhere made part of the broadcasting industry more concerned with attracting and retaining subscribers than with solely attracting audiences to sell to advertisers.

It would be a mistake to conclude that advertisers are the only key to understanding the influence of ratings or their purpose or, indeed, that advertisers are the only users of ratings. Ratings became integral to the work not only of programme-making, but broadcast scheduling and planning. Audience ratings were created at the same time as their twin, public opinion polls, and, indeed, were instigated by the same people who were involved in both. In societies with millions of people there are limited ways in which to read the public mind. Ratings and polls have become, universally, the accepted way to represent the public in democratic societies, outside of traditional voting cycles and participatory tools on the internet. The methodologies behind those techniques, therefore, have, equally, become very important as they determine whether or not the public and its governments or businesses trust them. Unlike commercial-in-confidence non-public research, audience ratings and public opinion polls require scrutiny.

What is clear from the historical record is that broadcasting, and television in particular, made the ratings its own. Print never caught up with broadcasting in the audience measurement stakes. It had circulation audits and readership surveys but it could not match the system that quickly grew around broadcasting. Figure 1.3 (on page 12) shows the rapid adoption and diffusion of the radio in the home during the 1920s and the 1930s in the United Sates, compared with other household purchases. Remember, 'radio homes' in these early days were exactly that – homes. People would come home to their families, lie on the living-room floor, switch off the lights, and listen to the latest drama or comedy. Radio was cheaper than other household appliances, even compared with the telephone, vacuum cleaners and irons. The dips in the sales, of course, represent the impact of the Depression.

Table 1.2 Advertising expenditure 1928–37 (millions US$)

	Newspaper	Magazines	Radio	Outdoor	Farm	Total
1928	720	190	20	85	30	1,045
1929	760	210	35	80	30	1,115
1930	670	180	50	65	25	990
1931	590	150	70	50	20	880
1932	470	110	75	35	10	700
1933	430	100	65	30	10	635
1934	470	125	90	30	13	728
1935	500	130	110	35	14	789
1936	550	150	135	45	17	897
1937	570	165	165	50	18	968

Source: Dygert 1939

The popularity of radio shifted advertising expenditure between media as radio grew from a US$20 million advertising revenue industry in 1928 to a US$165 million a year industry in 1937. As this occurred fan mail, one of the major ways of determining radio programme popularity early on, gave way to new measurements of radio-listening behaviour which gave advertisers and sponsors relatively quick feedback on the success or not of particular programmes. Table 1.2 shows the increasing radio revenue, compared with its counterparts (in percentage terms print did not change much over the same period). The ratings with its quick feedback loops and quality demographic data very became radio's advantage and selling point amidst stiff media competition.

If we flash forward to today we see a very different and more complex advertising media mix. The parallel to the advent of radio as a commercial medium in the 1930s is probably the internet today. It has emerged as another medium that splits the advertising revenue pie as Figure 1.3, drawn from the British telecommunications and broadcasting watchdog, Ofcom shows. At the same time each medium is becoming increasingly more complex as convergence increases (for example, Internet radio; IPTV). What Table 1.3 also shows is that there are large variations among the larger western countries in terms of their advertising mix which have consequences for the kinds of audience measurement services provided.

When we combined these figures with the huge proliferation of media within each of the main advertising categories we can get a sense of the problems facing both advertisers and media companies. Comparing 1985 to 2008 in the United States is especially instructive as to how complex things have become, in terms of choice of medium for advertising, since Creamer's day.

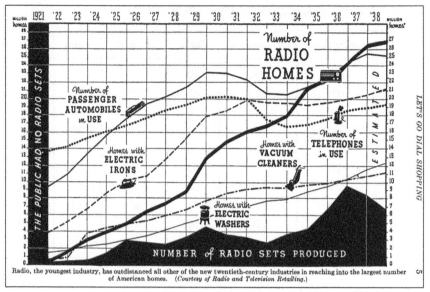

Figure 1.3 Radio homes in the United States, 1921–38
Source: Dygert 1939

In 1985 in the United States there were 3 Networks, 7,744 Radio Stations, 2,722 Print Options and 4 Outdoor Forms with analogue terrestrial, satellite and cable systems. By contrast in 2008 there were 7 Networks (plus Video on Demand,

Table 1.3 Distribution of advertising expenditure, 2007

	Net	Outdoor	Cinema	Radio	TV	Magazine	Newspaper
UK	14	7			28	13	34
FRANCE		10		8	32	20	26
GERMANY		5	26			18	43
ITALY					54	16	20
USA	10			11	38	10	27
CANADA	9			12	32	11	33
JAPAN	8	12			44	9	23
POLAND		6		8	51	15	16
SPAIN	6			9	45	10	27
HOLLAND	7	4		7	22	21	39
SWEDEN	12	5			21	11	48
IRELAND		9		8	21		59

Source: Ofcom. The International Communications Market, 2007

DVD and [H]DTV), 12,718 Radio Stations, 12,709 Print Options, 150+ Cable Networks, 500 Digital Channels, Digital Cable, Interactive TV, IPTV, Gaming Internet, Podcasting Email, Video Ads Mobile, Virtual Communications, Advergaming, Social Networking, Widgets, Twitter (microblogging) and Search.

This expansion of media channels has also seen an expansion in the measurement of different audiences as audience measurement companies have struggled to keep up. Nowhere is this more evident than in the proliferation in the number and range of panels that Nielsen alone uses to cover different types of media and circumstances in which media might be used.

The problem with this diversity of measurement across many different types of media is, as Gale Metzger points out, that not everyone now agrees with the efficacy of the *single number* of Creamer's day, when there were fewer media and more homogenous audiences. For Metzger, the major problem today is one of trying to 'measure microscopic shares' whereas once these were 'big' audience shares. He observes:

> If you're the Campbell's Soup advertising manager, and you advertise and want a measure of the audience reached, today's challenge is different than yesterday's. In the old days Campbell's Soup had a 40 per cent share of the soup market and they were getting 20 television ratings. The random duplication of those two phenomena is the cross product of 20 per cent and 40 per cent, or 8 per cent. Today, a media plan that reaches 10 per cent of the market and a brand that's got a 5 per cent share, you're dealing with less than an expected 1 per cent incidence within the population of people who use both the brand and that medium.

And because that dimension is very hard to measure with any kind of precision, it is the major issue of the day. Metzger goes on to wryly observe that the main reason 'we know less about the computer world than we knew about the slide rule world … is largely because of the size of things; it is easier to measure huge entities than microscopic elements' (Metzger 2008).

Moreover, the very ways of measuring audiences have come under the microscope, not least in the internet environment, which has grown very rapidly as an advertising platform. In 2009, according to the *Independent*, internet advertising revenue exceeded television advertising revenue for the first time in the United Kingdom. Internet advertising grew 4.6 per cent in the first half of 2009 to £1.7 billion, or 23.5 per cent of the total market, compared with television's £1.6 billion, down from £1.9 billion in 2008. Total advertising spend in the United Kingdom fell 3.5 per cent to £17.5 billion (Clark 2009). You might think that it is easy to measure what people do on the internet: you simply track where people go and what they

Table 1.4 Nielsen panels

	Year	Households in panel	Location
National Peoplemeter	1987	14,000	US
Local Peoplemeter	2002	600–800	US in 13 markets
Set Metered Markets (Electronic boxes that track viewing but information about the view is in a diary)	1959	21,000	US
Hispanic Peoplemeter Supplement	1994	270	US
Out of Home (Measures TV viewing at work, bars, airports, and so on, using sounds from the programmes that are recorded automatically by special mobile phones)	2008	4,700	US
Homescan Global (Purchasing behaviour)	1988	135,000	27 countries
Homescan US consumers	1988	125,000	US
Homescan Hispanic	2007	2,500	US/Latin America
FANLinks (Cross-references Homescan with their fan interests)	2005	50,000	US
Project Apollo (Multimedia consumption and purchasing – now cancelled)	2006	5,000	US
Nielsen BookScan (US book industry data) (booksellers)	2001	12,000	US
Your Voice (Online community for opinions)	2000	500,000+	Global
Nielsen Mobile Bill Panel (Activity on mobiles) (mobile bills)	2005	20,000	US
Hey! Nielsen (Website where users rate TV shows, movies and so on)	2007	30,000	US
NetView & MegaPanel (Offline and online audience and market research)	1997	475,000	US and 9 other countries
Pine Cone Research (Product and concept surveys)	1999	173,000	Global
The Hub (Former members of other panels who allow Nielsen to track them)	2008	1,000	US

Source: Adapted from Story 2008

purchase. But it is not that simple. Take the example of Meebo – a service which was designed to fill a gap in the market for an instant messaging service which would enable the interoperability of the different messaging services.

Life is good for 27-year-old Seth J. Sternberg. A year ago, he dropped out of Stanford Business School to work full-time on Meebo Inc ... Today Meebo is going gangbusters. It has raised $3.5 million from the Silicon Valley crème-de-la-crème, including Marc Andreessen of Netscape fame and venture capital heavyweight Sequoia Capital. More impressively, the service attracts almost a million people every day, who swap more than 60 million messages.

However the company finds it difficult to prove its site is as popular as the company says it is. As the *Businessweek* article noted:

Look up Meebo's Web traffic using the comScore Networks Inc. service, and you'll find that a European competitor eBuddy.com is four times as big. Alexa, a competing Web measurement service owned by Amazon.com Inc., shows Meebo is bigger. Which is true? Probably neither. Sternberg's best guess is that the two rivals are about the same size. Yet even he doesn't know for sure. (*Businessweek* 2006)

There is no agreement on metrics for the internet. This is precisely why agreements emerged on radio ratings in the 1920s – at the time various stations claimed that they had the best radio station but each would use a different way to measure the audience. A standard way of measuring was required.

Knowing, measuring and understanding media audiences have become a multi-billion dollar business. But the convention that underpins that business, audience ratings, is in contention. Joseph Creamer today would find a crowded market and he would be scratching his head about which business model might work. Audiences are no longer limited to watching television via cable, terrestrial and satellite broadcasts. The legal and illegal viewing of television content on the internet is rapidly increasing, and internet protocol television (IPTV) is growing in popularity. These developments have created the need to measure smaller, more fragmented audiences and more and more everyday exposure to media. There is now heated industry debate and experimentation with new and controversial ways of innovating the collection and analysis of the ratings to deal with this new reality. Sampling in its turn has also become the subject of political and methodological battles over how to best represent people, in the census, on the internet and as audiences for broadcast television. At the same time, audience participation in research is declining. The traditional ratings convention is under pressure from all sides.

The chapters ahead demonstrate why and how audience ratings research became a *convention*, an agreement, and interrogate the ways that agreement is under pressure and is seeking to innovate to meet these challenges. With Google in alliance with Nielsen, one of the world's leading media researchers, planning to literally auction audiences off to the highest bidder, there are now attempts to establish new ratings-based coordination rules and currencies. At the same time the survey and sampling methodologies that produce audience ratings, and the various technologies from Art Nielsen's original 'black box' – the Audimeter – to the contemporary peoplemeter and its rival – the personal peoplemeter – are often in public dispute. The practices of ratings measurement have become the subject of court cases in the United States as different media companies seek ways of reshaping the ratings in ways that better reflect their view of their audience. The crisis in the ratings convention matters because who is and who is not measured affects all aspects of media production, funding and consumption. The value of services, advertising expenditure, funding for content, technological developments, and the delivery and circulation of programming, are all dependent, to some degree, on the measurement and valuing of audiences.

As you will see, the contemporary controversy and crisis in the ratings convention recalls earlier controversies and crises, where there was the same querying of methodologies and technologies of counting and the same emergence of serious rivals using different methods from incumbent providers. What is different today are the ways in which *all aspects* of the ratings convention are in dispute at the same time rather than one particular issue dominating debate. Previous studies have tended to see the ratings from one particular angle, for instance, measurement, to the exclusion of others. Now is the time to see audience ratings as they are, as a complex set of formal and informal agreements, a compact that governs a multibillion-dollar business. The authors will show how new uses for the ratings convention developed over time. We analyse how the ratings have been used not only in commercial broadcasting, but also in public service broadcasting, in subscription TV and on the internet. And we demonstrate how the ratings have served as the coordination rule and currency for diverse industry stakeholders, in the process becoming integral to the ongoing operation, planning and development of the media industries.

Summary

Audience ratings are important because they permit agreement among parties involved in the creation and use of ratings that audiences exist and that the numbers produced from ratings surveys represent what those audiences watch or listen to.

The ratings numbers from surveys are then used as currency in media buying. This is called *syndicated research* because a range of clients, from advertisers to stations, buy the ratings. The syndication reduces the cost to subscribers because they do not have to conduct their own research to get a picture of the whole market – unless, of course, like Joseph Creamer, a new entrant with a new technology (in this case FM), there is a need for *customized* research to convince clients there is an audience. Customized research, of course, is often used for other things, like getting feedback on pilots for TV programmes and other types of in-depth programme- or station-specific work.

As Gale Metzger, Art Nielsen's protégé in the 1960s points out, audience research is not like other types of social-science survey research. It is a special type of measurement in that the estimates it produces of the number of people reached are bought and sold. Consequently, 'the number of people reached is a key fact about how well a media outlet is doing its job':

> Effectively, the numbers are the product. The numbers dimension and value the audience. Research on the sales of soap or cars or any other commodity or service or business, may provide insights on why or how people buy. But soap and cars are what is sold. With media audiences, users have a greater stake in the results. Accordingly, the estimates are subjected to closer scrutiny than statistics that only provide commentary about a product. Therefore, media audience research is generally of a somewhat higher quality than other measurements. The fact that the numbers are the product brings pressure for better quality. (Metzger 2008)

Chapter 2 provides a detailed introduction to the rise of the audience-ratings convention and the rules, established very early on, that have grown to define expectations among the different players in each market.

Chapter 3 looks at the history of the different ratings methodologies, especially panels and surveys, and how the early ratings intellectuals shaped their development and use. Broadcast ratings have a close resemblance with public polling and voting. This is not surprising. The ratings intellectuals who designed the ratings also created the first opinion polls. Audience ratings as a particular form of humanistic social research also adopted the revolutionary panel-based survey research technique using probabilistic representative samples. This enabled the media industry to see 'audience flow' over time and to estimate 'audience share' of a broadcaster. Sampling and surveys in audience ratings have, therefore, a dual identity. They are a public interest vehicle showing the public vote for programmes and media providers, and a market mechanism for making decisions on the media dollar. Ratings are part of politics because they represent the public and the market at the same time.

Chapter 4 maps the rise of formal and informal ways of auditing audience ratings. Various ways of checking the way audience ratings are collected and used have emerged. These range from in-house research by ratings agencies, competitors or technical committees of commissioning organizations like the Broadcasters' Audience Research Board (BARB), to public forums like the American Association for Public Opinion Research (AAPOR), to ad hoc Congressional Committees in the United States and public inquiries in the United Kingdom, through to legal action and ratings councils. These formal and informal ways of checking on audience ratings have had a dramatic effect on the content we end up with, either on our television screens or through our radios. The process of auditing is never ending in the ratings convention. It works out who is accepted as an audience, what is accepted as a reasonable sample or measure, and so on, and it is integral to the maintenance of confidence in the adequacy of methods of data collection and analysis.

Chapter 5 looks at the technologies of counting themselves, from the early use of the telephone for aided-recall and telephone coincidental research techniques, the development of the 'mechanized' Audimeter and the paper diary, to the development of the personal peoplemeter and finally digital set-top boxes designed to monitor contemporary media use. These technologies of counting have been the subject of continuous innovation under constant industry pressure, technological advances and the weight of changing media environments. This chapter examines the ratings as an innovation system. It explores the emergence and deployment of particular technologies in response to technological advances, changes in patterns of media use, and the different needs of the various parties to the convention. Modern technologies of counting have also expanded to ratings-like innovations for subscription television services such as Sky in the United Kingdom and Foxtel in Australia, and the different metrics for online audiences.

Chapter 6 provides an historical overview of the rise of the ratings provider as the key knowledge broker. The ratings provider is most likely the organization to be used, criticized, threatened and cajoled, both within the industry and from without. The ratings provider's strengths and vulnerabilities alike are an important part of our story. In this chapter we explore why ratings providers look the way they do.

In different ways similar concerns have been expressed in Australia, the United Kingdom and continental Europe around 'single ratings providers', with a clearly discernible trend first evident in the United Kingdom in the 1950s with the introduction of Independent Television towards industry-sponsored services whose form and organization are decided by committees comprising broadcasters, advertisers and advertising agencies.

Chapter 7 shows how the content providers became the fulcrum of the ratings convention. Although the larger and more dominant broadcasters initially were often not supportive of the ratings, they have been among the principal beneficiaries of systematic audience measurement. Television networks brought the ratings into media economics and, with advertisers, built a system for buying and selling audiences and content. The chapter outlines the challenge to the convention in each country, arising from the introduction of subscription services as an alternative economic model for television, and examines the ways that the responses of traditional broadcasters to the needs and demands of subscription television providers shaped research and ratings methods, approaches and debates in each country. In the United Kingdom, for example, public service management at the British Broadcasting Corporation (BBC) actively resisted the development of systematic ratings, preferring self-selecting listener panels. In the end, however, audience ratings became central to all broadcasters – commercial, public service providers and later cable TV (subscription TV) networks. We will see how the ratings benefited networks and later independent operators and cable TV. This central reliance on ratings among broadcasters in their competitive strategy has, at the same time, become a problem as ratings map the decline in free-to-air audiences. Ratings have, as a result, entered into the 'life and death' struggle of broadcast networks and other media.

Chapter 8 provides a detailed insight into the analytical techniques and vocabularies built by the advertisers to sell audiences around ratings as currency. Advertisers in the early part of the twentieth century were heavily involved in research and housed many of the research intellectuals, not least J.B. Watson, the behavioural psychologist and his work with JWT (formerly J. Walter Thompson). Advertisers were responsible for the development of the first ratings surveys in the United States and were critical in the early development of ratings in Australian radio. They have traditionally been among the most sophisticated users and critics of the ratings. And they have also been the group most likely to experiment with different sorts of research. We will look at the combination of declining media advertising spend and allocation of advertising spend away from broadcasting. Advertisers have flagged a lack of confidence in traditional advertiser-supported media and an intense interest in how newer media might provide more appropriate vehicles. With media advertising revenue either static or even declining and below-the-line advertising, such as trade shows and promotions, increasing, there is now considerable ferment within the advertising-marketing-promotions field about the best strategies for reaching consumers and the best methods for interacting with consumers.

Chapter 9 turns to the audience, an important but often unacknowledged partner to the audience-ratings convention. When Nielsen and Arbitron joined forces to set up the experimental Project Apollo in 2005 they expected to capture all of the everyday behaviour of audiences, from reading papers through to using mobile phones and buying food. To their surprise they found that people did not want to participate. The more they were asked to do and to provide, the more they resisted and refused. Increased interest in the 'fusion' of different sources of data was a result, together with increased understanding of audience behaviour. This is just one of the ways in which the audience has a 'voice' in how audience ratings are developed and how the audience as informants and respondents actively sets limits to what information can be collected and how it can be collected. Audience consent to research has been essential to the success of the ratings industry.

Chapter 10 investigates the different types of criticism of the ratings from the point of view of one of the most famous internal critics of the ratings, Leo Bogart. Audience ratings are structurally different from other market phenomena, because the audience market is separated from the media content market, and politically different, because audience ratings are perceived as a public service. Within this context there is a range of criticisms Bogart raises, from the modern dependence on secondary data and computation through to a perceived deprofessionalization of media research.

Chapter 11 peers into the future of the audience-ratings convention. Audience ratings remain a gilt-edged, gold-standard form of survey and panel research. The chapter reviews the key element of the audience-ratings convention and tensions that exist in the contemporary moment.

2 The Convention

n Chapter 1 we saw how a new FM station, when FM was itself new as a technology, needed to demonstrate the existence of its audience. If W71NY had already been recognized in the radio ratings of the time, then the work of demonstration of an audience would have already been done. However, FM was new and the popular stereotype was that it appealed to a very narrow, classical music-listening demographic. The customized, commissioned study by WOR showed that its audience was both more diverse and more valuable than this. The need to measure audiences and to agree on what counts as an audience has continued unabated since the early days of broadcasting media. In this chapter the authors provide a detailed introduction to the rise of the audience-ratings convention and the rules, established very early on, that have grown to define expectations among the different players in each market.

'The Crossleys' – Archibald Crossley

My father would bring them home, interview cards, and he trained me how to do tabulate data from them – 1, 2, 3, 4 across, 1, 2, 3, 4 across, to make bunches of fives that could be added up by hand. I got into that by the time I was 10. I remember that there were four radio networks across the top of the sheet, and you put your check mark under whichever network the listener was reporting, so when you added them all up and counted them in piles of five, you knew how many listeners you had out of 20 calls. Helen Crossley (Crossley 2008)

Helen Crossley is here recalling working for her father as a child, in the first weeks after Archibald Crossley set up his system for measuring the radio audiences of national radio networks. He had decided to measure 'exposure' in his radio ratings analysis – who listens, for how long and with what regularity. His calculus at first glance might look simple, but the environment in which it was agreed on was not. The alternative possible measure was 'engagement' – how involved people are in their radio programmes. However, there was no agreement on how engagement might be used let alone charted as a universal measure. For example, one person's 'like it very much' might be another's 'like it'. Exposure, on the other hand, delivered a more comparable objective measure. A person listening to the radio for ten minutes was directly comparable to another person listening to the radio for five minutes. This did not mean that audience researchers did not collect data on whether people did or did not like the radio programmes. But for the purposes of buying and selling radio airtime, or programmes, a metric that showed the fact of tuning in to a programme and the amount of time listening to a programme had a simplicity that was essential for bargaining in highly competitive environments. All competitors, though, had to agree to the measure being used.

The first ratings convention was not a broadcast station initiative but an advertiser initiative. Archibald Crossley was hired in 1929 by an organization of radio advertisers, the Cooperative Analysis of Broadcasting, Inc. (CAB), to measure the 'unseen audience'. The radio advertisers had an interest in a single rule and an authoritative audience measure covering those radio stations, particularly the national radio networks, that were relevant to the larger mostly national advertisers. They wanted a measure to enable them to pick and choose among broadcast outlets and, since this was an era where advertisers were also programme producers, an instrument to gauge whether they were getting their target audiences.

Crossley was a methodologist in his own right, working with George Gallup on public opinion polling, and experienced in the development and application of statistical sampling methods which he adopted to the audience ratings. With no prior methodology to work from, he created basic measurements for CAB that covered over 80 US cities for 16 years. His employees thumbed through telephone directories, called subscribers, and asked them what programme they had been listening to – a technique called telephone recall. Crossley's ratings estimated the number of telephone subscribers tuned in to any show. This approach provided timely survey results ensuring that they could be used iteratively by advertisers and their programme producers. But this relative immediacy came at a cost. As telephone ownership was limited to those who could afford it these ratings were skewed by its sample with the result that particular audiences, most especially regional, minority and African American audiences, were under-represented. (This skewing gave rise to criticism, which persists to this day, that the ratings discriminates and disenfranchises minority audiences.) The CAB ratings became known as the 'Crossleys' and were the currency for determining the popularity of programmes. 'Even top stars like Jack Benny and Edgar Bergen worried more about their "Crossleys" than their hairlines,' *Time* magazine reported in 1946 (*Time* 1946).

Archibald Crossley is the acknowledged founder of broadcast ratings (Beville 1988). His exposure measure quickly became the *standard* for measuring ratings. Crossley soon found that the demand for his radio ratings was extraordinary. Initially only made available to the advertisers participating in CAB, a bootleg market for radio ratings emerged among radio networks, stations and advertising agencies. Warren Dygert, in his 1939 advice to 'radio men' in *Radio as an Advertising Medium*, shows why:

> The old-time advertising man ... knows if he buys advertising space in *Redbook, True Story, Business Week, Country Life*, he buys a ready-made type of reader. The publisher can tell him the reader's buying habits, income bracket, even the group age and sex. This solves a big problem in periodical advertising. In radio, with the exception of foreign-language stations, the advertiser has no such help. Rich and poor, employed and unemployed, educated and uneducated, moron and Solon [the ancient Greek lawyer] listen to the radio and are no respecters of stations. The radio advertiser has the added task here of picking out the group he wants and building his program to attract and hold that group. If he wants both mass and class, he may do as the Ford Motor Company did in building a special custom-made program for each group. Or he may attempt to build one program for all, a difficult feat for, as already pointed out, no one program can possibly suit everyone. (Dygert 1939: 11)

In a broadcast environment where audiences could not be easily classified in the same way that subscribers to print could be, radio ratings provided the stability and certainty by providing authoritative measures of audiences for time segments and programmes. What Archibald Crossley set up was the core of the modern audience-ratings convention:

1 Exposure is the key measurement;

2 The inherent correctness of that measurement must appeal to all parties;

3 The ratings deliver a 'single number';

4 A probability, statistical, sample is used for data collection;

5 Distortion of the ratings by the research provider or by subscribers is unacceptable and requires monitoring and control.

Both formal and informal arrangements emerged to deal with how this agreed measure was collected, used and distributed. Conflict over accuracy and outright cheating had to be dealt with. However, one of the biggest problems was *hypoing*, where a systematic attempt is made to distort ratings figures. This might involve simple means like running competitions during ratings sweeps. C.E. Hooper, whose ratings later replaced those of Crossley and CAB, banned radio stations or others that attempted to distort ratings from participating in the survey. This threat to exclude organizations that were blatantly hypoing was remarkably successful, although, as we shall see later, more complex means of distorting the ratings numbers in favour of providers emerged.

Hooper replaced Crossley as the major ratings provider in the 1940s. CAB was seen as less reliable in its methodology and approach and, because of its close association with advertisers, less independent. Hooper's innovation was the 'telephone coincidental' method. It involved telephoning the household at the same time that the programme was running. By the time Crossley decided to adopt Hooper's technique it was too late, and subscribers had moved to Hooper's service. This did not change the industry agreement that exposure should be the core measure for audience ratings. After all, only the means of collection and the group that collected the ratings had changed. While methodological questions would continue to be raised, the ratings were now mostly accepted as a convention – an industry-wide agreement on how audiences would be measured and valued. On a day-to-day basis, radio ratings were used in a variety of contexts. They were combined with other information to help organizations make decisions on everything from programming to sponsorship and talent.

If Crossley instigated the first revolution – audience ratings themselves and exposure as the key measure – then it was Art Nielsen who embedded technology into audience ratings. Crossley, like Hooper, used self-reporting by audiences as the key technique for collecting the data on ratings. Nielsen thought that there was another step to take which would remove self-reporting altogether. He developed mechanical devices to register whether people indeed had the radio set turned on and tuned in to a particular station.

Arthur C. Nielsen (and the 'Black Box')

Arthur C. Nielsen set the scene for Nielsen's dominance of national audience ratings in the United States when he tied technology to the measurement of exposure. The legacy in the United States of this move has been to create, to use the economists' phrase, a path dependency in American audience measurement. Technology became with Nielsen's introduction of the 'black box', the Audimeter, an intimate part of the data collection process and of the convention itself, in the 1940s. In 1936, Nielsen acquired the Audimeter from two inventors, Bob Elder and Louis Woodruff, who had developed it to pick up and record frequencies tuned on a radio (Beville 1988: 20). The compiled information was stored on a wax drum then transferred to film and ultimately solid state memory. Nielsen then spent the next few years developing the technology and proof of concept for its use as an alternative ratings technology to measure radio and later television set on/off status and channel/station tuning. Nielsen began providing audience estimates to the radio industry in December 1942; by 1946 he had coverage of 63 per cent of all US homes, and by 1949 the company had 97 per cent (Beville 1988: 21–2).

Prior to his involvement in broadcast ratings Arthur Nielsen ran his own market research company specializing in testing the viability of new products and determining the market shares of products in retail stores. Nielsen is credited with formulating, popularizing and institutionalizing the concept of market share through his Drug Index and Food Index, established in 1933 and 1934 respectively. A.C. Nielsen was a well-established market research firm before it moved into broadcast ratings. The company's move into ratings was a natural extension of Arthur Nielsen's longstanding concern to measure market share in its various manifestations and to measure, as Gale Metzger recalls, 'the whole marketing process, step-by-step'. Metzger reckons that Nielsen was one of the first who 'wanted to report on all elements of the marketing process in a single measurement'. He also points out that Nielsen came at the ratings from a different position. Unlike the other notable audience researchers Nielsen was not an attitude researcher:

> In the early days, there were attitude researchers who became involved with media audience measurement. George Gallop is one name that comes to mind. The social research approach involved asking people what they did; what stations or programs they listened to. That was in contrast to an engineering perspective where a meter was used to record what was happening in the home. Art believe the metered measurement was more precise and a superior technique. He sold that point of view effectively.

For Metzger the turning point for Nielsen's metered approach came with the Advertising Research Foundation's review of audience measurement, which concluded that the meter measurement of set tuning was a superior way to estimate audience size:

> They affirmed that audiences should be defined by set tuning. That conclusion created great turmoil. There were very angry exchanges. Some in the industry objected strongly to the ARF taking that position. They felt it was highly prejudicial and wrong. Their feelings were expressed in angry terms. The appendix to the ARF report includes a strongly expressed minority opinion.

For his part Beville reckons Nielsen won 'handily' because of a superior product offering greater coverage: 'he had a continuous meter service that operated around the clock, 48 weeks a year' (Beville 1988: 22). Whatever the sources of 'industry endorsement', Nielsen was able to expand its media services in size and scope after 1950. Its national sample size was increased and with the development of TV as a mass medium it extended its coverage to television eventually moving from radio to television as that medium came to dominate broadcast advertising revenues. Nielsen was able to use its radio sample to leverage its television coverage, as Gale Metzger observes:

> When television came in the early 50s, Nielsen had a national panel of radio homes. At the time, they were measuring in-home use of radio. Television was measured by metering television sets that were purchased by the radio sample homes. As 10 per cent of the homes got a television set, they measured those 10 per cent. The sample size grew as television ownership grew.

But Nielsen was not able to organize the convention in quite the way he wanted to: he, like Metzger, felt that the major users of the ratings – the media companies, the advertising agencies and the advertisers – should equally contribute to its support. But this is not what emerged. It is worth quoting Metzger in full here:

> The history has been that the rating services' revenues have been at least 80 per cent from the media. Media often pay 90 per cent or more. For network radio, they paid about 95 per cent of the bill. Others paid what amount to token fees. The agency/advertiser perspective is that they pay for audience measurement when they buy the media. But their voice at the table is effectively a secondary voice rather than a primary voice. I've always felt and Art Nielsen advocated originally, that the bill should be split up a third, a third, a third – a third by the media, a third by the agencies and a third by the advertisers. That was never achieved. The Nielsen national service had relatively more revenue from the advertisers and agencies than other services. For print, publishers paid virtually the entire cost for audience measurement.

For Metzger this financing structure privileged the media companies' voice at the expense of the advertiser and advertising agency/market research voice. He sees this as the conceptual flaw in this financing structure:

> It puzzled me because of the interest in the return on investment for advertising. If one is spending hundreds of millions of dollars on advertising, it seems obvious to me that better, more accurate measurement would pay for itself. If advertisers could get an extra 5 per cent or 10 per cent efficiency out of advertising budgets, it would be an extraordinary return.
>
> I believe many advertiser research personnel see that potential also, but they were never able to sell that to the management. Art Nielsen worked very hard to achieve closer advertiser involvement. Whenever he had something new or different, he would always get on a train and go

to Cincinnati. That was the home of Proctor & Gamble. They were the industry bellwether – in his mind. If you could sell Proctor & Gamble you could sell anybody. They would set the pace. Proctor was more active in the earlier days and, at the same time, very guarded because they didn't want to 'throw their power around' and be exposed to accusations of anti-trust activities. So anyway the funding issue was a significant focus. We had advertisers who wanted to put up money, but instead of millions of dollars they were putting up tens or hundreds of thousands of dollars. While that is different dimension, it was moving in the direction of getting them more involved. (Metzger 2008)

Nielsen's Audimeter did not just suddenly appear without debate among those who had an interest in its use. Audience ratings are not just numbers and data collection techniques but a complex convention. C.E. Hooper sold his methodology in academic papers and in the commercial market. His telephone coincidental technique was, he argued, a better way to capture exposure than Crossley's telephone recall method. Nielsen did not change exposure as the core metric – he changed the technology for counting it. Nielsen funded his own innovation out of his own pocket and had a very different relationship to advertisers and other clients compared with Archibald Crossley. Crossley was employed by CAB but did not own CAB. Nielsen, however, had to convince parties to the convention that this new way of measuring exposure was superior to previous methods. This did not mean that Nielsen did not use diaries or other techniques to capture audience engagement with programmes or their demographics. It did mean that he set up the machine as an independent error-free source. Measuring radio exposure in a diary or by telephone appeared by contrast to be unreliable, because people might not fill out the diary at the time of listening to programmes or they might misremember or mis-record which stations they were listening to at particular times.

Nielsen emerged as a near monopoly player in the metropolitan television markets in the United States along with Arbitron in the radio markets. While there continued to be a range of smaller audience ratings providers, the United States became characterized by monopoly provision in broadcast ratings with the ratings and Nielsen becoming synonymous. The historical experience of Australia with audience-ratings methodology, technology and ratings firm provision was significantly different. Exposure was still the core measure, but technology was not seen as the answer to error. While Nielsen was consolidating its market power as a near monopoly provider of television ratings Australia supported two competing ratings firms operating in the same market.

Bill McNair and George Anderson

Rather, as commodities themselves, the ratings were constructed in response to market pressures, including competition and monopolization as well as continuities and discontinuities in demand. The ratings producer was no scientist motivated by curiosity, but rather a company seeking its self-interest through the profitable manipulation of demand. E.R. Meehan (Meehan 1984: 201)

Meehan gives the impression that audience ratings emerged in an uncontested way, part of a capitalist engine that discovered research and measurement and simply adapted them as a way of increasing profit. However, audience ratings and survey forms of media research undertaken for advertisers, producers and broadcasters have been an integral part of our broadcast system for so long that it is difficult to see how much work had to go into constructing them, and then having them accepted and utilized by the different industry players. In the case of Australia, compared with Archibald Crossley's experience, early promoters of ratings and media survey research more generally had to invent, and then sell, the very concept of ratings and survey research to reluctant radio stations, advertisers and advertising agencies. Like Crossley, Hooper and Nielsen, what they were selling were new forms of knowledge, practices and techniques associated with the application of social survey research techniques as integral to the very management and orientation of the businesses associated with broadcasting. Typically what was being promoted and accepted was the general concept of 'scientific research' – market research.

Bill McNair, the founder of the McNair ratings system, gave his account of the need for audience ratings in his 1937 work, *Radio Advertising in Australia*. McNair lamented that in Australia 'systematic research has hardly been tried. The agencies with competently staffed research departments are in the minority; and on matters affecting newspaper and magazine circulations and radio owners' listening habits very little information has been collected' (McNair 1937: 44). Of those who tried to survey audiences, 'in most cases the results have not been published, this has been of little use to the great body of advertisers. The few surveys on which information can be obtained have differed widely in method and scope' (McNair 1937: 248). At the same time, McNair noted the inappropriate uptake and problems of market research in the United States, where market and audience research had just taken off.

In America when consumer research first obtained recognition, the new technique was quickly abused. Business executives with no statistical training would run off long questionnaires abounding in irrelevant and ambiguous questions, and have them taken by untrained interviewers from door to door through all sorts of unrepresentative localities. Completed questionnaires which showed unfavourable results were freely discarded in order to make the final percentages more impressive. Such methods could not but cast discredit on the whole practice of consumer research. (McNair 1937: 248)

Bill McNair saw himself as promoting audience and market research that was independent and rigorous. His book is a report on his own surveys of radio audiences and listening habits of the time, pitched to convince the media industry of the need for sustained independent research. McNair attempted to establish the academic credentials of audience ratings by submitting his 1937 book as a PhD to a university in the United Kingdom. His application was knocked back but his academic interest in audience ratings remained, like that of his competitive counterpart George Anderson. Bill McNair's study was the first to touch on specifically 'audience' issues. But there were attempts at audience segmentation before McNair's survey.

J. Walter Thompson (JWT), McNair's employer at this time, hired psychologists A.H. Martin and Rudolph Simmat to measure consumer attitudes towards advertising. Simmat was research manager for JWT in Sydney in 1929 and began some of the earliest research into the segmentation of audiences. Simmat divided Australian society into four market segments based on income and housewives. Classes A and B were high income housewives; C and D were average or below average income housewives. Class D was 'barely sufficient or even insufficient income to provide itself with the necessities of life. Normally Class D is not greatly important except to the manufacturer of low price, necessary commodities' (Simmat 1933: 12). Simmat standardized interviewing techniques because experience had shown him that women were usually more effective as fieldworkers than men: 'Experiments have indicated that persons with a very high grade of intelligence are unsatisfactory for interviewing housewives ... usually a higher grade of intelligence is required to interview the higher class of housewife than is required to interview the lower grade housewife' (Simmat 1933: 13). Simmat and his team had interviewed 32,000 Australian housewives by 1932. Advertising was then targeted to specific audiences, with sophistication 'definitely soft-pedaled' for Classes C and D: 'We believe that farce will be more popular with our *Rinso* [detergent] market than too much subtlety.' Soap and detergent were the major advertising markets during the 1920s and crossed all market segments.

McNair does not mention Martin or Simmat's work in his book, even though he was familiar with it as JWT also supported the McNair radio survey. McNair used similar stratification variables, with the home as the key focus. Gwen Nelson, arguably the first Australian woman in a senior capacity within audience ratings research, managed Bill McNair's sampling, fieldwork and interviews. Nelson spoke to us about her experience of audience measurement. McNair used interviews and recall methods to ascertain audience ratings:

> The household was a household, it was a family. They weren't scattered here, there and everywhere. There was one radio set and the family sat around and listened to the radio. The advertiser thought it was ridiculous, nobody would sit around and listen to a voice. They'll read it when they see it in print, in the newspaper, and they'll believe it, but they won't take any notice of an odd voice talking to them over the radio. And also, the housewife was always at home, or mostly at home, we had no problem with what we would do with all the outs we found. We were able to get a very reasonable cross section of all the groups and all social structures, which was ideal for personal interviews.

For Nelson at that time the interview had several advantages over its Australian alternative of the diary:

> I was brought up on personal interviews, and I left on personal interviews. I didn't like diaries, I never liked diaries. Though I must admit, today you couldn't possibly work as we worked. It would be an impossibility to do house to house interviews. You wouldn't find the people at home. As for phones, we didn't use them at all. The phone ownership wasn't very high, and it was so impersonal that your interview had to get the confidence of the person you were interviewing, and make them feel that they were really contributing to something. Which I think they did. And they're the early days. They were the days … I staggered for 28 years, but I mostly … was in Sydney quite a lot, but I did mostly interstate work. Every month I went somewhere. We were doing three surveys a year in Melbourne, two in Adelaide, two in Brisbane and one in Perth. I went to Perth every year for twenty years. And we had teams of interviewers. We did quite a lot of New Zealand. But I suppose we had two hundred casual interviewers throughout Australia and New Zealand, and we just called on them whenever we needed them, and we paid them at a casual rate and they were thrilled to work for a week or so. (Nelson 2000)

At a time when the United States was using telephone interviews and telephone coincidentals as the standard, McNair was using door-to-door interviews. In a way they had to: telephone penetration in Australia was much lower than in the United States ruling out as Bill McNair observed that method for Australian conditions. At the same time the cost of these interviews meant that ratings sweeps would be more limited than in the United States. Finally, for decades in the twentieth century, Australia was not able to be grasped as a 'national audience' in any media or in any media organization conceptualization. There are various historical reasons for this arrangement. First, there was an industry resistance to measurement of audiences; ironically from the media itself, like radio. Second, there were, over time, limitations in what ratings could do in their classifications or which areas, geographically, they could reasonably cover in frequency. This meant that particular cities and regional markets were always the targets with the consequence that a national ratings figure was not the focus of the research as in the United States; the focus was instead on individual markets – the domain, in the United States, of 'local ratings'.

Bill McNair, however, never gained the ascendancy over the Australian ratings market that Art Nielsen achieved in the United States. McNair's chief rival was George Anderson.

George Anderson had a background in regional and then Sydney radio where he acted as station manager of 2GB and sales manager of the Macquarie Radio Network. Don Neely, one of his executives, recalls that Anderson became interested in media research, because he wanted to know 'who was on the other end of the microphone, listening':

> He corresponded, I believe, with some of the Americans who were active at that time, including Hooper, who was doing his Hooper ratings, and so George struck out on his own with a capital of fifty pounds. He founded the company and started measuring radio audiences. In between times, he'd found time to be a Colonel in the army, so he was a busy man and a real character. A very determined man. (Neely 2000)

George Anderson started with personal interview and recall, but after talking to colleagues in the United States and reading the research of the National Association of Broadcasters and C.E. Hooper, he settled on diaries as the preferred method of data collection. In 1947 Anderson wrote a confidential report to the Australian Association of National Advertisers, *Report on the Effectiveness of the Radio Listener Diary in Measuring Radio Audiences in Australia*. The extract at Figure 2.1 shows that he was familiar with all the major methods, including Nielsen's Audimeter.

Anderson concluded in his report to the advertisers that the Audimeter solution was too capital-intensive, and that the most reliable method for Australia was the Radio Listener Diary, used by C.E. Hooper as an adjunct to the coincidental

---

2. When, in June 1944, The Anderson Analysis of Broadcasting commenced to measure radio audiences in Australia, there were two methods in general use, viz:-

   (a) The Telephone Method, by which people with telephones were contacted by telephone and asked what radio station their radio set was tuned to:-

      (i) at the time of the call (the Co-incidental Telephone Method) and/or

      (ii) during a short period prior to the call (the Recall Telephone Method.)

   (b) The Personal Interview Method, by which people were interviewed in their homes to find out:-

      (i) The station being listened to at the time of the interview (the Co-incidental Personal Interview Method) and/or

      (ii) The stations which were listened to during a period prior to the interview (the Recall Personal Interview Method.)

3. At the same time (June 1944) two other methods were being developed as follows:-

   (a) The Mechanical Recorder Method, by which a mechanical recording device was attached to a radio set and, by means of a moving tape, recorded the times when the set was switched on and off and the time when each station was tuned in and tuned out.

   (b) The Radio Listener Diary Method, by which people in their homes kept a record, in diary form, of their listening during a number of consecutive days.

Figure 2.1 Extract showing description of methods
Source: Nielsen Historical Archive

telephone method. Anderson attached a sample diary for the advertisers, shown at Figure 2.2.

As we have seen, Bill McNair, by contrast, came to a completely different conclusion and settled on personal interview and recall. No doubt Anderson hoped that his report to the advertisers would knock McNair out of the race. However, quite the opposite happened. Both methods, personal interview and recall and diary, ran side by side as audience measurement technique until the two firms merged in the 1970s. For the whole period from 1944 through to the merger, the debate about the two methodologies was both personal and public. Bill McNair's son Ian McNair, himself a major figure in Australian audience research, takes up the story:

It was an argument that went on between the two research companies. It was a very public argument, because my dad liked sending out circulars and letters, and quotations and methodology arguments and George responded in his way, so the argument was going on all the time.

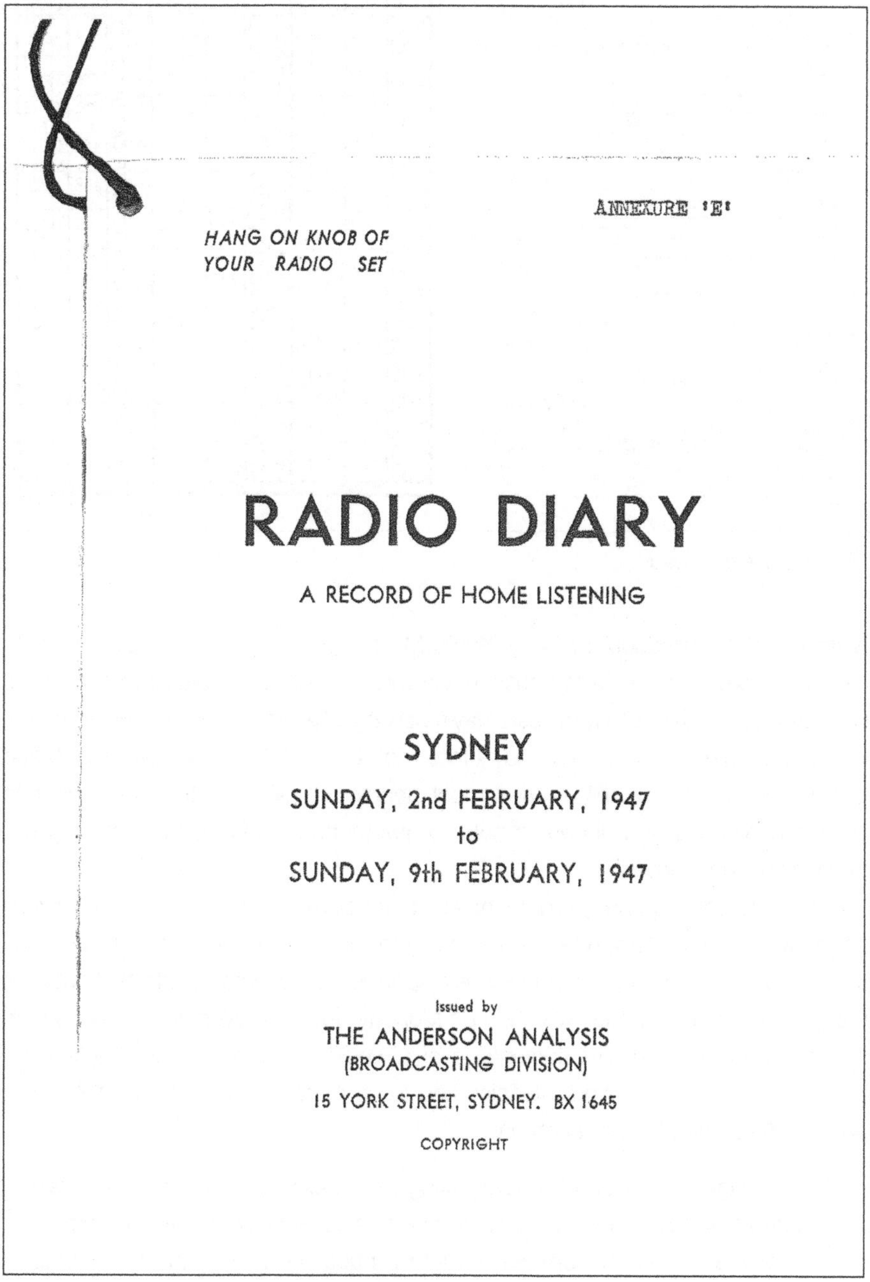

ANNEXURE 'E'

HANG ON KNOB OF
YOUR RADIO SET

RADIO DIARY

A RECORD OF HOME LISTENING

SYDNEY

SUNDAY, 2nd FEBRUARY, 1947
to
SUNDAY, 9th FEBRUARY, 1947

Issued by
THE ANDERSON ANALYSIS
(BROADCASTING DIVISION)

15 YORK STREET, SYDNEY. BX 1645

COPYRIGHT

Figure 2.2 Early historical example of Anderson Analysis Radio Ratings Diary
Source: Nielsen Historical Archive

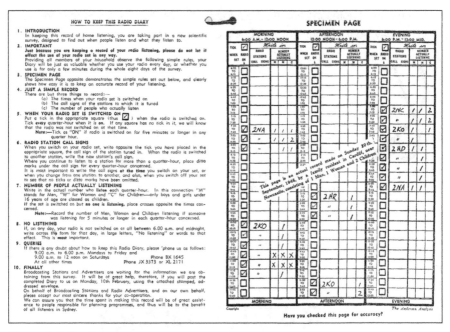

Figure 2.2 *Continued*

From the 1940s through the early 1960s McNair did personal interviews for both radio and television, house to house, using very controlled samples and concerned with 'yesterday's listening and yesterday's viewing'. The McNair company argument was that because it was 'yesterday's listening' it was 'fresh in people's mind, and they would be able to tell us, and most people do tell, exactly what happened yesterday. Not exactly, but quarter hour by quarter hour, as far as their listening and viewing was concerned'.

The Anderson Company argument was that people do fill out diaries reasonably diligently. For Ian McNair, what 'won the day for diaries was the fact that by getting seven days of recording from the same respondent they were able to find out from the same people what they watched on Monday, Tuesday, Wednesday and so on, and get a good cumulative audience over a week'. By contrast with the face-to-face, one-day recall method, samples had to be matched each day so there was going to be a sample error each day.

So you might have got a 30 news rating on 7 today, but it might have been 35 tomorrow and 37 the next day, and no one never knew if that was sample error or real. Some stations still bought it because they might have come out better on that survey than they did on the Anderson. So there was still a market for it. And the argument that we – McNair's – tried to put very strong was that ours was more reliable because it was what people remembered yesterday, and it wasn't just the people who filled out a diary. (McNair 2000)

The motives for collecting audience ratings were also personal, which often left Anderson especially on a financial tightrope because of George Anderson's commitment to methodology and service. Don Neely recalls Anderson over-providing to country TV stations 'for the reason George said, "it's their livelihood. Forget the agencies, it's the station that's got to live or die by these numbers, and I want them to be right".'

> The fact that we've quoted a price and are providing a service which was more expensive than we got was quite irrelevant to George. As long as he was right. And that's why the company was never really financially flush. McNair's on the other hand tended to go the other way. And I noticed this when we got together, for example in regional television, they only did it one year, and the spread of diaries they used was abysmal. They might have used twenty drop points in a market, ours would have used sixty. So you can imagine the cost differential. (Don Neely 2000)

By the mid-1960s McNair moved, under industry pressure, to adopt the diary system. For nearly the next decade there were two providers operating two systems based on the same ratings instrument. This dual system of audience ratings and its ongoing public display, including the arguments over methodology that were presented in many public fora, had practical purpose for clients. One system was a check on the other. No client bought one set of ratings without buying the other. The ratings could be used to present a case to advertisers as to why they should advertise on a station or be used in programming decisions. Only a minority of stations would ignore the ratings surveys, as Des Foster, general manager of 2GB at the time, notes:

> They weren't cheap, and some stations, I recall, who didn't do well in the ratings and were not doing well, revenue wise, would say 'we don't want them', they didn't have the surveys, they didn't want to know about them. My recollection was that 2KY might have been one of those stations at the time, and they took that view that surveys only damaged them. They're far better off going to clients and talking to them and selling them advertising and not raising the question of surveys. The big problem with surveys – there's always a debate in the industry, of course – not a problem with surveys, a problem with the way you deal with them. That is, when you have a good survey from the stations point of view, the station's sales people all want to race around the advertisers and say 'look what a good survey we've got'. And then, three

months later the positions reverse, they're telling you something else and perhaps one of the negative effects of that over the years is that there has been not enough selling of the radio ... the merits of radio as a medium ... there has been a much greater emphasis, unfortunately, in selling the merits of *my* radio station as a medium. And I think the industry has suffered to some extend because of that. (Foster 2000)

As the Australian market grew, including the introduction of new media like television, so did the cost of collecting audience ratings. Who should bear this cost, as mentioned by Gale Metzger in Chapter 1, is an ongoing debate in the ratings convention. McNair and Anderson finally merged in 1973 because of industry pressure to do so and affordability. The diary method then became the main method of data collection.

The main single reason was that being seven days, from the same respondent, we're able to work out reach frequencies much better than we could with the single day samples. And it wasn't so much personal interviews versus anything else, it was the fact that you got data over a whole week from a diary, that really persuaded us to continue on with that method for both radio and television. That's what we did, right from 1973 onwards. Anderson's were in town and they came across to the same building as us, 40 Miller Street North Sydney, and no one was sacked or anything because of the merger because McNair's continued doing their market research as well, and so we're able to employ everyone in the merger without laying off anyone. We're very proud of that. A lot of the market research that McNair's were doing was able to continue throughout the seventies. (McNair 2000)

Interestingly, the diary system ran in Australia up until 1991 when peoplemeters were finally introduced for the television market. Diaries, however, are still used for many remote parts of Australia and in Darwin, and remain the only means of collecting audience data for radio broadcasting markets. Commercial Radio Australia's *Global Overview & Australian Industry Position* emphatically stated in 2007 that 'Australia currently uses the diary system, the only proven and reliable ratings method used around the world at present. Electronic measurement is currently not in use country-wide anywhere in the world as the sole radio audience measurement system, nor is it regarded anywhere as industry currency, except in a few areas in Switzerland and one city, Houston, in the USA' (Commercial Radio Australia 2007).

Arbitron, the monopoly provider for radio ratings in the United States, has, by contrast, for many years been trying to replace the paper diary with a Personal People Meter (PPM). The PPM is like a pager. It can pick up digital codes from different media and send the information to a database. Arbitron has used paper and pencil diary systems for radio since 1965. But the Australian radio broadcasting market continues to reject the technology push. Australia's Commercial Radio Australia, however, argues that the PPM:

- Costs 2 to 3 times the cost of the diary system

- Has no real evidence of long-term compliance across all demographics – e.g. once listening is lost, it is lost and cannot be regained

- Drops in breakfast listening have been recorded in trials with no valid evidence provided for device purveyors' explanation that 'people must have been over-reporting breakfast listening'! And industry does not accept this explanation as no other daypart has been supposedly over-reported. We do not believe that tens of millions of diary keepers across the world over the last 50 years have all over-reported breakfast and no other daypart. (Commercial Radio Australia 2007)

The Australian situation gives us some tantalizing insights into the complexity of the audience-ratings convention and how formal and informal agreements work within this compact. While both the US and Australian markets agreed on exposure as the core measure there were fundamental differences between them in the *speed* by which new innovations or technologies were adopted and arguments about the validity of different technologies. In the United States the machine is still seen as the best solution to capturing exposure. However, competitive pressure in the United States – with Arbitron seemingly under-reporting radio audiences – has led to radio networks putting pressure on Arbitron by inviting Nielsen to introduce a paper diary system. The entry of Nielsen into the diary radio market, however, is more likely to be a stalking-horse attempt to force Arbitron to change its methods. This type of intervention itself is also not new, and often functions as an 'informal' way of creating change, as we will see later.

While the recall and diary methodologies continued to run side by side in Australia until the merger of McNair and Anderson in 1973, the underlying conceptualizations of the audience had changed during the 1950s. Programming formats and attention to demographics became interlinked. There was, by the time television became standard, no radio or television manager that was not looking carefully at the demographics of their audience and measuring their performance by the audience ratings. Australia also differed from the United States in its methodology and approach. As you can see from the accounts of senior participants in the creation of the audience ratings system in Australia, there was a dedication to the art of audience ratings in and of itself, to the point where a company was willing to lose money to ensure accuracy. Why did Australia keep two competing ratings systems, both of which collected data from the same audiences? Why would hard-nosed station managers and media magnates use two methodologies that produced different figures and were expensive?

The answer lies in the character of the competition between McNair and Anderson. Both thought that their methods were the best. Both were respected in the media industry and both were trusted. When the audience became more fragmented and there were more stations to measure, the economics of keeping two ratings agencies changed. But embedded in that older system was a perception of checks and balances, even if it was costly to run two methods of audience measurement. Those checks and balances, interestingly, did not disappear when the two companies merged in the 1970s. Don Neely recalls:

> The merger happened at the end of 1973, which saved the problem for the industry, because there was still an amount of sympathy for McNair, and because he'd been in the industry for so long, having been dumped in the tendering situation. So they were delighted when we announced that we were getting together. But they insisted that the methodology be the Anderson methodology, the format was the Anderson format, in fact it was an Anderson show. Except that McNair was part of the deal. And that really did help, having the two got together. There was never really enough market for two companies in Australia. One company made a lot more sense. So the industry was happy. They had a research committee, they and we agreed to have an auditor, Dr Arthur Meadows was the first auditor, and he would come in and go through all the diaries and all the paperwork to see if we did what we said we'd do. And I believe today there still is an auditor. (Neely 2000)

The shift to an audited regime in radio audience ratings in Australia, the authors would argue, is a direct consequence of the way that McNair and Anderson developed over time. The dual system of audience ratings acted as a default audit and indeed as an integral part of the audience-ratings convention.

New Forms of Knowledge about Audiences

The measurement of audiences led to the creation of a whole new language and form of knowledge centred on media buying as a speciality. Once all the results could be received in a form that was easy to manipulate by slide rule and then computer other kinds of pictures of the audience could be created. As we have seen, decisions about what counts as correct measurements in the world of audience ratings are negotiated. A method such as telephone recall might be argued as valid at one point in time and invalid at another. Ironically, C.E. Hooper, for example, returned to recall later in his career, despite arguing strenuously against it when Crossley ran recall and Hooper ran telephone coincidental. Arguments about methodology, of course, are also arguments about what to accept as methodology and what trade-offs to make in the process. Choosing exposure itself is a trade-off in that it is an indirect, not direct, measure of audience like or dislike of a programme or station. It is automatically assumed in exposure that ten minutes of listening is ten minutes of listening, when in fact people may have done other things or, indeed, very little listening at all.

The audience ratings numbers, however, did not only affect commercial decisions on media buying. The whole process of using audience ratings created a new type of knowledge to deal with the complexities of translating audiences as raw figures into analytic categories.

On the media side, for example, media analysis tools were created to assess the reach and frequency associated with different media and the costs to be charged against them. Reach refers to unduplicated exposures or gross impressions and the number of different people exposed to the message. Frequency refers to the average number of exposures and how many times an audience is exposed to a message. Outdoor, newspapers and magazines tend to be the best media for frequency. Broadcast advertising and magazines tend to be the best for reach. The best combination is found in radio.

A cost per thousand (CPM) calculation is made on how much it costs to deliver 1,000 gross impressions or to reach 1,000 listeners, viewers, readers, households and so on. CPM allows media planners to compare media based on audience and cost. The lowest cost per thousand medium therefore is the most efficient.

For print, when the cost of the advertisement is known: the CPM is the cost of advertisement x 1,000 circulation; when audience data are known: the CPM is the cost of 1 advertisement x 1,000 readers reached; with broadcast media: the CPM is the cost of 1 advertisement x 1,000 homes reached. Suppose that an advertiser can buy a television commercial minute for US$1,200 during a situation comedy that reaches four million people and a commercial minute for US$1,000 during a football telecast that reaches only one million people. When the costs per minute are compared the situation comedy seems to be a better buy:

Situation Comedy:	Football Game:
$1200 = $0.3 CPM	$1000 = $1 CPM
4000 (000) total audience	1000 (000) total audience

But if an advertiser's target is men aged 18–49, the situation comedy may not be so attractive. If only one million men watch the comedy and all the football viewers are men, the football game is a better buy.

Situation Comedy: Football Game:
$1200 = $1.2 CPM $1000 = $1 CPM
1000 (000) men (18–49)   1000 (000) men (18–49)

The comedy costs US$1.2 CPM and the game only US$1. Thus, football is a better buy for the advertiser because it reaches the target audience at a lower unit cost. Lest this hypothetical example prove misleading, it should be emphasized that it is deliberately simplistic. Many other factors may be taken into account when measuring an audience and in general prime-time Australian television audiences don't normally subdivide so markedly. In prime time stations are competing for the whole family. They normally attract the middle to lower income groups, as those on higher incomes tend to watch the Australian Broadcasting Corporation (ABC) or be relatively 'light' television viewers. The most desirable age group to reach may be the 25–39 demographic as it delivers the best combination of viewing numbers, spending power, flexibility of attitudes and predictability of tastes.

Again speaking generally, a show must score high ratings to survive in prime time – between 6 p.m. and 10 p.m. If it is rating less than 'twenties', or 20 per cent of homes with televisions, it probably won't survive. If it is screened on a commercial station and scores ratings of between 20 and 30 it is probably getting a fairly even share of the market in Sydney, Melbourne, Adelaide and Brisbane. If it is getting 'thirties' it is probably doing very well indeed as the ABC typically accounts for between 10 and 20 per cent of the homes using television and Special Broadcasting Service (SBS) for around 5 per cent. When an ABC public service show goes into 'thirties', commercial station managers often complain that the corporation is not serving its minority audiences. Ratings of programmes outside prime time are another matter. Off-peak ratings of only 2–3 per cent of sets are common and 10 per cent might be considered good. Sets in use vary according to the time of day, the day of the week and the time of the year (higher in the winter, lower in summer). They also vary by city.

All stations seek high rating shows because they tend not only to attract viewers to that particular programme but also to hold them for other programmes. Many stations, for example, often spend more than they reap on the main evening news bulletin because it marks the beginning of prime time and may lock in its audience for the evening. Thus, the sequence of programmes is important because a show following a high-rating programme tends to do better than it otherwise might have done. A series rating thirties can lift a channel out of the economic doldrums by attracting viewers to the channel itself. The station management may then bargain with advertisers, offering them good 'positioning' in the highly rated shows if they will agree to fill several less favoured time spots in slack periods.

Series and serials are the dominant programmes on most prime-time commercial television. But because of the spectacular successes of a handful of drama programmes, many of them produced overseas, it is easy to overrate the viewing loyalties of series. A series is a drama programme in which the same characters appear in successive episodes, each with a self-contained plot. A serial differs in that it has a continuing story line. Such programmes are normally shown for a certain number of episodes at the same time each week, with relatively few changes throughout a TV season. Such repetitive programming gives television viewing a firm structure, attracting viewers back night after night or week after week at the same time. They also know what to expect when they return. Producers in particular like serials because they are cheaper to make than 'episode' or one-off dramas, as they can use the same sets, cast and crew.

But it does not necessarily follow that the viewers of one episode of a series or serial will automatically watch the next, even though they may like it very much and even though they may say they watch every episode. In *Television Audience: Patterns of Viewing* Goodhardt, Ehrenberg and Collins showed that at that time only about 55 per cent of viewers of one episode of a programme would watch the following episode, no matter what the type of programme or content or even when completely different programmes (with similar ratings) were shown in the same timeslot each week. 'Repeat viewing,' they argued, 'therefore appears to be more a function of social habits (i.e. people's availability) than of programme content' (Goodhardt, Ehrenberg and Collins 1975: 125). They also found that the extent to which different programmes share the same viewers also follows a simple pattern. They called this 'the duplicate of viewing law': 'for any two programmes the level of duplication in their audiences depends on the *ratings* of the programme and not on their *content*. One pair of programmes generally has the same degree of audience duplication as any other pair of programmes with the same ratings' (Goodhardt, Ehrenberg and Collins 1975: 126). They also worked out a multiplier constant for audience overlap in the second programme of a series. For example, if the constant or 'proportionality factor' for Nine Network programmes is 1.4 and the rating of the second programme is 20, then the duplication of viewing law states that about 20 x 1.4 = 28 per cent of the audience of the *first* programme will have watched the second programme. That is, the audience overlap generally depends only on the proportionality coefficient (here 1.4) and the programme's rating (here 20) and *not* on programme content. Summing up their findings, the authors say very few viewers of any series see all or most of its episodes. Even self-proclaimed 'regular viewers' are not all that regular.

With the introduction of computers a range of permutations of individual variables is possible. Moreover, with the introduction of peoplemeters, near

Figure 2.3 Sample of in-house and fee-based analysis services

instantaneous data collection became possible as the time of exposure can be transmitted directly to databases. A large range of software packages quickly became available to analyse ratings and other audience research data on users' desktops. In an earlier era there was no intermediary between the ratings firm and their clients. But now media buying, whether in-house or as a separate agency, provides a raft of analytical services that interpret the ratings. The people who do this interpretation are no longer, necessarily, methodologists: they are knowledge brokers in the real sense of the word. Nor is the manipulation of audience data limited to simple classifications.

The early ratings methodologies used families and social class definitions to segment the audience. McNair and Anderson, surprisingly, ran different definitions of the audience up until 1963. McNair used A,B,C,D,E and Anderson used A,B,C (upper, middle, industrial). The age categories for television were also different. For example, in reporting on audience ratings for television Anderson did not use age breakdown in reports until 1961 and then reported on the age ranges 1–15, 16–24, 25–39, 40–54 and 55–99. McNair also did not use age categories until 1963 and then reported on the age categories 0–11, 12–19, 20–35 and 36+. By 1970, however, both McNair and Anderson were using the same age categories for radio and television: 10–17, 18–24, 25–39, 40–54 and 55+. Housewives were their own category in this period, together with reporting on 'housewife lifecycles'. The use of social class definitions also affected the 'argot' or local language for reporting audience ratings. The term 'AB', for example, was first used in one of McNair's reports in 1959; previously the categories had been separate.

Once the audience ratings structure was in place and once it was established by McNair and Anderson and accepted as the currency, changes in the machineries of knowledge became intimately linked to changes in demographics or technology or the needs of stations and programmers. The first big change in the 'simple model' came with the introduction of the transistor radio in the 1950s, and, of course, with television:

Radio was a medium for groups. That's peak time radio. Very few car radios and virtually no portables. So it was all done in the home. Then there was the invention of the transistor. The transistor suddenly made it possible to produce a light little tiny radio set that you could carry around with you. So the technology gave us very very quickly the capability to transform the medium from a group medium, a medium for a family, into a medium for a person, one person. And so that was highly significant. Portable, you could have it in your car, you could take it to the beach, you could do what you like. Portable, personal medium. You don't have one radio in the household. Whereas in the household you might have had a big one in the living room, perhaps one in the kitchen for mum. Now junior's got his own radio, and sis has got her radio and they could all be doing their homework in their different rooms, listening to different programs. This mobility allowed a switch of focus from nighttime radio and radio was never ever to dominate at night again. So what they were able to offer in the daytime was programs for individuals in the daytime and for people on the move, and for people at the beach and for people at leisure, mobility, individuals in their own rooms, in the garden. Suddenly the medium began to transform. And the major emphasis was on music formats.

I think that gave a shove along on the concentration on demographics, also. Suddenly the 12–18 year-old group became a very identifiable segment, 12–18, whatever you like. But I mean all these age demographics became very very relevant and it was possible to tailor programs for them. And instead of thinking in mass terms, mass audience, it was no longer quite so important to be number one in the ratings if you could be number one in 10–17. (Foster 2000)

The whole practice of radio, in this case, changes because of both a new technology and a newly defined and differently valued demographic. At the same time, more data are collected as categories expand and time of collection expands. Diaries collect data in 15 minute segments. Peoplemeters collect it by the second. Agreements on the valuable demographics, however, are not accidents of history, accidents of technology or accidents in measurement. The agreements are a part of ongoing debates within the audience-ratings conventions.

Theorizing the Convention

In modern marketing circles there appears to be a visceral reaction to continuation of the use of A,B,C,D classifications:

> As far as marketing jargon goes, nothing bothers me more than use of the term AB to refer to a demographic target audience. As far as I'm concerned, all it stands for is Absolute Bollocks. The term originates from the social-economic classifications of the English class system. It could never have originated here as Aussies have no class ... When was the last time you heard a consumer self-refer as an AB? Just imagine the scene in a restaurant: 'Waiter, why is my main course taking so long you lowly D, and tell the chef he's a useless FG. This is outrageous – I'm an AB don't you know!' (Joseph 2008: 17)

Joseph is not disputing exposure as the key measure in ratings, but rather aspects of its use. The early regime in audience ratings may appear to be a simple model, but in fact it was and remains a complex agreement between many often conflicting parties on what should be counted and how frequently, even if there are different ways of 'cutting up' the demographics of exposure. The need for standards or conventions governing measurement is not new, as Stigler has pointed out (Stigler 1999). Stigler uses the 'Trial of the Pyx' to show the differences between 'standards' and 'statistics' and the role of sampling. The Trial of the Pyx system was created in 1150. The trial was where the mints' coinage was put to test: there were standard and statistical methods. A standard was needed for comparison to tell if a newly minted coin was as promised. For example, as a standard of fineness, a bar of gold was retained as a reference. Statistical methods were needed because the sheer volume of the coinage makes the individual weighing of a coin impossible. Tests of fineness were destructive and made tests of each coin impossible. Sampling, as a consequence, was absolutely necessary.

> The earliest documents are not specific about how the samples would be drawn, but it is impossible to believe that the different (and very suspicious) parties would have been satisfied with a noticeably biased selection, and the documents support this. But sampling was not the only statistical method born of necessity in this trial; there were two others of note. One of these was the mean. In order to avoid having vaguely understood uncertainties of weighing mask major variations in the weight of coins, the coins (like Kobel's feet) were measured in the aggregate, say 100 at a time – essentially it was the average weight of the tested coins that was compared with the standard. Of course from the point of view of experimental design, this was admirable – the aggregate was subject to one measurement error rather than 100. And

there was yet another statistical method employed, an allowance for variability: because mint technology was not perfected, it was granted by all that some allowance had to be made for variability. If the coins weighed too little, the barons were being cheated and the acceptance of the coins in circulation was jeopardized. If the coins weighed too much, the larger coins would be culled from circulation, melted, and recoined, with the profit going to the merchant. Neither situation was tolerable. The allowance that the contract specific was called the 'remedy,' since measures outside these limits would need to be remedied by the master of the Mint. (Stigler 1999: 367)

'Allowance for variability' that was made in the case of the Mint is no different from the 'allowance for error' in modern audience surveys, which will be discussed in the next chapter. What is important from Stigler's history of sampling is the recognition that agreement on measures and standards may not only be a scientific matter. The negotiations around standards are often complex and who is accepted as arbiter equally complex.

Exposure as the core measure in modern audience ratings has often been debated by the ratings methodologists and its weaknesses betrayed, yet the parties have agreed to accept the weaknesses. Where improvements have been proposed, like Art Nielsen's Audimeter, the 'superior' method of measuring exposure has to be argued and sold. New categories of audience, likewise, are not static or immediately universally accepted, and agreement is needed on any changes to the convention. The measure and the standard remained much the same for many years because more complex analytics were not required, and not because early audience ratings experts had no idea how to create more complex definitions of demographics based on exposure data.

There are two levels at which exposure, the standard, can become contested:

1 the method by which exposure data is collected (the measuring instruments, like telephone coincidental versus recall); and,

2 the analysis and classification of that data (demographics, sizes of audiences, and so on).

The dynamism and ongoing fact of this contestation is little talked about and only sometimes comes to the surface in key debates about audience ratings and their validity. What has to be recognized, however, is that this dynamism has an inherently democratic aspect to it and is built-in to the convention. In particular, the adoption of modern audience ratings means that the data collection methods and analytics need to be transparent. Hypoing is still not acceptable in the convention. What this means in practice is that countries like China are adopting measures and standards that will affect the presentation of their audiences to the global market. If China seeks to distort its audience for national purposes or to influence the international market, then it will be seen to be breaching the ratings convention.

China is quickly becoming an established ratings user. China originally teamed up with one of the largest ratings providers, Taylor Nelson Sofres (TNS). Chinese TV viewers are measured by peoplemeters and the radio users by diary (as they are in western countries). There is one panel (sample) of 4,000 households to represent 1,199,564,000 people in China, as the national panel. There is also measurement at city and province level and where peoplemeters are not possible for television measurement diaries are used (in Australia cities like Darwin are still measured by diary for television).

It is not at all clear how a global audience-ratings convention might work, but there can be little doubt that audience ratings are expanding on all continents. What we do know is that audience ratings as they have developed in western industrial countries have a *dual identity*. Audience ratings are not like other forms of social science survey research because they require a higher level of scrutiny than other types of research. They are at one moment a standard by which media markets

Table 2.1 Structure of China's TV panels

	Number of Panels	Sample Size	Universe '000
National Meter	1	4,000	1,199,564
City Meters	43	9,950	103,042
Provincial Meters	4	2,050	155,969
City Diaries	125	15,500	106,612
Provincial Diaries	21	12,400	917,077
Total	194	43,900	

Source: CSM Media Research

Table 2.2 Structure of China's radio panels

	Number of Panels	Sample Size	Universe '000
City Diaries (constant)	13	3,900	32,216
City Diaries (3 sweeps)	6	1,800	13,386
City Diaries (4 sweeps)	13	3,900	14,758
Total	32	9,600	

Source: CSM Media Research

make financial decisions and at another moment a public agreement, a convention, on what counts as an audience.

Summary

Broadcasters, advertisers, universities, media, ratings firms, government and equipment manufacturers, among others, are all involved in both the creation of audience ratings and their use. In Chapter 3 we will see in more detail how ratings intellectuals crossed over from university to industry. The broadcast audience-ratings convention, or standard, on the authors' historical analysis, has had several important components. The convention:

1 is based on exposure as the key measurement;

2 must appeal to the inherent correctness of the measurement;

3 uses a probability, statistical, sample;

4 delivers a 'single number';

5 is syndicated to reduce costs to subscribers;

6 has generally been third-party (the ratings firm, except in the case of Crossley, has been separate from the advertisers or the stations);

7 is expected to work in the public interest (that is, accurately to represent the public audience).

Unlike McNair and Anderson, Archibald Crossley did not have the same control over his destiny even though broadcasters and advertisers could and did put pressure on the two Australian broadcast ratings companies over time. By the 1940s the principle of 'current opinion/view/actions' based on probability sampling principles as the basis for future estimates was established in the United States and Australia. The broadcast ratings built by Crossley drew on the credibility of opinion polling and came to occupy a similar position as regular repeatable information to be used predictively (Beville 1988).

The early ratings methodologies used families and social class definitions to segment the audience. McNair and Anderson even ran different definitions of the audience up until 1963. The age categories for television were also different. The aim of this methodology was to produce relatively simple data for the production of figures for buying and selling data.

The United States and Australia did not differ significantly on this side of the methodology – the 'single number' principle governed media buying. However, as discussed, the audience ratings differed significantly. The history of audience ratings is not therefore simply a history of the statistics of ratings. We have seen that there are significant differences between the American and Australian audience-ratings conventions in practice even though they share a very similar overarching convention. The United States for much of its history has had a 'competitive' model in which Nielsen came to dominate as a free-standing company, now owned by private equity shareholders. Australia has had a succession of models: first competing providers with different methodologies pursued with integrity; and then a broadcaster-defined ratings contract which ratings companies tender for and in which broadcasters call the shots, with ratings owned by the networks but subject to auditing. In Australia the broadcast ratings companies themselves went out of their way to make public the 'black box' of ratings and how the methodologies work.

We can see glimpses of the convention in operation when the audience and media technology context changes or when the methodology is questioned and the measure – exposure – or sampling become an issue. We can see it when the currency appears to be failing or when proprietary control of audiences and their information is queried or problematic. The gradual erosion of the standard broadcast model and the evolution of niche broadcasters alongside a variety of platforms including YouTube demonstrate an increasingly more complex and mixed set of televisual arrangements and business models. In this context audience measurement is becoming more complex and recalibrating its instruments to meet the new challenges of covering more and also different kinds of viewing. At the same time the relation between the audience market defined by advertising and the content market defined by sales of media product including cable TV, DVD and downloads of programmes is entering a new and radical phase.

3 The Panel and the Survey

The claims that have been made for political opinion polling have not been modest. George Gallup has said that the 'modern poll can, and to a certain extent does, function as a creative art of government', and refers to political opinion polls as a 'sort of American equivalent of a vote of confidence in the government'. Catherine Marsh (Marsh 1984: 32)

There is no logical difference between the study of voting or of buying. In each of these areas, the final goal is the discovering of regularity in social life. Hans Zeisel (Zeisel 1968: xvii)

National television ratings should not be confused with public opinion polls or election forecasts or surveys of how much of what consumers plan to buy. Ratings are better than such estimates, because they do not have to deal with confusions introduced by phrasing of a question, or difficulties in predicting who will vote, or the chance that economic conditions will change. They seek only to measure only a very simple piece of behaviour at or close to the time that it occurs. Martin Mayer (Mayer 1966: 23)

In Chapter 2 the authors argued that audience ratings are not only a measure; they are a convention that brings together many parties in its creation and use. The most important aspect of this convention is that audience ratings have a *dual identity*. They are a public interest vehicle showing the public preference for programmes or media channels and a market mechanism for making decisions on the media dollar. Ratings are part of politics because they represent the public and the market at the same time. In this chapter the authors will show how the ratings intellectuals created the surveys and panels that have become part of the audience-ratings convention. We will also show the changing pressures on the panel as demands increase to represent increasingly demographically defined publics. These demands are a part of broader survey and sampling wars. The US Census, for example, under-represents its minorities, and the role of sampling and the survey has become the subject of battles over ways to count them, to the point where the Republicans vetoed the commissioning of a Census Director's appointment because of his association with previous plans to use statistical sampling to represent minorities in the Census. Audience ratings panels are based on establishment surveys using ... the Census.

The Ratings Intellectuals

George Gallup and Archibald Crossley gave speeches after the 1936 US presidential election in which they stressed that techniques used in political polling were applicable to market research. They did not say this as a commercial plug, pushing their own commercial interests that they had in developing and applying public polling techniques. Both made the link between public opinion polling and markets because, like other contemporary experts in methodology, they had an intense interest in the use of advanced survey research techniques in enhancing democracy, and markets, for them, were an integral part of democracy. The idea of surveys as genuinely being able to represent the 'public vote' was no accident. The dual identity of audience ratings as public vote and market measure was a part of the ethos of Gallup and Crossley's intellectual contemporaries. At the heart of this dual identity was 'scientific sampling' and methodological and popular understanding of what it was and its limitations. As Crossley wrote:

> In the early days of sampling there was, and it may be noted that there still is occasionally, a tendency to think of cases taken 'at random' as being typical or representative of a universe, although the term 'universe' was not used. When the transition was made from 'at random' to true 'randomization', the lily was gilded with the phrase 'scientific sampling'. This gilding, I would say, was done at the time of the introduction of the national polls on political issues in the mid-thirties. Actually, however, reasonably reliable stratified or quote sampling methods were in use in marketing research ten to fifteen years before this. Already at that time the effort was to establish what George Gallup later so aptly called a 'micro-America', by selecting the sampling so it would be representative of all possible breakdowns, as shown by the latest census. To the best of my recollection this use of the word 'scientific' was the first of a long string of competitive catchwords which has so thoroughly characterized claims about sampling and interviewing methods. While the bruiting of the word 'probability' did not achieve this fanfare until the 1948 nadir of the polltakers, the word had been used considerably earlier, and many probability principles had been used for a long period – e.g. rotation and randomization of blocks, road segments, homes, and individuals, and the assignment of specific locations to interviewers. (Crossley 1957: 162)

Crossley's point about 'competitive catchwords' taps directly into concerns from survey research methodologists of the time about how an essentially probabilistic approach might be used to deliver precision statements. Statistics delivered from samples are inferential and have an element of *error* associated with them. Calling them 'scientific' does not make that error less certain. Using decimal points in polling figures or ratings figures as exact when there is a possibility of 5 per cent sampling error, for example, is ludicrous, but advertisers and marketers do exactly this, regardless of sampling error estimates. This problem exploded in the 1960s with the US Congressional hearings on ratings, which the authors deal with in the next chapter.

Crossley was also highlighting the major transition from 'random' as an attempt to remove bias in earlier studies and 'randomization' as the mathematical attempt at representation, a major advance in polling and ratings and methodology and little understood in the industry (something Bill McNair and George Anderson knew very well in their attempts to sell randomization and the extra costs that it might incur).

Gallup and Crossley are what the authors call 'ratings intellectuals'. They were not just academic in their work, publishing academic papers, but interested in all things ratings or polls – working within the industry itself, developing the very techniques they critiqued and publishing seminal papers along the way. They also participated in the fierce politics involved in the application of the techniques and any public arguments about them. C.E. Hooper co-authored a book outlining the deficiencies of Crossley's telephone recall method but also took the argument to industry forums and the industry press. Bill McNair and George Anderson in Australia, likewise, saw themselves as academically interested in the methodologies and not mere technicians. They also saw themselves as taking on the broader role of informing the industry and the public on how audience ratings worked.

Crossley worked with Gallup on public opinion polling after leaving audience ratings in the 1940s, and had maintained his interest in public opinion polling while working with CAB. Gallup himself, of course, was not only interested in public opinion polls. He launched the Audience Research Institute (ARI) in 1940 in the West Coast headquarters of Young & Rubicam; 'a cozy reciprocity' (Ohmer 2006: 79).

> ARI conducted a quarterly study that it called the 'continuing audit of marquee values'. The audit asked the public whether seeing a particular person's name on a theater marquee would in itself induce them to buy a ticket to the film. ARI compared these studies to the ratings that Archibald Crossley had carried out for the Cooperative Analysis of Broadcasting, so these audits represented a direct transference of personality ratings from radio to film. (Ohmer 2006: 79)

It was not Gallup or Crossley, however, who developed the underlying sampling techniques that came to dominate audience survey research, survey methods generally and, especially, longitudinal research. Paul Lazarsfeld studied the effects of radio in 1937 and discovered that radio listening created no public records, such as circulation records in the case of print. He took the public opinion poll and ratings methodology and by the multivariate analysis of responses developed ways to measure the impact of radio on attitudes. 'This transformation of the opinion poll into multifaceted survey research constitutes one of Lazarsfeld's major accomplishments' (Sills 1987). But Lazarsfeld's work on longitudinal methods itself fed back into audience ratings methodology. The *panel* was a revolution in collecting data about the same people over time.

> A major finding of Lazarsfeld's research on radio listening is the tendency of audiences to be self-selected; that is, to tune in to programs that are compatible with their own tastes and attitudes. Accordingly, in order to sort out the causal sequences of such problems as the effect of listening upon attitudes versus the effect of attitudes upon patterns of listening, a method of determining the time order of variables was required. Drawing on his research in Vienna with the Biihlers, in which repeated observations were made of the same children over time, as well as on the earlier research of Stuart A. Rice among Dartmouth College students and Theodore M. Newcomb among Bennington College students, Lazarsfeld developed what he called the panel method, in which a sample of respondents is reinterviewed at periodic intervals. The panel method is a form of longitudinal research; it is essentially a field experiment in which a 'natural' rather than an experimental population is studied. Although Lazarsfeld cannot be said to have invented the panel method, it was his imaginative use of it, and particularly his innovative ways of introducing control groups into the analysis of panel data, that made him its earliest and most effective exponent. (Sills 1987)

Lazarsfeld

Paul F. Lazarsfeld ... virtually created the fields of mathematical sociology, multivariate survey analysis, and the empirical study of both voting behaviour and mass communications.
David L. Sills (Rogers 1994: 244)

Theodor W. Adorno, Hans Zeisel, Herta Herzog, Robert Merton, Bernard Berelson and Leo Lowenthal were all famous colleagues of Lazarsfeld. All conducted research on media and new methods emerged from the research. In the case of Merton, a lifelong friend and associate of Lazarsfeld, his focused interviews and focus groups technique became a standard part of industry data collection as well as of qualitative methods generally. Adorno provided the bridge with European critical approaches and drew the famous distinction between 'administrative research', which served government and industry, and 'critical research', which sought to critique the whole capitalist enterprise and the role of ideology. While Adorno saw Lazarsfeld's work as primarily of the former rather than the latter kind, Adorno and Lazarsfeld shared a common interest in making research methods democratic, transparent and hybrid – making sure that qualitative research informed quantitative research and vice versa. Lazarsfeld, Berelson and Gaudet's seminal work *People's Choice* (Lazarsfeld, Berelson and Gaudet 1944) is a classic example of hybridity and the application of the panel method to assist with explanatory research.

The 1940 presidential election in the United States presented to Lazarsfeld an opportunity to undertake a study of voting intentions in new ways. Voting records were until then the only material used for analysing voter behaviour. These records made it possible to study the geographical distribution of voting results as well as individual votes. Public opinion polls went a step further and correlated political opinion to the characteristics of the individual voter. Gallup and Crossley's opinion polls, however, were normally conducted with different people and *not the same people over time*. What Lazarsfeld decided to do was to trace a person's voting intentions over the course of a political campaign. To do this he created a 'panel' technique using the same set of voters over the period of the political campaign and election.

Lazarsfeld's broader research aim was straightforward: 'We are interested here in all those conditions which determine the political behaviour of people. Briefly, our problem is this: to discover how and why people decided to vote as they did. What were the major influences upon them during the campaign in 1940?' (Lazarsfeld *et al.* 1944: 1). Within this broader aim, Lazarsfeld asked, 'What is the effect of social status upon vote?' 'How are people influenced by the party conventions and the nominations?' 'What role does formal propaganda play?' 'How about the press and the radio?' 'What of the influence of family and friends?' 'Where do issues come in, and how?' 'Why do some people settle their vote early and some late?' 'In short, how do votes develop? Why do people vote as they do? By inference and by direct accounts of the respondents, we shall try to show what influences operated' (Lazarsfeld *et al.* 1944: 6–7).

Lazarsfeld and his colleagues had a specific *sampling frame* and *variables* in mind for measurement. Erie County was chosen for the study 'because it was small enough to permit close supervision of the interviewers; because it was relatively free from sectional peculiarities, because it was not dominated by any large urban center, although it did furnish an opportunity to compare rural political opinion with opinion in a small urban center' (Lazarsfeld *et al.* 1944: 3). Three thousand people were chosen to represent the county and a *systematic* sampling technique adopted. Trained local interviewers, mainly women, visited every fourth house in the county. Four groups of 600 persons were selected by *stratified sampling* and of these only three were re-interviewed once each. These were control groups to test the effect that repeated interviewing might have on the panel (Lazarsfeld *et al.* 1944: 3). The fourth group, the *panel*, was interviewed once each month from May to November 1940.

Operationalization of 'social and economic status' gives the reader an insight into how the study went about quantification. The interviewers were trained to assess the homes, possessions, appearance and manner of speech of the participants. The interviewers then classified them into a stratum according to a set quota: 'The people with the best homes, furniture, clothes, etc, i.e., the ones with the most money, would be classed as As; and the people at the other extreme would be Ds. In Erie Country, the quota was approximated in the following distribution: A, 3 percent; B, 14 percent; C+, 33 percent; C-, 30 percent; and D, 20 percent' (Lazarsfeld *et al.* 1944: 17). This was in an attempt to reflect the broader sampling frame. The study used simple and more complex measurements for analysis. For magazine reading, the respondent was asked about several specific articles appearing in current issues of magazines. The resulting index was a count of the number of articles on political affairs that a person said that they had read. In the October interview each person was asked whether they agreed with eight arguments then current in the political campaign, on a scale of -8 to +8. One of the eight arguments was 'Roosevelt has great personal attractiveness, capacity for hard work, and keen intelligence'.

One of *People's Choice*'s main findings was that media appeared to have little influence on changing people's voting intentions. Media had a reinforcement not a transformative effect. 'The first thing to say is that some people *were* converted by campaign propaganda but that they were *few* indeed' (Lazarsfeld *et al.* 1944: 94). Interpersonal influence emerged as a key factor. 'Whenever respondents were asked to report on their recent exposures to campaign communications of all kinds, political discussions were mentioned more frequently than exposure to radio or print' (Lazarsfeld *et al.* 1944: 150). The voters most likely to change their voting intentions in the political campaign 'read and listened least' (Lazarsfeld *et al.* 1944: 95). The study also found that opinion leaders had a dramatic influence on people around them. Print and radio did not change behaviour because 'the people who did most of the reading and listening not only read and heard most of their own partisan propaganda but were also most resistant to conversion because of their strong dispositions' (Lazarsfeld *et al.* 1944: 95).

Lazarsfeld and his colleagues' study has all the elements used in modern broadcast ratings, including not least the panel. However, before proceeding to discuss issues in sampling in more detail, it is worthwhile revisiting how quantitative methods and probability sampling work. The authors italicized some of the concepts that are basic to quantitative methods. Operationalization is an overarching concept that describes quantitative, variable-analytic, method. Wanting to operationalize 'gender' as a nominal variable measured by the categories 'male' and 'female', for example, is unlikely to encounter significant resistance. But not all constructs or phenomena are this easy to measure or indeed to reach an agreement on. Social scientists use language to describe and to define the phenomena that they measure and this language has to be accepted by others to be valid. The social scientist tries to measure constructs described by language that they argue corresponds to the phenomenon of interest.

The Very Idea of Measurement

In the case of audience ratings *exposure* is the phenomenon of interest. Have audiences been exposed to the radio channel and the radio programme, the television and the television programme? This construct might be described in natural language as: 'The stations and programmes listened to, the times that they were listened to, and the demographics of the audience.' This description might then be broken down into various variables that represent real, observable, measures, such as those outlined in Frank Stanton's 1935 doctoral dissertation:

1 When does the listener use his receiver?

2 For how long a period does he use it?

3 To what station or stations does he listen?

4 Who listens (sex, age, economic and educational level)?

5 What does he do while the receiver is in operation?

6 What does he do as a result of the program?

7 What are his program preferences?
   (Stanton 1935; cited in Webster, Phalen and Lichty 2005)

How these questions are operationalized as variables becomes very important. For example, question 2 could be operationalized as a nominal/categorical variable or at a higher level of measurement:

'For how long a period do you use your radio receiver?'
A long period
Not at all

This answer, you might tell the authors, is inappropriate. It gives the analyst too little information. You might propose a set of answers like:

'For how long a period do you use your radio receiver?'
Monday   Tuesday
Number of Hours   Number of Hours, etc.

The definition of the construct and the level of measurement of the question are analytical choices of the researcher, but they must be useful to the research and have validity. If you have noticed, Stanton's questions 5–7 go beyond exposure in our definition of the construct. These are the kinds of decisions Archibald Crossley had to face. What definitions and measurements of exposure would ratings intellectuals and the industry accept? Which measures were seen as more objective than others?

Figure 3.1 summarizes the relationship between construct and measure. If the authors were to define exposure as 'how engaged the listener is with the radio programme' then a whole new set of variables would be needed. Is 'engaged' related to length of time that a person listens to the programme or the amount of attention that they show? Crossley, not surprisingly, tried to steer clear of this question of attention. Exposure was measured by whether the listener said that they were listening and for how long, not 'how much attention the listener paid to the radio programme'. The problem of engagement versus exposure is a contemporary debate but, as the authors want to show you, it is also an old debate and one faced by the early ratings intellectuals. The comment by Martin Mayer at the beginning of this chapter, that 'they seek only to measure only a very simple piece of behaviour at or close to the time that it occurs', is highly misleading as it is not a simple behaviour. For example, Nielsen would contest that the problem with self-report, the listener telling you when they turned on the radio set, is itself not reliable and thus his mechanical measure was more valid than self-report. Even the 'simple behaviour' can become contestable.

Audience ratings therefore do not escape the same problems faced by any social phenomenon. The construct itself requires qualitative description, in natural

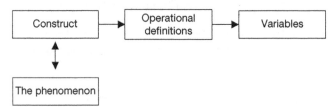

Figure 3.1 From construct to measure
Source: Balnaves and Caputi 2001

language. That construct has to reflect a phenomenon in the real world that can be observed. The methods and the measures chosen need to reflect the phenomenon accurately. Agreement on the measure is not necessarily easy. A construct like 'child abuse' could have many measures, but each could also be contestable. For instance, 'smacking a child five times a week' might be defined by a researcher as child abuse, but the question might be asked, 'Of what does the smack itself consist? And how can it be observed?' In television viewing, having the station switched on is no guarantee that anyone is in the room. Or they might be in another room listening to the television, partly. Or they might be in the television room, talking to other people and not listening to the programme at all. As we can see, this is the type of trade-off that Crossley had to make in his pioneering efforts to create the measure. What do I count? And how do I count it?

The 'construct' therefore is your idea about the phenomenon that you want to measure. The operational definition is the statement about how you want to measure the construct. 'The construct "delinquency", for example, might be operationally defined by "being arrested more than once prior to the age 18". In a questionnaire you might have the question (your variable), "Have you been arrested more than once prior to the age 18? Yes. No." This is a nominal level question. This is one variable. It is also possible to imagine other definitions and operational definitions of the construct that might be useful' (Balnaves and Caputi 2001).

In general, social science assumes that attributes of a phenomenon are measurable. 'Male' and 'female' are, for example, attributes of 'sex' and as categories can be assigned the numbers 1 and 2. Notice, however, that we can only derive frequencies from this measurement, called a nominal or categorical measure. We cannot derive an average of males and females on this measure. If, however, one was to ask each male and female their ages and they gave them to me as '17', '18' and '36', then one would be able to derive averages from this higher level of measurement. Variables embody both constructs that we want to define and the numbers that we use to represent them.

Variables can be operationalized at various levels of measurement, and traditionally textbooks have listed four levels of quantification or measurement – nominal, ordinal, interval and ratio measurement. *Nominal or categorical level* measurement consists of categories that can be given a name or a number. *Ordinal level* measurement has the same properties as nominal scales with the additional property that the categories can be rank-ordered. In audience research, getting people to rank their preferences of programmes is an ordinal scale. Note, however, that the distance between intervals is not necessarily equal. A person who ranks their programmes 1, 2, 3 may like number 1 significantly more than 2 and 3.

Interval level measurement assumes equal intervals on the scale represent equal amounts of the quantity being measured. If we are measuring household income in dollars, then the difference between annual income of US$60,000 and US$65,000 is the same amount as the difference between someone who earns US$70,000 and US$75,000. One could ask viewers to rate the content of three television programmes in terms of humour using a 5-point scale where '0' means 'not at all funny' and '5' means 'extremely funny'. If we can demonstrate that the difference (in terms of the amount of humour represented in the variable) in ratings between '0' and '1' is the same as the difference between ratings of '3' and '4', then we are using an interval scale. Clearly, establishing this property in this case may be difficult. It is possible to try to establish what properties the observations should have in order to lead to the interval scale measurement and then to investigate whether these properties are in fact met by the observations. Cliff argues, however, that in the social sciences we can only achieve ordinal level measurement (Cliff 1996).

Ratio level of measurement has all the properties of ordinal and interval measurement with the additional property that equal ratios between numbers on the scale represent equal ratios of the attribute being measured. Height measured in centimetres (cm) is an example of ratio measurement. Someone who is 180 cm tall is twice the height of someone who is 90 cm tall. The levels of measurement represent the mathematical possibilities available for quantitative analysis such as adding, subtracting, multiplying and dividing – when it is decided how one wants to define the phenomenon one wants to study; how to measure one's observations. Definition, as we have seen, precedes measurement.

It takes students of statistics in the social sciences and media a little time to get their minds around the idea that there are in fact different levels of measurement and that choice of measurement must relate directly back to their definitions of the constructs. There may be logical limits on which measures correspond to which defined phenomenon. Modern sampling, no less, creates similar difficulties. Modern sampling requires a *sampling frame* and this frame (population or universe) and the sampling technique(s) to be used are decided upon by the researcher, as you saw in the case of Lazarsfeld in *People's Choice*.

Constructs and variables are defined by the researcher. Populations and sampling frames are also operationally defined by the researcher. A sampling frame must be accessible and quantifiable, and related to the purpose of the research. 'All households in New York' is a definition of a sampling frame, with households as the unit of analysis. But, one would correctly ask, what counts as a 'household'? Is it any dwelling, including the boat in the backyard that one's relative lives in? If it is, then this example needs to be included in the definition of the population, the sampling frame. If a sample of households was drawn from New York, then 'New York' also needs to be defined. Is New York defined by local government boundaries? Is it defined by census boundaries?

When one has decided on all these definitions then every household that meets one's definition is on the list. That list is called a *sampling frame*. It is called a sampling frame because it constitutes a defined universe or population of elements that is to be studied. Without this kind of defined list modern probability or random, sampling selection procedures cannot be used. 'Probability' is perhaps better than 'random' as a term for modern sampling, as Crossley pointed out earlier. It is called random because it is supposed to be non-biased in the selection of the sample. In the popular mind, however, 'random' means 'arbitrary', which modern random sampling certainly is not. This confusion has affected the media industry perception of sampling because 'random' has never been well understood. McNair and Anderson in Australia had to continuously argue, reargue and explain modern sampling techniques, because industry commentators or ratings users found the idea that a thousand households could represent a million households almost impossible to accept.

You can number each household in New York and put them in a large hat. If you drew out ten households then you would have a *Simple Random Sample* (SRS). You know that there was no bias in your choice and each element, each household, had an equal chance of being chosen. You would be more likely to use a table of random numbers and select 50 households out of 1,000 households. In this case you would number each household from 000 to 999 and then select 50 numbers from the table of random numbers. In Table 3.1 below, a shortened version, you start anywhere in the table of random numbers and then, proceeding up, down or diagonally, select the 50 numbers needed. In this case, the selection starting from 284 downwards would be 284, 361, 779, 176 and so on. Each of these numbers would represent a real household.

By chance you might have selected 50 households that only included people who lived in boats in the backyard in New York. You have not represented *all* households in your sampling frame, only boats. An additional probability technique

Table 3.1 Table of random numbers

2	8	4	9	8	8	9	9	5	5
3	6	1	9	0	3	0	1	1	1
7	7	9	9	7	8	3	3	3	2
1	7	6	9	2	4	1	8	6	7

might be required – stratified random sampling. You can break the sampling frame into different strata and then conduct a simple random sample with each stratum. The strata might be divided, for instance, into single-level households, double-level household, boats and other classifications. There may be very few boats-as-households in the sampling frame, let us say 2 per cent. If we wanted to represent the 2 per cent in our sampling frame, then 2 per cent of your stratification would be boats. This is called a proportionate stratified random sample representing each type of household proportionately. A simple random sample from each separate list of types of household would be required. Sometimes we might want to over-represent a particular stratum, especially if there are very low numbers, and this is called disproportionate stratified random sampling. In audience ratings, which often use census data for creating establishment surveys, marginal groups are often under-represented because they are not in the census. In the United States, Hispanics have traditionally been under-represented in the census and consequently severely under-represented in the audience ratings panels.

Large-scale national studies use different types of units of analysis in their sampling frame, or their list. In cluster sampling, for instance, we select groups or categories. In Figure 3.2, representing New York, we could break the list up into suburbs and randomly sample those suburbs. We could then break up those suburbs into census collectors' districts and then randomly select from those districts. We could then select streets and *systematically* sample those streets, as Lazarsfeld did in his study. A systematic sample is when every *n*th unit of analysis is selected – every fifth house in the street, or whichever interval the researcher thinks is best. Once the researcher has selected the sample of households, then they might select a demographic quota from those households (people of a certain age or sex and so on). In order to randomly select the participants the researcher could again use a table of random numbers. For example, the interviewer could ask, 'How many people are there in your home aged 15 or older?' If the first participant says 'three people', then according to the table at Figure 3.3, the second oldest person is chosen.

Simple, stratified and multi-stage cluster sampling are forms of probability sampling, although there is sometimes debate about whether systematic sampling is genuinely random. When probability sampling is not possible then alternative sampling strategies can be used. For instance, it would be hard to get a list of 'heroin users who watch television'. There is no Association of Heroin Users Who Watch Television (although such an association would constitute a valid list). Going to a shopping mall and talking to someone believed to be a heroin user who watched television is *not* random sampling but it is a form of non-random, non-probability sampling. A 'mall intercept' like this might be useful for research, but the result could not be generalized to the population from which it is drawn, firstly

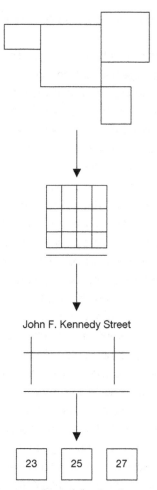

John F. Kennedy Street

Figure 3.2 Multi-stage cluster sampling – following the census tracts

No. of people in household

	1	2	3	4	5
Person to interview	1	2	2	4	3
		1	1	2	5
			3	1	4
				3	1
					2

Figure 3.3 Random selection from households for interview

because there is no sampling frame and secondly because defining the population is not simple either.

The argument of modern researchers is that good sampling reduces the chance that we have picked the wrong people, reduces error and maximizes external validity. Internal validity deals with the logic and construction of your research questions, variables, and so on. External validity deals with the construction of the sampling technique. Statistics that make judgements about the relationship between samples and their sampling frame are called *inferential statistics*. Modern audience ratings figures are inferential, relying on samples drawn from sampling frames.

As might be guessed, advertisers and others had and still do have some difficulty in swallowing the argument that 1,000 homes could represent over 50 million people, which is the national television ratings panel size that Nielsen ran in the United States in 1966. Because a probability sample is a sample, and not the full sampling frame, there is likely to be an element of error. Understanding this error is important because a rating point is a probabilistic estimate, not a certain figure. If Nielsen interviewed each of the 50 million or so television viewers, then it would have a census, a full population. This, of course, is too costly to do as well as time consuming. There is also an element of *intrusion*. A probability sample or panel could limit the amount of intrusion into households. A panel could collect longitudinal data and minimize privacy intrusion and increase the speed by which ratings could be measured. In 1966 the Committee on Nationwide Television Audience Measurement (CONTAM) that represented industry and government conducted a major study to see whether sampling theory was correct. Could 1,000 households properly represent over 50 million households with minimum sampling error?

Ten programmes were selected from the rating weeks, ranging from *The Beverly Hillbillies* (a rating of 50.7 in the 56,386 diaries ARB received in the March 1963 ratings period), *Dr Kildare* (a rating of 37.0) through to *Eyewitness* (7.1) and *Voice of Firestone* (3.0). Eight hundred samples were drawn in computer table of random numbers – 100 samples each of 25, 50, 100, 250, 500, 1000, 1,500 and 2,500 diaries. There were then 8,000 samples, 800 for each of the programmes.

Statistical sampling theory says that about 5,460 of these 8,000 samples should produce results falling within the first standard error. The study produced 5,475 within that range, and the appropriate proportions for the other standard errors. The standard error is a statistical measure of dispersion: under normal circumstances approximately 68 per cent of all cases will fall within one standard error of the mean, about 95 per cent will fall within two standard errors, and 99.7 per cent will fall within three standard errors.

CONTAM had shown that sampling theory does apply to television viewing behaviour for a universe or sampling frame of 56,386 homes and that similar results would be obtained for a sampling frame of over 50 million homes, although this remained to be demonstrated. The part of sampling theory that is most difficult for people to understand is that the accuracy of results obtained by sampling is independent of the size of the sampling frame or the universe from which the sample is taken. A sample of 1,000 is just as accurate for a population of 50 million, the number of television homes in the United States in 1966, as it would be for 50,000. To demonstrate this, CONTAM again took 8,000 samples, 100 each of 8 sizes for 10 programmes from 4,927 diaries from one section of the United States, shrinking the universe to see if the sampling produced the sample results as those produced for sampling the whole universe.

The 8,000 samples from the large population produced 5,475 results within one standard error of the true result and the sample from the shrunk universe produced 5,528 cases. Bar charts were produced to show the actual results from the samples of 1,000 for each of the 10 programmes studied. On each chart the normal curve of the distribution around the true value was superimposed to show the degree to which the bar chart met the predictions of the theory. Each test showed that there was no unusual factor about television viewing that made sampling less effective than in other domains. A sample of 1,000 homes could represent 50 million homes.

In the United Kingdom in the lead-up to the broadcasting of Independent Television (ITV) for the first time in September 1955, and in the period immediately afterwards, the most important issue for the new public regulatory body, the Independent Television Authority, was one of *exposure*: how many homes were equipped with sets able to receive ITV programmes. Television sets in Britain in the mid-1950s either had to be fitted with a new station selector switch or viewers had to buy new sets, and many homes needed new aerials in order to receive a signal from the ITV station in their region. In the period immediately following the commencement of the ITV service, a controversy blew up over differences in figures for ITV's share of the evening audience in multichannel homes in the London region.

Table 3.2 Panel result differences between providers

	BBC Audience Research	Gallup TV Research	TAM Machine Panels
All Week	44%	49%	59%
Monday to Friday	41%	45%	53%
Saturday and Sunday	52%	57%	73%

Source: TV Research (Gallup Poll) Ltd, 'Enlightenment on the Controversy following Publication of BBC and ITV Research', ITA Archive, Audience Research – Gallup Poll 301/4, 6 December 1955

Research in December 1955 by the BBC Audience Research Unit, under Robert Silvey, was broadly consistent with independent research by the Gallup group in findings about the average number of viewers for each network. Research by Television Audience Measurement Ltd (TAM) indicated higher viewing figures for ITV than those recorded by Gallup and the BBC, particularly on the weekend, when TAM recorded a 20 per cent jump in ITV's share compared with weekdays. Gallup and BBC also recorded a rise in ITV's share at weekends, but much smaller in size. Both the BBC and Gallup used personal interviews and aided recall, almost 5,000 in total per week, to ascertain results. Gallup also used the telephone coincidental method to check audience figures. TAM used a panel of about 100 homes, fitted with machines to record the station to which the television was tuned.

In commentary on the discrepancies between the figures, Henry Durant, the director of the British Institute of Public Opinion (BIPO) which conducted the Gallup polls, noted that unlike the BBC and Gallup, which offered no inducement to their respondents, TAM 'as a minimum' maintained the television sets in panel homes to ensure that they could receive the ITV signal. This was considered potentially likely to produce figures that were unduly favourable to the ITV programmes, or as Durant put it, 'Where a man's treasure is, there is his heart also'. Durant also pointed to the potential for the ideological leanings of the respondents to skew the machine panel figures, noting that, 'It needs precious few of [panel members] with a feeling for "free enterprise rather than the BBC monopoly" to produce a slant in the figures' (Durant 1955).

Despite these criticisms, the ITV companies, advertising agencies and advertisers agreed at an early stage to use one source of statistical information about television, and selected TAM with its metered system, supplemented by diaries, over a rival meter system operated by Nielsen and a variety of survey and interview systems operated by BIPO and other organizations. In January 1957, TAM was awarded the industry contract for an initial period of five years. The contract was extended by the Joint Industry Committee for Television Advertising Research (JICTAR). The issue of discrepancies between BBC and TAM/Audits of Great Britain figures for audience share arose on various occasions until the creation of the Broadcasters' Audience Research Board (BARB), jointly underwritten by the BBC and ITV, in 1981, although as Ehrenberg and Twyman noted in 1967:

> Stories of gross disagreement between the BBC's results and Tamratings would appear to have been due largely to the frequently ignored difference in technical definitions (the two systems set out to measure slightly different things and express the results in rather different ways) together with the incidence of sampling errors which in regional comparisons can be particularly large. (Ehrenberg and Twyman 1967: 15)

The audience-ratings convention around sampling and panels is well established, including the formats for reporting audience results. There is basic agreement that probability sampling works. All of the ratings figures can now be produced quickly in standardized formats with a range of permutations possible. You might think that this is the end of the ratings intellectual and that all is well with sampling and surveys in the audience-ratings convention. But this is far from the case. The modern ratings intellectuals, like Gale Metzger and Peter Miller with his colleagues at Northwestern University, while not in the milieu of Lazarsfeld, Zeisel, Crossley, Gallup and others, still have a major role of critique of both the industry and the methodology. There are additional biases that might affect sampling and panels. This includes the problems of multiplication of channels and programmes as well as non-cooperation of participants.

Single Source: 'The Holy Grail'

Audience ratings panels and survey research generally have always had problems with non-response or non-participation in research, even in the days of Archibald Crossley and Paul Lazarsfeld. However, there has emerged an erosion of the ability to get people to participate in surveys or to give more data about themselves at the very time when there is today an explosion in demand for more measurement. Project Apollo is the paradigm example of an attempt to capture everything people do in one panel. When Nielsen and Arbitron joined forces to set up the experimental Project Apollo in 2005 they expected to capture all of the everyday behaviour of audiences, from reading papers through to using mobile phones and buying food. To their surprise they found that people did not want to participate. The more they were asked to do and to provide, the more they resisted and refused. The current situation involves many separate panels for separate activities, for example, a panel for outdoor advertising, a panel for mobile phones and so on, as we found in Chapter 1. There is also access to 'buyer graphics' such as actual purchases of, for instance, books.

In television ratings the longitudinal aspect has been fundamental to the operation of the business of ratings as it has provided the users of ratings with the capacity to map audience flow and to get a sense of what is happening to audiences over time. The process of selection of panels and their retention over time is therefore key to the quality of data that are retrieved. Television ratings panels may obtain an appropriate sampling frame but that is not the end of it. If not all the 'basics' – those on the list – do not want to participate, as Nielsen found in the 1990s, then the alternates, those who say yes, may not be representative of the panel originally chosen. In the case of Nielsen, the 'alternates' ended up having fewer televisions and were heavier television viewers than the 'basics'. There end up being key trade-offs if an appropriate statistically representative group cannot be found.

Table 3.3 from Peter Miller's work provides a summary of those trade-offs. The ultimate in survey research is gaining a Data Rich and Case Rich outcome. Data Rich means that the information coming back from the audience is extensive and has qualitative depth. For example, information on Facebook is Data Rich – there is significant information posted by people on to their sites that can be used to understand audiences and what they think or do. However, it is very difficult to establish from Facebook an appropriate sampling frame or probability sample that allows researchers to generalize their findings. At the time of writing, Facebook has 500 million users. These 'users' do not form into well-defined and easily accessible lists. There are, as a result, problems in establishing or verifying identities of users and creating an acceptable list where a random draw or stratification can be made. Facebook, therefore, is Data Rich but Case Poor as an audience and as a source of information. The traditional panel for television ratings, by contrast, is Case Rich but Data Poor.

The Data Poor nature of the television ratings measured by exposure – who watches, where, for how long – was made up by the fact that users of the ratings found them practical and acceptable as a form of currency (a trade off). Miller would call this part of the 'coordination rule' in audience ratings. There was in the past confidence that the television ratings panel indeed reflected the population from which it was chosen. Through peoplemeters the television ratings panels have provided information about an audience's *exposure* to television. If a company or a researcher wants more information about whether the audience actually like programmes then customized Data Rich studies are often required. Modern syndicated ratings research therefore has often been complemented by customized studies seeking more detailed information about audiences.

If there is significant non-cooperation in television panels, however, it is only so far that a trade-off can be accepted. Miller conducted a major independent study, the first of its kind on non-response bias, for Nielsen in 2009, and its results give an insight into the role of the modern audience in survey research and the limits the audience itself puts on participation. The study consisted of 2,300 basics,

Table 3.3 Trade-offs in audience survey research

	Case Rich	Case Poor
Data Rich	Single source (the Holy Grail)	Custom
Data Poor	Syndicated	Quick and dirty

Source: Adapted from Miller 2009

with 1,000 responding households (a 95 per cent return rate) and 1,300 refusing households (a 62 per cent return rate). Special in-person follow-ups were made with those households that did not respond. Few studies have followed up with non-responding households on why they have not participated or given data, and this is what makes this particular study important. Table 3.4 shows the difference between responding and refusing households by day-part. The p values are significant for the 8–11 pm day part, with the possibility of differences in the 5–9 am day-part.

Table 3.5 in comparison shows refusing households by channel, with significant differences for Cable News Network (CNN) and Home Box Office (HBO), with MTV (originally Music Television) and Fox approaching significance.

Table 3.4 Day-part comparisons

Day-part	Per cent Response	Per cent Refuse	P value
5–9 am	41.9	45.8	.11
9 am–4 pm	56.1	56.3	.94
4–8 pm	67.4	69.7	.46
8–11 pm	71.2	76.2	.04
11 pm–2 am	39.3	39.7	.89
2–5 am	10.2	12.3	.18
12 am–12 am	91.5	90.1	.41

Source: Miller 2009

Table 3.5 Channel comparisons

Channel	Per cent Response	Per cent Refuse	P value
ABC	70.3	73.7	.19
CBS	68.7	73.2	.12
Fox	68.4	72.7	.11
NBC	71.2	73.3	.38
Univision	7.6	6.7	.52
BET	11.3	12.5	.52
CNN	37.7	45.2	.00
HBO	17.4	27.9	.00
MTV	15.5	19.1	.09

Source: Miller 2009

Table 3.6 Equipment comparisons

Device	Per cent Response	Per cent Refuse	P value
Big Screen	22.6	41.2	.00
Cable	61.9	69.1	.00
Satellite	24.7	28.5	.18
DVR	9.7	20.1	.00
Hi Speed Web	72.9	75.3	.30
Web TV	63.6	69.5	.15
3+ TVs	46.1	60.2	.00

Source: Miller 2009

However, it is the figures in Table 3.6 that start to show why many people do not want to participate in modern audience panels and audience ratings survey panels especially. Nielsen found that technology-rich households did not want to participate in research – the very demographic that modern marketers want to grab. There are various reasons for this, ranging from an unwillingness of households to allow increased intrusion into their lives across a range of technologies and, of course, the simple fact that the technologies themselves need to be intruded upon in order to gain data (for example, additional wiring) and participants do not want their expensive technology tampered with in any way.

In summary, Case Rich studies are those that use statistical sampling methods to derive their samples from sampling frames. Case Poor studies are those that have not deployed statistical sampling methods and therefore their samples cannot be used to represent the populations from which they might have been drawn. Data Rich studies are those that yield detailed data or accounts from participants. In the case of television, for example, an interviewer living with a television household for a month is getting fine-grained qualitative data. Data Poor studies are those that gain minimal information back for their purpose. In the case of television ratings, exposure gives the media industry basic information about who is watching, when and for how long. Those studies that do not gain an appropriate probability, statistical, sample, and do not gain particularly rich and detailed information, are both Data Poor and Case Poor. The modern problem for syndicated research is that participants do not want to participate, especially those who are of most interest to media researchers. If panels are failing to adequately represent the modern audience, then they are Case Poor. The data, as a result, are not generalizable to the defined population.

Gale Metzger also sees the pursuit of single source as impossible for very human reasons that do not only include non-participation – the limits on human patience:

Before the peoplemeter, the 'people' part of the measurement was based on a diary. Nielsen had a meter-diary combination measurement. The set tuning came from the meter and the persons-per-set from a diary. And you combined those two to obtain a projected audience. The peoplemeter brought the people measurement into the meter itself and people had to push buttons to register themselves as viewers. We did a lot of experimentation with passive measurements, voice-based systems or even passive recognition systems. The proliferation of outlets and fragmentation of the TV medium has several measurement implications. It is easier to measure a big thing than a small thing. It is easier to measure a 30 per cent market share than a 3 per cent market share. A relatively small and crude sample can provide a reasonable estimate of a dominant phenomenon. But when you have a single digit share, larger and better samples are required for reasonable precision. Network ratings have gone from the 20s and 30s to twos and threes. Today, there are many stations and outlets that are unmeasurable.

Today, samples of tens of thousands of respondents are needed rather than one thousand – the US national sample size for decades. For our RADAR [Radio's All Dimension Audience Research] service, we went from a sample of 4,000 in 1969 to – I think we ended up in 2001 – a sample size of 16,000. We progressed in stages from 4,000 to 8,000 and then to 12,000. The price for the service related to sample size. We sold the increases to the industry by demonstrating the loss in precision of audience estimates due to audience fragmentation.

RADAR technique: the RADAR interview involved a one-week period where we would contact a person ideally eight times. Each time a respondent was asked about his/her activity from the time of the last contact up until this contact …

The easiest way to get out of the interview is to say, 'I didn't do anything. I'm done.' That makes for a very quick interview. If people learn that, the result is under-reporting. The objective is to cultivate complete and accurate reporting. That is a core reason why you don't want to throw a lot of other peripheral stuff on to a media measurement. By doing so, it creates fatigue factor; you cause people to be discouraged to ever say they do anything. They come to know that if they say 'yes', they get more questions. Once they learn that, you're in trouble as a researcher. So you want to keep the burdens light. By doing so, a better measurement is achieved. If a respondent is subjected to a two-hour interview and then you come back the next day and want to talk again, a likely response is, 'Are you nuts? I just gave you two hours yesterday.' If you can complete an interview in three or four or five minutes, it's a different matter. You can give them some small incentive and they'll stay with you.

A truism in research is that the more you ask, the less you get on any one subject. By that I mean that a properly defined survey dedicated solely to the measurement of television yields one result. In contrast, if an attempt is made to measure four or five media and product information, a natural result is to find less usage of each component … In general, more questions per subject will yield more activity; fewer will yield less. That is one element.

The other element is the so-called fatigue factor.

A respondent may begin a survey by wishing to be helpful. As more and more is asked, the mind set changes from 'how can I be helpful' to 'how can I get out of this'… it makes life easier to say 'no' than 'yes' – in order to get to the end of the process. Multimedia measurements are not as accurate as single subject surveys – assuming all else is equal. When recruiting someone to be part of a survey, you necessarily have to tell something about what is coming. If you tell them you need to move in for a few days to get all your questions asked versus proposing a 15-minute survey, different responses result. So there are many things that mitigate against multi-faceted studies.

We have learned that the so-called single-source data where you try to get it all will not hold up over time. The quality of information is not up to what it should be, or not up to standards. So to this day, notwithstanding the fact that in this country we've had 30, 40 maybe more measured efforts at doing multimedia product media surveys, none have succeeded. One of the more recent ones was Project Apollo by Arbitron – which one of my friends called 'Project Appalling'. (Metzger 2000)

Metzger is highlighting what the authors call underlying survey wars. Everyone in the industry knows that non-participation in surveys has become a major issue and that attempts at single-source data are fraught with methodological difficulties (simply fusing the data from a sample from one panel with a sample in another panel is not going to solve the problem). Creating more measurements of exposure does not create single source data. Simple categories that showed a critical mass of an audience are now competing with thousands of categories attempting to demonstrate a market. This puts the original agreements on exposure as the standard under pressure, as it does the Mint Master, that is, the organization that produces the audience ratings.

For ratings intellectuals like Leo Bogart the single source pursuit and the role of computers have displaced the role of the ratings intellectual; computation has come to replace good judgement.

The universal use of the computer in business prompted a desire to crowd the maximum amount of information onto a single spreadsheet, and thus to squeeze an ever-greater variety of acts about product and media consumption out of a given database. Advertisers have become more and more obsessed with the idea of the 'single source' – the dream of getting all the information on what individuals buy and on all their media experiences from one giant research service, so that cause and effect can be clearly measured. Presumably such a service would end the deplorable present necessity of putting together the data derived from different research organizations, with all the inevitable inconsistencies that result. The underlying premise is that the quality of information from a single source could be equivalent to what can be obtained by specialized studies that focus on just one subject at a time. The premise is incorrect, but good judgement, experience, knowledge, and common sense are commonly overruled by the desire for convenience. (Bogart 2000a: 132)

Summary

Strange are the uses of radio statistics. Last week in Variety two double-page advertisements appeared. One tried to prove by Cooperative Analysis of Broadcasting figures that CBS [Columbia Broadcasting System] was the leading network of the land. The other, also using C.A.B. figures, advanced the proposition that NBC's Red Network led all the rest. Not responsible for interpretations of its figures is C.A.B. Having used them against each other, the networks last week united in using C.A.B. statistics against their common foe ASCAP, the cooperative which controls most U.S. music. The networks claimed that according to C.A.B. figures radio listening had not decreased since their contract with ASCAP acrimoniously expired Dec. 31. Promptly they were jolted with the news that in its regular report C.A.B. had checked the popularity of 91 evening programs, discovered that since the New Year 52 were down, 35 up, four unchanged. Anon. (*Time* 1941)

The 1941 *Time* story tells us a lot about how broadcast ratings can be used as a tool to influence the media industry and, indeed, public perceptions about what is happening with networks and programming alike. CAB was the Cooperative

Analysis of Broadcasting, an advertiser-led consortium that produced the first radio ratings. At first glance, the use of CAB ratings looks like manipulation of industries and audiences. In this case, the ratings are used to argue that one network is better or more popular than another or that network popularity has not suffered because of unfortunate contract events in their programming. This is perhaps the most common type of example that people are familiar with in arguments about ratings. But ratings have always been more than that. They have a close resemblance with public polling and voting. This is not surprising. As we have seen the ratings intellectuals who designed the ratings also created the first opinion polls. Audience ratings as a particular form of humanistic social research also adopted the revolutionary panel-based survey research technique using probabilistic representative samples.

The ratings intellectuals have been and remain essential to the audience-ratings convention. They originally had a bridging role, working across private and university sectors. They were creators of methodology as well as users of the methodology, fierce critics and often businesspeople with vested interests in the very markets they studied. Most importantly, however, they anticipated the world of multiplication of publics and a world where large populations needed to express their preferences or voting intentions. Modern discussions on the multiplication of publics, like those happening now on monitory democracy (Keane 2008) and the role of the internet in gift economies and participation, have their precursor in the practical work of the ratings intellectual. Public polling and audience ratings were not created simply to be a capitalist tool of domination. Quite the opposite. The early ratings or survey intellectuals, especially those like Hans Zeisel and Paul Lazarsfeld, who followed a strong socialist tradition, worked purposefully in the media field to develop methodologies that enhanced, from their point of view, democracy. Likewise Gallup and Crossley did not see their activities as purely commercial but intimately tied to developing methodologies to enhance the 'public vote'. Samples and panels were methodologies developed to ensure representation of the public through small samples. This dual identity of the ratings, rarely acknowledged, is undeniable.

The modern era in audience ratings, however, is marked by underlying survey wars. Traditional audience research has relied on statistical sampling that provided Case Rich foundations for syndicated ratings. Exposure has been the key measure, even though it is Data Poor compared with sites like Facebook. However, the traditional panel is under threat because of problems of non-response bias, among other things. This situation is unsustainable because in the long term the media industry will end up with Case Poor and Data Poor delivery of ratings. The alternatives, like drawing information from sources like Facebook, are also not sustainable. These alternatives would most likely be Case Poor and Data Rich. The idea of having non-representative population data for ratings would be an unacceptable trade-off from the point of view of currency. It is one thing to make the trade-off with exposure as a measure and keeping the study Case Rich and another to have data that does not represent statistically defined populations.

In the meantime, the demand for more measurement is increasing. Collecting data from proprietary set-top boxes, for instance, is growing, but that faces all the difficulties of privacy and intrusion that are emerging, apart from the fact that each proprietary system will have its own measurements. Google has combined with Nielsen to try to capture the tail of small audiences in television and to auction off those audiences. What all these attempts at new measurement are encountering is what the authors have identified in this chapter – the audience. The audience is an integral part of the audience-ratings convention and its assent is essential to the overall working of ratings industry.

4 The Audit

Ratings methodology came into the United States public spotlight for the first time on a large scale with the quiz-show scandals of the early 1960s, even if it was not responsible for the scandal. The US Congress brought in its expert statistical methodologists to check out what the ratings companies were doing. In effect Congress undertook a formal audit. Auditing takes a number of forms. Sometimes it takes an informal turn as when there are methodological debates among proponents of different ratings systems. This happened in the 1930s when C.E. Hooper went public with his arguments for the superiority of his telephone coincidental method over CAB's recall method. It happened in the United Kingdom following the commencement of the ITV service in 1955 when Nielsen, TAM and the BBC's survey unit were engaged in very public debates over methodology and audience size. It is happening today as Arbitron promotes its portable peoplemeter technology (PPM) as an alternative technology of the ratings. Sometimes the auditing process is conducted by independent or joint industry bodies such as the Media Rating Council (MRC) in the United States or the Broadcasters' Audience Research Board (BARB) in the United Kingdom. And sometimes, as in the case of the Congressional inquiry following the quiz-show scandals of the 1960s, auditing can be conducted by or through government processes.

In this chapter the authors look at some of these audit processes and the impact they have on how the media industry runs. It is not only research methods that are inside the black box of audience ratings. There is a whole array of groups, expert and non-expert, that monitor syndicated research. The different parties to the ratings convention need to have confidence in those carrying out the survey, in the quality of the instruments being used, and in the integrity of the results. In short, there needs to be integrity in the practice of the ratings and surveys and this integrity needs to be publicly demonstrated. Forms of public auditing provide this. Today, this auditing function has become increasingly contested.

Taming Error

In the United States the development of audience ratings has been the subject of extensive historical study (Beville 1988; Webster, Phalen and Lichty 2005). However, there have been few studies on the ratings as a social convention. A notable exception is ratings intellectual Peter Miller, who concluded that audience ratings involves an arrangement where all parties have a common interest in a coordination rule, none has a conflicting interest and none will deviate lest the coordination is lost (Miller 1994). This arrangement dictates that in the operation of the ratings there must be: firstly, an appeal to the inherent correctness of the measurement; and, secondly, a demonstration that the information that emerges from the measurement process is eminently practical for day-to-day purposes.

The discussion on the audience-ratings convention in the previous chapters raises some important issues for the development of an overarching theory of audience ratings. We argue that the empirical evidence on how the ratings operate points to a pluralistic rather than a constant-sum view of power. In the case of Australia, the ratings firms had to lobby forcefully in order for a systematic ratings system to be adopted. These firms then had primacy in the definition and adoption of ratings for many decades. In the United States, competing ratings providers gave way to monopoly. MacKenzie's idea of markets – particularly market information – as engines rather than cameras is important to the understanding of the audience-ratings convention because individuals like Hooper and Nielsen, and the structures established, can transform the field and have an effect on individual and corporate actions.

In Chapter 2 the authors outlined Stigler's example of the Trial of the Pyx, where all the specialized techniques used were subject to debate and decision among different parties. Because each coin of the realm could not be tested individually, a sampling system was required. Likewise, audience ratings, the coinage of the media realm, brings with it particular measures that are often contested and used in particular ways. The corporate decisions that developed around the operation of the Mint formed into ongoing agreements on measures. The decisions made about coinage were linked in a complex web of ideas on measures and standards.

The auditing in the Trial of the Pyx has its analogy in the audience-ratings convention. The powerful rationale behind audience ratings is that it is both a *public vote* and a *market measure*. The Mint, likewise, was both standard coin for the realm and linked to individual baron's interest in its accuracy and use for trade and, of course, for reserve. No baron wanted another baron to have an advantage in coin because of manipulation of the measure and the weights. Ratings methodologists such as Art Nielsen, Bill McNair and George Anderson had no interest in providing bogus data or in taking short cuts that might devalue the accuracy of the ratings. However, the United States did not have a system, like the one that had developed in Australia, where clients bought both sets of ratings, McNair and Anderson, as a default audit of one on the other. Nor did the United States have the equivalent of the Australian Broadcasting Control Board (ABCB), an independent government body that kept an eye on both what the ratings reported and how they were used.

Importantly, also, McNair and Anderson decided very early on to provide detailed information about procedures in the ratings books themselves, including estimates of error. These qualifications on the data and the decimal points are important because they allowed clients to understand that ratings points numbers were probabilistic and that their interpretation required skill. This did not stop some clients treating the figures as precise estimates, but the provision of this advice within the ratings books only became mandated in the United States after a major scandal.

The corporate ethos associated with interpreting audience ratings in the United States compared with Australia was different in the period leading up to the 1960s. In the United States a corporate approach of *taming error* dominated. Audience ratings figures were often sold to clients as though decimal points represented the real numbers of listeners or viewers, regardless of statistical variance. Some companies, moreover, would sell audience data from surveys that had not been conducted. There was an additional problem. As the value of ratings grew so too did the motivation of organizations to 'hypo' the ratings. In the cases of deliberate deceit it was impossible for ratings companies like Nielsen to stop it. Gale Metzger recounts his personal involvement at the time when scandal hit:

> In 1957, a congressional committee had stimulated a review of media rating services by the American Statistical Association (ASA) ... This was followed by the Congressional Hearings of 1963, a major episodic event. At least two underlying factors served to generate interest in the Congress. First, many in the Congress owned broadcast facilities. Lyndon Johnson was one. He and his wife prospered through their ownership of broadcast stations; they were not unique. Those involved individuals had a personal interest in the ratings; they realized that ratings determined the value of their assets. They also recognized the social importance of ratings insofar as they allegedly reflected the tastes and interests of the American people.
>
> The ASA tactical review was directed by Bill Maddow and Morris Hansen. Hansen, Hurwitz and Maddow were renowned US statisticians. The three of them wrote an important text in the United States, *Sample Survey Methods and Theory*. They worked at US Bureau of the Census. They were not just great theoreticians. They had first-hand experience ... in the 1960s, they were hired by Nielsen as consultants. I was the liaison between those gentlemen and the Nielsen Company for about ten years.
>
> The conclusion from the 1957 report was that the methods and procedures were reasonable. Some were not satisfied with that conclusion. A few years later, there was a quiz show scandal in the United States. A very popular quiz program, 'Twenty-one' was found to be rigged. Contestants

in sound-proof booths were found to have been given the questions in advance. This was not the pure measurement of knowledge and skills and understandings that was represented. Rather it was something that was being set up by the producers to create drama; the results were preordained. It was realized that producers were doing this in order to get higher ratings – more measured audience and to sell more advertising at higher prices. This re-raised the question of … 'What are these things called ratings?' So there were Harris Congressional Hearings to consider the quality of ratings. Congressman Oren Harris was the committee chair. In those hearings it was determined that some measurement companies were bogus; i.e. were in effect making up numbers. Others were not forthright about their methodology – effectively not disclosing what they were doing and thus handicapping users in their efforts to understand the derivation of numbers that affected their businesses. A number of companies were examined, maybe ten, and some went out of business almost immediately.

Because Nielsen was the primary game in town, Nielsen was a focus. Two of the committee investigators, Messer's Richardson and Sparger, camped out at Nielsen. They befriended many of the Nielsen people. In the meantime they were engaging in investigative techniques, which included going through the office trash cans. In the actual public hearings, Nielsen was handled harshly. It was determined, to the embarrassment of many of their clients, that Nielsen was not being totally forthright in their disclosure of their methods. Nielsen was not telling the clients all that they were doing or where they may have made compromises. It appeared to be more than just 'putting your best foot forward'. Important network clients felt that they had been misled – effectively betrayed.

Henry Rahmel, the head of the Media Division, and Warren Cordell, the Chief Statistical Officer, were two people who testified for Nielsen. Arthur Nielsen Jr was in Europe and was not available to testify … It was a traumatizing event for the Nielsen witnesses because both were aware that Mr Cordell had written a 13-page memo to Art Nielsen Sr justifying his appeal for a higher budget and more people in his department by citing weaknesses in the systems. He knew what was in the full memo. He did not know if they had the entire memo or just part of it or how they may have acquired what they had. It was a memo that was labelled 'highly confidential'. In subsequent days, they slowly fed limited parts back to him. They had found copies of parts of this memo in the trash … In those days we didn't shred waste documents; extra copies went in the waste baskets. So that was how the investigators had acquired what they had. Cordell still didn't know how much of it they had. The fact that the hearings were coming may have stimulated a desire to do better and straightening things up. If there was a cause and effect, I was not aware. My sense was that there was a natural progression in trying to do better. In any event, at that point I was doing a lot with the networks and I remember after these hearings were finished, one of the Research Directors stood over me, wagged his finger in my face and threatened that if I ever participated in misleading him, he would have me castrated. The problem was that they were embarrassed. That should never happen again. The networks were the primary funders of all this work; it served as their market currency and if their currency was devalued, sales would be affected. (Metzger 2008)

The fallout from the Congressional hearings was the establishment of a Broadcast Rating Council (BRC), now the Media Rating Council (MRC). The BRC was overseen by an industry board with Hugh Malcolm Beville, who wrote a major history of audience ratings, as the first Executive Director. Beville had been Head of Research for the National Broadcasting Company (NBC) before the Second World War. He had been a high-ranking intelligence officer during the war and when he returned to civilian life he returned to the NBC. The BRC's successor, the Media Rating Council, is a non-profit organization. Revenue raised from membership fees finances the work of the council, with any company that uses media research eligible to become a member. Research providers like Nielsen and Arbitron are, however, expressly prohibited from becoming members. Today the MRC has almost 100 members drawn from the television and radio broadcasting, subscription television, print media and internet sectors, as well as advertising agencies. The MRC has a three-fold mission, as outlined by George Ivie, the council's Executive Director and Chief Executive Officer, in evidence to the Senate Committee on Commerce, Science and Transportation Hearings on the Fairness, Accuracy, Inclusivity and Responsiveness in Ratings Act in July 2005:

to secure for the media industry and related users audience measurement services that are valid, reliable and effective; to evolve and determine minimum disclosure and ethical criteria for media audience measurement services; and to provide and administer an audit system designed to inform users as to whether such audience measurements are conducted in conformance with the criteria and procedures developed. (Ivie 2005: 3)

The MRC conducts annual audits of rating service organizations which voluntarily submit to the auditing process. The MRC can also accredit new services, although the rating service organizations are neither required to submit their services for accreditation, nor prohibited from operating a new service that has not received

MRC accreditation. This became a major issue in 2004–5 when Nielsen expanded its rollout of Local People Meter, as we describe below. The MRC audits cover:

- Sample design, selection, and recruitment
- Sample composition by demographic group
- Data collection and fieldwork
- Metering, diary or interviewing accuracy
- Editing and tabulation procedures
- Data processing
- Ratings calculations
- Assessment of rating service disclosures of methodology and survey performance

Ratings services that submit to the accreditation process are required to disclose methods and performance measures, which may include:

- Source of sample frame
- Selection method
- Respondents by demographic group versus population
- Response rates
- Existence of special survey treatments for difficult to recruit respondent groups such as young or ethnic persons
- Editing procedures
- Minimum reporting requirements for media
- Ascription and data adjustment procedures employed
- Errors noted in published reports
- Data reissue standards and reissue instances
  (Media Rating Council 2010)

Congress did not legislate to regulate procedures but set up this industry watchdog to oversee the ratings services. The rating council had and has a limited role, to check that the ratings services 'say what they do and do what they say'. This includes disclosure standards. The label on a ratings book was required, like that provided by McNair and Anderson, to show what the ratings service did, how it got the sample, how it processed the data and so on. This was and is a formal audit but it does not extend to performance standards.

The second part of the post-hearings mission was to do methodological research to try to improve the systems. The Justice Department gave the industry a waiver to allow working together on methodological research. Statistical Research, Inc. (SRI) filled the void left by Nielsen's exit. SRI was created in 1968 by Gale Metzger and Gerald Glasser, a statistics professor at New York University. SRI took over Radio's All Dimension Audience Research (RADAR) three years later. SRI provided independent biannual reports on radio network audiences and, as Metzger recounts, launched a major initiative, Systems for Measuring and Reporting Television (SMART), as an alternative to Nielsen:

> They formed a group called CONTAM, which is an acronym for Committee on Nationwide Television Audience Measurement. There was also a parallel group called COLTAM, Committee on Local Television Audience Measurement, and COLRAM for Radio. Our firm was formed in late 1968, just after the hearings. My partner Gerald Glasser was from NYU. I left the Nielsen Company to join him and set up the firm. A good part of our work was with the networks in doing research on television audience measurement. We worked to assess how things could be improved. We did experimentation for the industry and for individual companies. What's reported in that 30-year history is a series of large studies, studies that were in those days funded at the US$60,000 to US$600,000 level. Doing this work and publishing it and discussions of findings were considered within the industry as a means to pressure Nielsen to do better over time.
>
> But what really forced Nielsen to make changes was the threat of competition. When AGB [Audits of Great Britain] tried to come into this country with the peoplemeter, that's when Nielsen picked up a peoplemeter, not before ... Rating companies who have monopolies talk about conducting research to do better but they rarely change. They keep doing the same old, same old. There's a financial reality: the more you spend on methodological research, the less money goes to the bottom line. I feel that the Nielsen Company, so long as it was in the hands of the Nielsen family, was really driven by a broader principle ... The monetary objectives are secondary. Art Nielsen was a principle-directed person who was a shining star in my life.
>
> When Nielsen sold the company to Dunn and Bradstreet, it converted from being a research company to becoming a money machine. With the monopoly position, they were making very good returns and it became very attractive to Corporate America. Now they have been sold several times and are in

the hands of private investors who have no interest in research; they have an interest in getting some multiple of their money back in a limited period of time ... That's a big part of the problem with the quality of measurement over time ... Our firm was successful because the industry felt that we could be used to encourage improvements – to do better work. Anyway when the peoplemeter came in, there were many issues. We were retained in 1987 to do a peoplemeter review. The product was a 600-page, 7-volume report on all aspects of the peoplemeter. It was well received within the industry. We kept the industry quite widely informed and gave Nielsen basically an agenda for how to improve.

One of the major studies we did was a study on fatigue. We analysed TV tuning and persons viewing levels as a function of how long the meters had been in the homes. It was determined that the longer the meter was in the home, the less button-pushing occurred; that is, fewer people were reported to be in the audience. That study was a landmark. I don't think the core issue of fatigue has ever been addressed effectively or the study updated. The research has been mimicked around the world ...

After a person is assigned a task they may be quite anxious to do it right; that motivation may erode over time. It is also true that the meter has certain prompts to encourage people to enter their viewing. It implicitly encourages a cooperator to 'feed the monster'. If you push one button it stops bugging you. And if two or three people are in the room there's nothing to motivate the entry of that second or third person. We work with imperfect devices.

Notwithstanding all the work that had been done in the 1970s and 1980s, the feeling was that Nielsen really hadn't changed and still was not responsive. Nielsen had a pricing philosophy which became more onerous over time. They charged for everything you accessed. You couldn't just buy the service and then use it. You had to pay for every piece of data you got. Special tabs cost a lot of money and time. During the 1980s, Nielsen sold the networks home-by-home data tapes. The networks bought those tapes and gave them to SRI. We developed a special analysis facility and as an outside company could process and produce reports faster than Nielsen could for less money. Nielsen became aware of our service but they never did anything about it – to my amazement.

NBC was primarily behind this work and then CBS got aboard. As experiments, NBC would place parallel orders at the same time from Nielsen and from us. They would receive the tabs the next day from us and two weeks later from Nielsen – at double the price. Anyway CBS heard about this and CBS wanted to buy access to our system. Nielsen forced CBS to buy the tapes even though we already had the data on our computer. CBS paid

Nielsen US$200,000 or US$300,000 so that they could access that data. Nielsen turned the cheque over, endorsed it and put it in the bank. There was no work done. They were selling the data by each point of access. This business policy was galling to the networks. I thought it was self-destructive. As a business, you want to provide good, easily accessible information so that it gets used well and everybody prospers. As the clients prosper, you can charge more. They will pay more if you help them prosper.

So in any event, after the peoplemeter review and the criticism around it, the networks decided that having this independent research to force Nielsen to improve wasn't enough. The industry needed to set up a better model. That began the SMART era … SRI was commissioned to build a better system. You could say that this commitment was evolving during the 80s. The project was actually launched in '89 or '90 …

We also had to negotiate an arrangement for the long term. AGB felt they were encouraged by the networks to compete with Nielsen and they lost a lot of money trying. Arbitron also claimed to have lost a lot of money trying to compete with Nielsen. If we built a large staff and the networks decided to walk away, we would be in the same position as AGB and ARBITRON. I was not prepared to get started in this and build a staff without having a fall-back position in case they did walk. Therefore, we had a cancellation clause which provided that if the project were terminated, we would be paid a shut-down fee. We negotiated a good contractual relationship.

In the almost ten-year existence of the project, there were three generations of meetings with the CEOs. We met with Larry Tische, the Cap Cities' team of Murphy, Burke and Sias and Bob Wright and the people at NBC. They collectively blessed the work and ultimately Fox joined the effort. Fox was growing during the 90s and we had a long negotiation over getting Fox in. There was a lot going on with the business side of SMART. The work itself meant that we built a brand new meter, we built an entirely new system; we put up a television audience measurement laboratory in Philadelphia and had it up and operating for almost a year.

An important business policy was that we charged a client one price and once they paid that price, the data could be accessed in any way they wanted. We also provided desktop reporting; the data were on your desktop computer and tabulations could be run at will. They could use the data effectively without incremental costs … Special analyses were not a profit centre; it was a service centre.

In 1999, the SMART laboratory was up and going and we were ready to go to a national rollout. The year 1999 was a crazy time. It was the era of the internet craze and extraordinary 20 per cent annual returns on investments. We joined hands with Anderson Consulting, a major consulting company, to help us rollout the service. We authored a $100,000,000 proposal; we proposed that $50,000,000 would be raised from within the industry and $50,000,000 from outside. The outside portion was said to be easy to get after we had the internal commitments. In 1998, the inside sale was said to be a slam-dunk. But in 1999 there were changes in management. Larry Tische sold CBS. He was very committed to this project. Mal Karmazin came in. At NBC, Jack Walsh was about to retire. There was a report in *Businessweek* magazine that said he had put out an edict that any NBC investments must bring immediate payout; there would be no diminution of the bottom line.

The payout on SMART was four years plus. The national rollout was scheduled over three years. At that point, there would be two national services. Once the second service was operational, a choice could be made to go with the best and, at that point, benefits begin to accrue. As part of SMART, we proposed an Industry Board of Directors to help direct the system. It would not be solely controlled by SRI. We were not able to get the internal industry funding and SMART was shut down in 1999. Nielsen continues to be the sole supplier to the industry. Occasionally, people will call me and lament the loss of SMART. The industry had the opportunity and they passed on it. It was a practical business failure; not a research failure. The research product was great and industry observers will tell you that. We delivered on our promises. (Metzger 2008)

It is worthwhile quoting Metzger at length from his interview not only because of his central role in audience ratings history in the United States but also because he provides a succinct overview of the role of his company as at one moment an independent provider of checks on audience ratings and at another a potential competitive player in the provision of ratings themselves. It is a signal of the respect with which all parties to the audience ratings convention held Metzger that they could accept him as both competitor and independent player. That said, it is difficult to know whether SMART was a stalking horse to try to force Nielsen to change and, indeed, following the demise of SMART, Nielsen took up many of the innovations created by Metzger. Nevertheless, Metzger himself emerged after the Congressional hearings as part of a semi-formal auditing system in the United States. He was a key part of the CONTAM research and reports, especially the major Peoplemeter review. His company's research did what the MRC did not do: SRI provided performance overviews of existing ratings research.

The outcomes of the Congressional hearings, therefore, had a formal aspect in the creation of an independent body that checked that the measures were what companies said they were and semi-formal encouragement at industry-research collaboration. There is, though, another semi-formal but nevertheless powerful means of auditing that affects the audience-ratings convention. This comes from litigation in the public domain. Once again, accuracy of the ratings is at the heart of the contest.

Invisible Audiences

If the ruler doesn't work, we can't use it to measure the room and know how much carpet to buy ... Radio was an effective medium and still is an effective medium – it is only the measurement that is not right. Ceril Shagrin, Executive Vice President, Corporate Research, at Univision Communications

Sample selection and accuracy in measurement have always been major issues for parties to the ratings convention. Occasionally disputes over methodology and participation in research can generate disagreements that call the credibility of research providers into question and threaten the very basis of the convention. Such disputes often arise from, or result in, the introduction of new measurement systems or technologies, and changes in the conduct of audience measurement services.

In 1999, for example, Nielsen began trialling 'local peoplemeters' (LPMs) in the Boston television market, with a view to replacing the longstanding Audimeter/ diary system. The LPM system was designed to provide detailed, year-round television audience data, and to circumvent the issue of errors in recall that are an almost inevitable part of the diary system. Nielsen chose Boston as a test market because it is less demographically diverse than other large television markets, which 'simplified the process of recruiting and maintaining a representative sample' and therefore helped keep costs down (Napoli 2008: 8). But this decision was met with immediate opposition from some broadcasters and advertisers who were concerned that the system would under-represent minority audiences, with implications for advertising revenue and programming. Nielsen continued to develop plans to rollout the system in other large markets including New York in 2004. But concerns about the LPM system's capacity to accurately measure minority viewing continued to simmer. In March 2004 Lachlan Murdoch, Deputy Chief Operating Officer of News Corporation, issued a statement condemning the preliminary results from the New York LPM trial, which appeared to show that audiences for some programmes aimed at minorities were significantly lower than under the diary system. New York Senator Hillary Clinton and two other members of Congress, along with a number of other leading New York political leaders, then wrote to Nielsen President and CEO Susan Whiting to voice their concerns. News Corporation subsequently hired three PR firms to organize a 'community organization', 'Don't Count Us Out', to campaign against the LPM system principally on the basis that it threatened media diversity. New York Assemblyman José Rivera outlined the case against Nielsen:

> This systematic undercounting [of minority viewers] could lead to the cancellation of numerous programs geared toward African American and Latino viewers, as well as impacting negatively on Spanish-speaking programming, dealing a serious blow to efforts to encourage diversity in the industry as a whole … Nielsen's decision to use LPMs in New York effective April 8th directly threatens minority-oriented television programming, employment opportunities for minority producers, directors, actors, writers, and related businesses including advertising and television production. (Quoted in Napoli 2008: 11)

In April 2004, Nielsen announced that it would delay the launch of its New York LPM system until June. The company also announced its support for the creation of an Independent Task Force on Television Measurement, chaired by former Congresswoman Cardiss Collins, to review the system and the complaints. In July 2004, the MRC audit committee voted to withhold accreditation of Nielsen's New York LPM, citing problems with minority audience measurement and fault rates. Despite the supposed confidentiality of the audit report, extracts had been published in the Los Angeles Times in June, including findings that 'one in six viewers was improperly classified as black and one in nearly 14 viewers was improperly labeled Hispanic' (Napoli 2008: 15). Spanish-language broadcaster Univision entered the fray, filing a suit in the LA Superior Court seeking an injunction against the proposed July rollout of the LPM system in Los Angeles. Univision argued that Nielsen's Los Angeles sample was flawed, that the LPM data would be misleading for advertisers and marketers, and that this could negatively affect the provision of programming dedicated to minority audiences. The request for the injunction was denied, but the LPM issue was now firmly on the political radar, with the question of the impact of the system on media diversity now central to the debate.

In July 2004, a subcommittee of the Senate Commerce Committee held a hearing on the LPM issue, with evidence given by the President of Univision, the Executive Director and CEO of the MRC, the President and CEO of the Advertising Research Foundation, a representative of Fox Television Stations, and Susan Whiting, President and CEO of Nielsen Media Research. Philip Napoli later wrote that, 'While the bulk of the hearing was focused on the issue of Nielsen's methodology and the possible undercounting of minority viewers, the obvious subtext of the proceeding was whether Congress should step in and impose some sort of direct regulatory oversight over the television ratings business' (Napoli 2008: 17–18). After the hearing, Nielsen announced that the William C. Velasquez Institute, a non-profit research organization specializing in research relevant to Latino Americans, would evaluate and make recommendations on its television audience measurement systems. Nielsen also provided an initial US$2.5 million in funding to establish a new joint research initiative, the Council for Research Excellence, to work on large, industry-wide projects.

Still the issue rumbled on. In July 2005, four Republican senators sponsored a bill to create the FAIR [Fairness, Accuracy, Inclusivity, and Responsiveness in] Ratings Act, which was referred to the Senate Committee on Commerce, Science and Transportation. The FAIR Act proposed to make MRC accreditation mandatory for providers of television ratings measurement systems; in other words, Nielsen would be prevented from continuing with any LPM trials that had not been audited and approved by the MRC. The Senate Committee heard testimony by George Ivie, Executive Director and CEO, Media Rating Council; Susan Whiting, President and CEO Nielsen Media Research; Ceril Shagrin, Executive VP for Research, Univision; Pat Mullen, CEO, Tribune Broadcasting; Kathy Crawford, President of the consultancy and media buying firm Local Broadcast MindShare Worldwide; and Gale Metzger, former CEO, SMART Media.

The accountability of Nielsen's services, the representativeness of the MRC, and the issue of accuracy of measurement featured prominently in witness testimony. Nielsen argued that mandatory accreditation would inhibit the development and improvement of services, while the company's critics argued that its monopoly position was the real threat to innovation. Gale Metzger went so far as to say that 'it would be difficult to have less competition or less innovation than we have now' (Metzger 2005: 3), and noted that in the past it had only been the threat of competition that had forced Nielsen to introduce new technologies. Susan Whiting pointed to Nielsen's intention to adopt a recently introduced MRC voluntary code of conduct, to the company's support for the Independent Task Force on Television Measurement and to its funding of the Council for Research Excellence as evidence of Nielsen's commitment to accuracy and accountability. 'Nielsen Media Research is in the truth business,' she argued, 'the truth of what people are actually watching on television, and how they are watching it' (Whiting 2005: 1).

While the catalyst for the introduction of the bill had been concerns that the LPM system under-counted minority audiences and therefore posed a threat to media diversity, the hearings and the debate around it revealed a great deal about the tensions and issues within audience measurement in the United States even though the bill ultimately did not enter into law. As Philip Napoli has observed, the introduction of the LPM, as with any new technology, changes the overall picture of the audience, with implications for all parties to the convention (Napoli 2008: 20–21). This was the case again in 2009 when the Federal Communications Commission launched an inquiry into the impact of the introduction of Arbitron's Portable People Meter (PPM) measurement system on radio stations targeting minority audiences.

Hispanic advertisers and radio managers had been shocked to find that Arbitron's Portable People Meter significantly under-reported the Hispanic audience, even compared with the US Census that also under-reports Hispanic households. Big money rides on radio ratings and if you do not have any ratings for your radio station or programme then you do not have an audience to sell in the market. The issue of Hispanic representation in the ratings went to court in 2009 and Arbitron subsequently reached agreements with the New York and New Jersey State Attorneys General. Arbitron agreed to change its ratings system to ensure that ethnic listeners were properly represented, including recruiting participants through a combination of telephone number and address-based methods and increasing the number of cell phone-only households.

The National Association of Black Owned Broadcasters (NABOB) and the Spanish Radio Association were required in the ruling to fund a joint project to support ethnic radio. This dispute gives an insight into the impact of the 'black box' of audience ratings as a sampling and a survey technology and the multiple interests tied up with them. It was a different insight than the US Congressional hearings of 1963. The issue at stake in this court challenge was not only the role of ratings companies in representing ethnic audiences accurately, but the role of the Census itself in accurately reflecting the US population. Ratings companies use the Census to construct the establishment surveys from which panels are drawn. If the Census under-represents particular groups or communities then the ratings panel will do so as well. In the case of Hispanic communities there are various reasons for under-representation, ranging from an unwillingness to complete the Census through to difficulties in finding the communities themselves. Some in the Census management have proposed using sampling techniques to represent the Hispanic community. A census, however, by its nature is a census, counting everyone, and that proposal has received strong resistance from political parties, especially the Republicans, and within the Census management itself. The US is not the only country that has difficulties counting its ethnic communities.

There are also audiences whose preferences are not expressed through the formal ratings system. The audience in the case against Arbitron was represented by legal means and specific organizations operating in the ratings market. Modern social networking media have encountered the voice of the audience in the market but not through legal parties. Facebook planned to exploit the private information of its 500 million members by creating one of the world's largest market research databases. It planned to allow multinational companies to selectively target its members in order to research the appeal of new products. Companies would have been able to pose questions to specially selected members based on such intimate details as marital status and sexual preference. In 2009 Facebook amended its privacy settings that allowed Facebook to take ownership of anything users posted on to their profile and even delete their accounts (Walters 2009). Facebook users were outraged and protested against the social networking giant. Mark Zuckerberg, the founder, issued a statement saying, 'trust us, we're not doing this to profit from you, it's so we are legally protected as we enable you to share content with other users and services' (Walters 2009). Needless to say, users were not happy to just 'trust' the CEO of a billion-dollar company and Facebook was forced to revert back to its old privacy policies. Zuckerberg subsequently set up a poll asking users to vote on new privacy policies as he still felt they need to be updated (Musil 2009).

What we see in the Facebook experience is what history has told us about audiences and the media industry. Audiences are sensitive about the ways they are represented and how information about them is used. The metrics associated with audiences – how they are measured and how the information is captured – are directly related to how decisions are made about advertising, programming and the provision of services. Facebook, in short, came up against what traditional broadcasting has experienced for decades. Particular agreements and arrangements have to be made when dealing with audiences that limit intrusion but still allow the interested party to gather information about them. Facebook, in short, was not part of an audience-ratings convention.

Facebook's experience is part of a trend towards the measurement and monetization of massive audiences online that are perceived to have economic value. Google bought YouTube in 2006 for US$1.65 billion when YouTube had over 100 million videos viewed and over 72 million individual visitors every day. Google makes its money from small text advertisements that appear next to Google search results. These advertisements deliver most of Google's US$16.6 billion in revenue. This is a different model from traditional audience measurement. Google started planning in 2007 to have advertisements that appear inside videos on its sites. Google's approach is to buy massive audiences and to experiment with them. It does not need panels or samples because it has either a record of what its users do, or a site like YouTube, where the audience gathers. That audience in itself has economic value. This idea of looking at the census and not the sample has not escaped dedicated pay-TV services. Ian Garland, formerly a senior director at Nielsen and now head of the Australian Subscription Television and Radio Association (ASTRA), outlines the pay-TV view.

I think that we've lived in this really interesting period, certainly in Australia from 1956 until 1996, when pay-TV started, when there was 40 years of oligopoly rule. From 1996 to 2000, and since 2007, we saw subscription TV primarily challenging it, and the advent of broadband means that there is now alternative challenges, not just to free to air, but also to pay-TV as well … I have a 13-year-old daughter, and last year she harvested all of *Chaser* [a comedy show] online. And, in fact, there was another example that came from that, even in our home, where we have Foxtel IQ, we came home to watch some live sport, and we didn't have a second unit, and she was halfway through a *Friends* episode. So she left that, went into her bedroom where she has a laptop, and broadband access, and she found the rest of the episode online. That, to me, says there's a mindset here, and this is, part of this is coming to an overarching model of how the consumer works, and just understanding the nature of the consumer, and then where the money comes with regard to that … Audiences can no longer just be assumed to be this passive mass which is sitting back there waiting for the seed, whether it's program or advertising, to fall on fertile ground. I think broadcast, the traditional model, it's throwing seeds as widely as possible, hoping as many [as possible] will take root. For us in pay-TV, it's about targeting. And, indeed, we talk about fragmented audiences or fractionalised audiences. But that is almost the negative. The glass half empty. The glass half full for us is all about targets. We know each of our customers. Austar, Foxtel and Optus each have one to one relationships with over two million subscribers today. They know more about those people than 7, 9, 10, the ABC [Australian Broadcasting Corporation] and SBS can know about their 20 million subscribers because, at best, they're throwing it out, hoping it lands somewhere, and there's no particular link back. Subscription TV by definition, the most important metric, is, 'are they paying to keep the service next month?' (Garland 2008)

In Australia Foxtel and regional pay-TV group Austar, in conjunction with Multi Channel Network (MCn), announced in 2008 the launch of a new digital television audience measurement system (AMS) that would, the group argued, be the largest measurement system in Australia, providing viewing results from a panel of 10,000 Australian subscription TV homes (Bodey 2008). The system is designed to give the pay-TV group information on how Australians are adapting to the digital TV environment, the acceptance of the new standard definition and high definition multi-channels, and trends in timeshifted viewing. 'No one was willing to admit it was a competitive service to OzTAM's, which measures free-to-air and pay-TV viewing. Rather the new system is seen as complementary' (Bodey 2008). (OzTAM is the Australian Television Audience Measurement.) This shift of pay-TV providers towards their own ratings is not only an Australian phenomenon, it is an international phenomenon.

There is nothing wrong with Google having proprietary control over its audience research. Indeed, there is nothing wrong with pay-TV controlling its own research. However, such an arrangement does not solve the problem of a universally agreed currency for the media trade or public transparency of research results. Historically, as earlier chapters have shown, hypoing or distortion of representation of the markets and audience are irresistible where formal auditing mechanisms are not there. The newspaper and advertiser experience in the United Kingdom at the beginning of the 1900s is a classic example of what happens when non-audited, non-public systems are the only systems of claiming audience figures. The US Congressional hearings on audience ratings were extraordinary not only because of the pressure on commercial owners who woke up to their public importance, but also because of the recognition that the conventions governing audience ratings were also in the public interest.

The British Broadcasting Corporation (BBC) never had in its early years the problem of trying to demonstrate an audience to a commercial market. Its brief was already one of having to demonstrate to the government that it was representing the public.

The BBC: Robert Silvey's Thermometer and Barometer

Audience measurement, properly used, can be a good servant; but it is a bad master ... the fate of the *Battleship Potemkin* shows what happens when the ratings take over. Robert Silvey, Head of BBC Audience Research, 1936–60

It is a remarkable feature of the early BBC that its broadcasters worked in almost complete ignorance of their audiences. None of those involved in making programmes for the British public had any systematic knowledge of the audiences for whom they were making these programmes nor the reactions of those audiences to the programmes they had made. As the BBC's first Listener Research Director, Robert Silvey, himself pointed out, unlike other inter-war mass media, the cinema or the newspaper press, broadcasting had 'no box office, no sales figures'; the 'link between microphone and listener ... carried only a one-way traffic'. Siân Nicholas (Nicholas 2006)

> **All the time there has been in the background, the inexorable tick of thousands of meters and the rustle of completed questionnaires – surely the most comprehensive cattle herding operation ever undertaken. Sometimes one is compelled to ask oneself whether it is not reminiscent of the Maginot Line – a magnificent structure but did it really serve any useful purpose?** Nigel Rogers (Rogers 1969: 31)

The United Kingdom has its own ratings intellectuals, not least Tony Twyman, Gale Metzger's counterpart in the United States. But, as Siân Nicholas suggests, it also had its 'anti-ratings' intellectuals (Nicholas 2006). Robert Silvey was an audience research methodologist and head of audience research for the whole of the early part of the BBC's audience research history and before competition entered the broadcast market. He may have been anti-ratings but he was certainly not anti-probabilistic sampling. The limits on Silvey's work were directly imposed upon him by his management. The BBC decided early on, and provided the direction to senior management and to Silvey, that audience research was *not* be used to determine future policy of the BBC.

The BBC started broadcasting in 1922 and was incorporated by Royal Charter in 1927, giving it independent status, at arm's length from government interference. In 1936 the BBC began systematic audience research when it set up the Listener Research Section (LRS) in the Home Intelligence Department of the BBC Public Relations Division. The LRS became the BBC Listener Research Department (LRD) in 1939 and in 1950 the LRD was named the BBC Audience Research, as television started to become a major medium.

We know from the historical record that the BBC had its own advisory committees, public meetings, personal contacts and listener correspondence – over 50,000 items a year by 1927 – that provided feedback on radio programmes. The BBC sought listener comments through radio appeals, advertising in the *Radio Times* and sometimes through 'programme consultants'. Outside of the BBC the press ran listener 'preference polls' and did their own listener surveys. The listener associations and the Radio Manufacturers' Association also collected listener views.

Silvey was 31 in 1936 when he started as head of research at the BBC. He had been employed in the statistical department at the London Press Exchange (LPE) and was the author of *News Chronicle*'s path-breaking 1931 'Reader Interest Survey of the British Press'. Silvey had also undertaken a survey of English-language broadcasts and advertisements directed at UK radio listeners from Europe. This audience was in the tens of millions.

Silvey was under no illusion about his brief at the BBC. It was not part of his section's role to apply its findings or even to decide whether research findings should be applied or not. 'This explicit separation of audience research from programme-making was crucial to its initial acceptance within the BBC; as Silvey later put it, "Map-making and navigating were quite different functions. Ours was map-making". Listener research findings were to be made freely available to BBC staff, but were considered to be confidential to the BBC and not to be published or otherwise disseminated in any way except in certain narrowly defined circumstances, usually publicity-related' (Nicholas 2006). This did not mean that the BBC itself did not have very precise views of what kinds of research interested it. Indeed, it was made clear to Silvey that a 'sociological' and not a 'statistical' approach should inform his research.

> In May 1930, Charles Siepmann of the Talks Department and Val Gielgud (brother of Sir John), Director of Features and Drama, both of whom had long expressed frustration at the lack of substantive information about the audiences for their programmes, strongly argued for a more systematic approach to audience research. In response to those who feared the tyranny of crude audience figures, Siepmann argued that what was required was not a 'statistical' but a 'sociological' approach. This point was subsequently reinforced by Hilda Matheson, former BBC Director of Talks (1927–31), who, writing in the *Sociological Review* in 1935, argued that information about the modes of presentation that audiences preferred were just as important as information about the types of programme they most listened to; further, that 'more attention was being paid to social change in primitive societies than to the social effects of radio'. One of the BBC's principal programme consultants, Filson Young, underlined this point, arguing that what was needed above all was an understanding of the role that listening itself played in people's lives. (Nicholas 2006)

Silvey's first work involved creating 'panels' – not of the Lazarsfeld kind and not probabilistic. The 350-member Drama Panel, for example, was made up of ordinary volunteer listeners who filled in qualitative questionnaires over a three-month period about each production of the Department of Features and Drama to which they had listened out of a possible total of 47 productions. This panel was considered very successful by the BBC and Silvey subsequently created other similar panels for other programmes, like Talks (spoken-word programmes). Silvey called this research the Listening Thermometer because it registered the 'temperature' of the audience response to a programme. Silvey understood, however, that the weakest part of the methodology was in estimating audience size for programmes and in his final report he advocated to BBC management that the principal need was for some way of measuring not only 'audience *opinions* about a programme but the actual *size* of that audience' (Nicholas 2006, emphasis added).

Silvey rejected the research methodology currently being developed for radio in the United States as one-dimensional and unreliable, including telephone coincidental, telephone recall and the Audimeter. Sampling methodology, however, Silvey had time for, even though the BBC itself considered modern sampling as dubious:

> Silvey's compromise was to draw up what he termed the Listening Barometer (i.e. it measured 'pressure rather than heat'), setting out to measure not a monolithic 'radio public' *per se* but the variety of 'radio publics'. The first such 'barometer', the Variety Listening Barometer, was established in the autumn of 1937, and comprised 2000 listeners randomly recruited from an astonishing 47,000 volunteers after a microphone appeal by Director of Variety, John Watt. These volunteers completed weekly logs specifically listing the Variety programmes they had listened to over the previous week (again, 'No Duty-Listening, please!'). After interviewing a parallel control group it was discovered that while the members of the Variety panel were, unsurprisingly, atypical of the average listener in the *extent* of their listening to Variety programmes, they were in fact quite representative in their relative *choices* of programme. The panel findings could therefore be used to register listener choice by estimating relative if not absolute audience size. On this basis, [the Listener Research Department] was permitted to extend the experiment and establish a General Listening Barometer of each day's listening, based on weekly returns from 4,000 volunteer listeners. (Nicholas 2006)

In 1937 and 1938, Silvey conducted the first national surveys of listening habits ever conducted anywhere in the world. His team recruited 3,000 households from the General Post Office's list of wireless licence-holders. The one-sheet questionnaire sought information on times of day people listened to the radio and what types of programmes they liked and when. Silvey received a 44 per cent return rate and found a pattern of daytime listening that peaked between 1 and 2 p.m., then again between 5 and 6 p.m. Listeners preferred light music in the middle of the day, with variety, plays and talks in the later afternoon, with a steady audience until 10 p.m. 'Members of the BBC senior management who had long argued that "nobody dines before 8" were shocked to learn that in fact most people had finished their evening meal before 7 p.m.' (Nicholas 2006)

As Nicholas points out, Silvey's work had a direct parallel with Tom Harrisson and Charles Madge's Mass-Observation movement that started in 1937 and Silvey's work meshed well with the research ethos of the time (Nicholas 2006). Harrisson and Madge's approach was quasi-anthropological and involved volunteer-based 'observation':

Hilda Jennings and Winifred Gill's impressionistic study of the impact of broadcasting on a working class area of Bristol, *Broadcasting in Everyday Life*, commissioned by Silvey, has distinct parallels of tone with Harrisson and Madge's Penguin Special *Britain, by Mass-Observation*, published almost contemporaneously. It took the Second World War however fully to vindicate Silvey's approach, and to give him scope both to consolidate his research and to extend it into previously forbidden territory. (Nicholas 2006)

By 1939 Silvey had restructured his General Listening Barometer from a weekly to a daily survey of listening, measuring audiences for all radio programmes in the schedule – a cultural marker of the move to 'statistical' audience research and evidence of the BBC's support for sampling as a research method (Nicholas 2006). In addition to the Thermometer and Barometer, Silvey expanded the range of Listener Panels and recruited a network of 2,000 unpaid 'Local Correspondents' who provided answers to monthly questionnaires.

While Silvey and his team's work before and after the war was not, by direction, supposed to influence BBC policy, there can be no doubt that it had its strategic use outside the BBC:

The LRD also proved useful to the BBC in another way. It provided the ammunition with which the BBC could counter the unreasonable demands of government, thereby preventing ministerial attempts to influence, for example, the selection of particular speakers, the choice of presentation style or the scheduling of particular programmes in which they had an interest. Tellingly, when in January 1943 Silvey offered to reduce LR's costs by discontinuing the Forces Survey, senior management rejected the offer on the grounds that this would leave the BBC with no means of countering unwanted interference from the Service ministries. (Nicholas 2006)

It might be argued that the United Kingdom did not have any formal or informal auditing of audience research in this period because it had in its early history no audience ratings and was not involved in any direct way in the development and application of audience ratings technology. This, however, is far from the case. Silvey, like his counterparts in the United States, had an interest in creating methods that could provide an overview of the audience and its preferences. Unlike his US counterparts, however, Silvey made study of *engagement* of the audience the key methodological issue, something that has returned as a key methodological issue in the contemporary moment. Silvey's methodology, of course, would not be accepted as currency for media buying because there is no way to get industry agreement on either the Thermometer or the Barometer as a universal measure. The BBC's approach to methodology, however, directly affected the auditing regime when the market became competitive and when audience ratings did enter the United Kingdom. Silvey was still involved with broadcasting research up until 1960 and the ethos of strong control over audience research remained.

Today the non-profit Broadcasters' Audience Research Board (BARB) oversees audience measurement for both commercial and public service broadcasters. BARB sub-contracts the actual data collection but keeps strict control over the processes. It was formed in 1981 when the BBC and ITV jointly established a ratings measurement organization. BARB is funded by the BBC, ITV, Channel 4, Five, BSkyB and the Institute of Practitioners in Advertising (IPA), and is the only provider of audience measurements for all channels across all platforms, including terrestrial, satellite and cable. This has not stopped other broadcasters or media content providers employing other measurement agencies to collect audience research data, but BARB is the formal authority. Australia, on the departure of McNair and Anderson, similarly maintained a strong auditing regime. OzTAM in Australia appointed Australian Television Ratings (ATR) to collect the data, later to become AGB Nielsen Media Research and now Nielsen. Nielsen still conducts the ratings for radio on behalf of Commercial Radio Australia (CRA). The Australian system employs a formal independent auditor to review the methodology. Canada has two ratings services, BBM Canada (originally known as the Bureau of Broadcast Measurement) and Nielsen Media Research. BBM is non-profit and owned and operated by broadcasters, advertising agencies and advertising companies. In July 2004 BBM and Nielsen announced an agreement to merge their TV ratings creating a single source of ratings. Like Australia, Canada ran for many years with competing ratings services, but unlike Australia these services were not used as a default audit.

Summary

The authors in this chapter presented an approach to understanding the audience-ratings convention that focuses on the types of agreements reached among the parties. Styles of reasoning are deployed in the audience-ratings convention, ranging from statistical reasoning through to marketing. In the United States the methodological styles of reasoning and the market styles of reasoning clashed in the public domain. The common practice of fudging audience figures presented to clients, as though they were scientific, came up against the methodologists in the US federal government.

Auditing regimes, whether formal or semi-formal, in the audience-ratings convention have the function of minimizing manipulation. Catherine Marsh makes a perceptive comment about manipulation in her 1982 book *The Survey Method: The Contribution of Surveys to Sociological Explanation*.

There are two quite distinct ways in which surveys, or social science in general, have been held to be manipulative. The first, which can be called 'abuse of power', recognizes that knowledge about the social world, in an analogous way to knowledge about the natural world, gives power to those who own or control it, and hence gives them the wherewithal to put it to ends of which one may approve or disapprove.

The second, which may be called 'ideological manipulation', asserts that the so-called 'knowledge' about the social world is not knowledge which is grounded in outside reality but is an ideological reflection of some kind, created through artefactual or reified means, whose acceptance furthers particular interests.

You cannot make both these criticisms at once: either some particular piece of knowledge is powerful enough to endow its owners with a real basis for action when they intervene in the world, or it is artefactual and serves as the basis for various ideological constructions. There has been a tendency to present both criticisms of surveys, especially opinion polls, alongside one another without facing this contradiction. Surveys of objective or subjective phenomena raise the possibility of the abuse of power, whereas opinion polls are the correct object of a criticism of artefactuality. (Marsh 1982: 125)

Audience ratings, with their dual identity, are capable of being classified under both forms of manipulation, in Marsh's sense. This is precisely why ratings fall into a different category from other forms of survey research. Ratings are continuously contested, within the industry itself and outside of it. If audience ratings seem to become more tied to private interests, at the cost of accurate representation, then the situation is pulled back by having auditing mechanisms that help with balance. If audience ratings are perceived as artefactual, then actions are taken to address methodological or application concerns, as in the case of the Hispanic audience.

But mostly the ratings' auditing regimes are behind the scenes. Auditing tends to be a vigorous, largely intra-mural conversation among the parties to the convention. The public rarely sees the memos that fly back and forth between television stations and ratings providers, advertisers and television stations, technical sub-committees of networks, and advertisers and ratings providers. Sometimes the public sees both the formal and informal types of auditing together when there is a bun fight – particularly when different parties to the convention take issue with ratings provision or when there is a move to 'new technologies of counting' which disrupt the market and broadcaster bottom lines. In the contemporary moment we are seeing a return to the highly charged circumstances of the early 1960s in the United States as parties to the ratings convention are now involving and enlisting external parties, including legal forums, Congressional members, foundations and other agencies. This is because the stakes are so high, whether for OzTam in Australia, BARB in the UK or Nielsen in the United States. These high stakes are a consequence of the 'single source' characteristics of ratings provision that can create a feeling among various parties to the convention that the other parties to the convention are exercising undue power and authority over it and are largely unaccountable with respect to it.

With quite different and even opposed interests needing to be taken into account protocols need to be developed to ensure that the ratings are not influenced – and are not seen to be influenced – by the action of any of the parties to the convention. The need for assurance that the ratings survey is being performed competently has been historically met through a combination of means:

- Accreditation for ratings systems secured from a media ratings council of some kind, with such accreditation being dependent upon ongoing oversight.

- The appointment of external auditors on both a continuing or an ad hoc basis to deal with particular problems.

- The establishing of ongoing high level technical committees acting as a liaison point between ratings providers and the parties to the convention providing an ongoing feedback and checking loop.

- The 'holding to account' of ratings providers and their instruments in regular public and industry forums such as the American Association for Public Opinion Research (AAPOR). Constant discussion and debate has been historically an important mechanism for improvement and innovation in ratings services. AAPOR has functioned as a discussion place for methodologies and their application. It functions to exchange ideas and stabilize 'data analysis' and the consideration of various forms of 'data collection' and the like.

- The public criticism of ratings providers by other ratings providers and would be providers. Different survey proponents favour their own system.

- The establishment of ad hoc inquiries, studies or hearings in which ratings practice and methodology is the subject of sustained interrogation. Studies might be commissioned by different parties to the convention, sometimes by the rating provider as with the recent Nielsen non-response survey, and sometimes by external agencies (such as Congress in the United States).

- The carrying out of regular research programmes designed to map the changing context of viewer use of media inside and outside the home to provide a check on the adequacy of the data collection instruments. With a constantly changing media scene there needs to be confidence that the methods of data collection remain adequate to the measurement of changing viewing and listening circumstances and accommodate the advent of new technology.

5 The Technologies of Counting

The need for industry cooperation seems more important than ever as online video is becoming a larger source of revenue. Hulu recently brought attention to the problems with online measurement when they publicly criticized Nielsen for under-counting its audience: In the month of March, ComScore counted 42 million Hulu viewers while Nielsen only reported 9 million. In a business based on CPM, a difference of 33 million viewers is unacceptable, even if online viewing only makes up a fraction of television revenue. Further, large-scale projects like television Everywhere will most likely complicate audience measurement even further as publishers and MSO's make television subscription content available on multiple screens with authenticated protocols ... The data is there and it's abundant, but the industry needs to create standards and protocol to measure the quality of that data if they expect to use at as a workable basis for negotiation. Sheila Seles (Seles 2009)

SanCom's patented solution combines powerful biometric authentication and efficient neural network processing to produce the only television Rating product that enables passive gathering of the following seemingly simple but highly elusive viewer data: (a) who is actually present in the television viewing area (b) who enters and exits the viewing area, and exactly when (c) what channels are being watched (not just tuned) and at what time (d) who changes the channel (e) who turns the television on and off and (f) the presence of a guest (an unrecognized person) in the viewing area. SanCom's hypersonic facial recognition technology (http://www.sancominc.com)

There has been an explosion of types of measurement. SanCom's promise is that its hypersonic facial recognition system will solve problems associated with exposure, showing, with reduced error, what people do. Self-report, like people filling out diaries, has often been seen as a more error-prone way of collecting ratings data compared with physical technologies that can remove the human element altogether. As Sheila Seles points out in her blog comment, however, the primary problem is not one of measurement but one of agreement, the topic of this book. Yet this does not make technology unimportant.

This chapter places the technologies of counting within the highly charged innovation system that is the broadcast ratings. While there has always been significant public debate about the methods of data collection and their relative merits – whether meters, diaries, the face-to-face interviews, telephone coincidentals or aided recall – the contemporary politicization of the 'technologies of peoplemeter counting' has brought with it new and previously unprecedented attention from new places and new people. This makes all the more necessary careful attention to and exploration of the ratings innovation system. In this chapter we will look at how the methods of data collection and their associated technologies are changing. Particular technologies of counting have emerged and been deployed (and in some cases redeployed) to meet both contingent circumstances of listening and viewing and to address different market contexts. It will be also shown how changes in the contexts of listening and viewing directly lead to the adoption of some instruments or technologies over others; how technological advances in both the household (the receiving context) and the 'production' context influence the form, direction, presentation and timeliness of data collection and its analysis; and how what can be expected of respondents enters into the very organization of data collection. The combination of collection friendliness and cost effectiveness has been crucial in the adoption of particular methods of data collection.

The Diffusion of Ratings Technology

Television ratings services are now rapidly diffusing worldwide. Russia and the former Eastern Bloc countries also have syndicated ratings, although these ratings do not necessarily have full coverage of television homes. Most of Africa does not have a syndicated ratings presence. Customized studies, by companies like Telmar, tend to cover those countries with emerging markets but no ratings. Keep in mind, however, that many African countries have major problems with basic infrastructure, making radio the major medium in rural areas in particular.

Table 5.1 shows when Peoplemeters were first rolled out in some of the established countries (excepting more recent Asian countries). Most panels collect data on individuals, timeshifting and guests to the home. The organizations in charge of ratings, however, can vary in structure, from joint collaborative industry committees, such as BARB in the United Kingdom, through to independent ratings company ownership of ratings, such as Nielsen in the United States.

The US Nielsen television ratings obtain data from a statistically selected sample of over 9,000 households, containing over 18,000 people. Nielsen also measures 210 local television markets in what it calls designated market areas (DMAs). The 56 largest of these DMAs are measured by Peoplemeter technology. Twenty-five are measured by Local People Meters. The remaining areas are measured by paper

Table 5.1 Establishment of Peoplemeter panels by country

Country	TV Homes (Million)	Start-up Organization	Meter Start Date
Australia	3.7	ACNielsen	1991
Austria	3.7	AGTT/GfK Austria	1991
Belgium	4.7	Audimétrie	1985
Bulgaria	2.6	TV Plan/TNS	1999
China	7.0	ACNielsen	1996
Croatia	1.4	AGB Nielsen Media Research	2002
Cyprus	0.3	AGB Nielsen Media Research	1998
Czech Republic	3.7	Mediaresearch	1997
Denmark	2.4	TNS Gallup	1992
Estonia	0.6	TNS Emor	2003
Finland	2.2	TV Mittaritutkimus/Finnpanel	1987
France	25.0	TRCC Médiamétrie	1989
Germany	33.9	AGF/GfK Fernsehforschung	1985
Greece	3.4	AGB	1988
Hungary	3.9	TNS	1994
Indonesia	7.34	ACNielsen	1998
Ireland	1.5	AGB Nielsen Research	1996
Italy	22.6	Auditel – AGB Italia	1986
India	135	TAM Media Research	1998
Japan	50.8	iNEX2/Videoresearch	1997
Latvia	0.8	TNS Latvia	1999
Lithuania	1.3	TNS Gallup	2000
Malaysia	3.1	ACNielsen	1995
Netherlands	7.1	Intomart/TV Times	1987
New Zealand	1.1	AGB McNair	1990
Norway	2.0	TNS Gallup	1992
Philippines	1.5	SRG	1994
Poland	13.4	AGB Polska	1996
Portugal	3.5	Marktest Audimetria	1993
Romania	6.9	AGB-TNS International	1998
Russia	50.0	TNS Gallup Media	1996
Serbia	2.4	AGB Nielsen Media Research	2002
Slovakia	1.6	TNS	2004
Slovenia	0.7	AGB Nielsen Media Research	1999

Continued

Table 5.1 Continued

Singapore	0.9	ACNielsen	1994
South Korea	2.8	MSK	1992
Spain	15.7	TNS	1988
Sweden	4.1	AGB Nielsen Media Research	1993
Switzerland	3.1	IHA-GfK Hergiswil	1985
Taiwan	5.4	ACNielsen	1994
Thailand	20.3	SRG Deemar	1990
Turkey	15.9	AGB	1990
Ukraine	16.5	GfK Ukraine (GfK-USM)	1998
UK	25.2	BARB/Ipsos RSL/RSMB/AGB	1981
USA	89.1	ACNielsen	1987

diaries. In 19 local markets Nielsen measures Hispanic audiences. In 14 of these markets diaries are used; in one market Nielsen uses meters and diaries and in four markets Local People Meters are used for measurement. Nielsen uses a special National Hispanic People Meter sample of 1,000 Hispanic households to represent the whole US Hispanic population. As discussed in the previous chapter, the change in counting technology in the transition from the Audimeter/diary system to the Local People Meter has not been without controversy, although in July 2010, the Media Ratings Council accredited all Nielsen's LPM systems in 25 markets.

In order to graphically compare television and radio ratings markets and the location of meters or diaries in a country with a geographically dispersed population, like the United States, with another, albeit one with a population less than one-tenth the size of the United States, it is worthwhile looking at Australia. OzTAM, owned by the three major free-to-air broadcasters, has appointed Nielsen to collect the television ratings data. Nielsen collects the radio metropolitan data on behalf of Commercial Radio Australia (CRA) and regional radio ratings data on an ad hoc commissioned basis. Households are recruited to OzTAM's panel from a large scale Establishment Survey that, based on the Census, defines the population to be represented and its characteristics. In 2009, there was a panel for each one of the 5 metropolitan markets, comprising a total of 3,035 homes (Sydney 765, Melbourne 705, Brisbane 615, Adelaide 475 and Perth 475). Figure 5.1 shows the distribution of meters. There is also a panel for the national subscription television market comprised of 1,200 subscription television homes drawn from the metropolitan and regional TAM services. Figure 5.2 shows the distribution of meters for this service.

The meter in the home records and stores all broadcast viewing: the time, date, whether the television set is on/off and the channel to which each television set

Figure 5.1 Television meters for the metropolitan market in Australia

is tuned. All residents and guests register their television usage using a remote control. The meter is connected to the telephone network and every night data is automatically and silently retrieved via the meter's internal modem. The production system performs the collection, processing, validation, weighting and final production of each household's data. Once the production processes have been completed, the television programme information and ratings are integrated. All data undergoes rigorous quality control both electronically and manually. All results are released the following morning and the data is made available to subscribers via a secure website.

The social stratification variables used by OzTAM below are no longer the A,B,C,D,E classifications of the past but, despite being called Occupation Groups, serve the same purpose as McNair and Anderson categories:

Occupation Group 1 (OG1): Managers, Administrators and Professionals

Legislators and Government Appointed Officials; General Managers; Specialist Managers; Farmers and Farm Managers; Managing Supervisors (Sales and

Figure 5.2 Television meters for National Subscription Panel

Service and Other Business); Natural Scientists; Building Professionals and Engineers; Health Diagnosis and Treatment Practitioners; Tertiary Teachers; Social Professionals; Business Professionals; Artists and Related Professionals.

Occupation Group 2 (OG2): Para-Professionals, Clerks, Teachers, Salespeople and Professional Service Workers

Medical and Science Technical Officers and Technicians; Engineering and Building Associates and Technicians; Air and Sea Transport Technical Workers; Registered Nurses; Stenographers and Typists; Data Processing and Business Machine Operators; Numerical Clerks; Filing, Sorting and Copying Clerks; Material Recording and Despatching Clerks; Receptionists; Telephonists and Messengers; School Teachers; Investment, Insurance and Real Estate Salespersons; Sales Representatives; Sales Assistants; Tellers; Cashiers and Ticket Salespersons; Personal Service Workers.

Occupation Group 3 (OG3): Tradespersons

Metal and Machinery Tradespersons; Electrical and Electronics Tradespersons; Building Tradespersons; Printing Tradespersons; Vehicle Tradespersons; Food Tradespersons; Amenity Horticultural Tradespersons.

Occupation Group 4 (OG4): Plant and Machine Operators, Drivers and Police

Road and Rail Transport Drivers; Mobile Plant Operators; Stationary Plant Operators; Machine Operators; Police.

Occupation Group 5 (OG5): Labourers and Related Workers

Trade Assistants and Factory Hands; Agricultural Labourers and Related Workers; Cleaners; Construction and Mining Labourers.

OzTAM can break down the audience by gender, income and a range of other variables. Table 5.2 below is an example of some of the breakdown as of 2009:

Table 5.2 OzTAM audience breakdown

Total Individuals		3,698	100.0%
Working 16+		1,720	46.5%
Not Working 16+		1,175	31.8%
Total Households		1,221	100.0%
1 Person Households		152	12.5%
2 Person Households		438	35.9%
3 Person Households		226	18.5%
4 Person Households		252	20.6%
5+ Person Households		154	12.6%
Grocery Buyers	18–39	366	30.0%
Grocery Buyers	18–54	804	65.8%
Grocery Buyers Age	25–54	765	62.7%
Grocery Buyers Age	40–54	438	35.8%
Grocery Buyers Age	55–64	227	18.6%
Grocery Buyers Age	65+	190	15.6%
1 television Households		239	19.6%
2 televisions Households		437	35.8%
3+ televisions Households		545	44.6%
Grocery Buyers		1,221	100.0%
Grocery Buyers Working		682	55.9%
Grocery Buyers Not Working		539	44.1%

In analysing audience ratings, as should have become clear in the chapter on sampling, the more the sample is broken down to analyse smaller groups, the more the sampling error changes. The samples for radio, as a result, are larger than those for the television panel. Australia has over 260 commercial radio stations. In metropolitan and major regional surveyed markets there are 53 commercial stations and all of these stations are included in the radio ratings sweeps. The balance of commercial stations is surveyed from time to time but not on a regular scheduled basis. Table 5.3 provides an overview of the radio ratings samples in 2006.

One of the obvious benefits of ratings is the same benefit that Silvey sought in his BBC research: an idea of when people used the medium. Australia, however, is experiencing, along with the United Kingdom, the United States, Canada and others, a decline in television free-to-air network audience share. Figure 5.3 shows the dramatic drop in share between 2000 and 2006 in the Canadian market.

Table 5.3 Australian radio diaries

Metropolitan Markets (53,904)
- Perth 8,829
- Adelaide 8,281
- Melbourne 11,895
- Sydney 11,454
- Brisbane 9,879
Regional Markets (15,557)

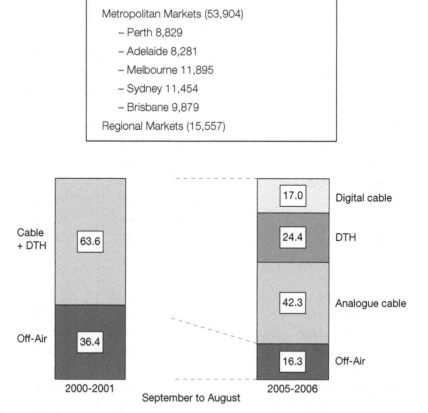

Figure 5.3 Canada's declining network audience

The decline in network viewing has had a corresponding effect on advertising and subscription television revenue, which today exceeds traditional advertising revenue in the broadcast markets of the United Kingdom and the United States. Advertising revenue has also shifted towards below-the-line advertising techniques, like direct selling.

Proliferation of Channels and Measurement

The type of measurement promised by SanCom at the start of this chapter – to closely monitor viewers' biometrics, or to capture data on who is watching and how engaged they are without relying on viewers reporting their presence by pressing a button or punching in a code – has been around for many years. It always flounders on the difficulty of recruiting a representative panel willing to be watched in this way. The evolution of set-top boxes has led to the development of technologies that can count and monitor viewing in ways that are less obvious and much less objectionable to viewers. They can also capture information on a scale not previously possible. The availability of these technologies led to changes in ratings measurement, as Alan Wurtzel, head of research at American network NBC, observed in 2009:

> A couple of years ago, Nielsen delivered a single television-rating data stream. Today, Nielsen routinely delivers more than two dozen streams (yes, we counted them) and countless more are available for any client willing to pull the data. Moreover, set-top boxes (STB), moving closer and closer to second-by-second data, will produce a staggering amount of new information. And, with internet and mobile metrics as well, it's not the amount of data that is the problem; it's the quality and utility. (Wurtzel 2009: 263)

Digital set-top boxes can now routinely gather and report enormous amounts of information from subscribers. However, few common standards exist, and proprietorial systems dominate. An independent report commissioned by the Nielsen-funded Council for Research Excellence in February 2010 described the set-top box as the '"wild west" of research' and raised concerns about the potentially unethical motives of some of the developers, about the lack of standard practices in the field and about the 'veil of secrecy surrounding set-top box data processing' (Brooks, Gray and Dennison 2010: 9). With the billions of dollars that ride on ratings data, and with the value of the data collected via set-top boxes for quantifying, monetizing and targeting the audience, it is highly likely that some of the key issues – inconsistent data formats creating difficulties in cross-referencing data across systems and different methods used to determine when the television is in use, for example – will be resolved, and the set-top box frontier will be tamed.

This frontier is increasingly being populated as these boxes rapidly become normal television interfaces. And the prospects, in terms of the size of the population whose preference data can be collated and distilled, are enormous. In November 2009, TiVo agreed to provide data from its 1.6 million direct subscribers in the United States to Google, which already had secured access to data from the four million subscribers to the dish satellite service to help develop Google's television ads service. This large survey group complements the data Google derives from Nielsen's panel under the terms of a 2007 deal. Unlike panellists or diarists for Nielsen, BARB or OzTAM, TiVo subscribers are not constantly reminded that information is being collected about their viewing habits. Subscribers are largely unaware of the value of their information, or of how much information they continue to provide after they initially 'opt in', agreeing to provide certain data when the contract of service was signed or accepted with a click. Viewers consent to provide feedback, whereupon tags are attached to the return path data – viewing choices and other information – for sorting and aggregating. The tagging system is proprietary, and not subject to an industry standard. Although TiVo makes clear that viewers must specifically 'opt-in' to provide 'Personally Identifiable Viewing Information', that information must be provided to access certain features of the TiVo service. This data is then compiled and provided to TiVo's many research partners including TRA (The Right Audience).

While small panel-based research projects like the BBC's 650 panellist Cross Media Insight survey are still very much part of the landscape, the advent of the digital set-top box has allowed the numbers of participants in such studies to be dwarfed by census-level data from surveys of millions of subscribers. Frances Bonner calculated that television requires something like 250,000 ordinary people each year as contestants, interviewees and audiences (Bonner 2003). The number and variety of ordinary people providing feedback to research organizations and market researchers is many times more than this, and still the audience remains the key uncertainty affecting the economics of the media industries (Napoli 2003: 39). Napoli argues that this fragmentation increases the disparity between the predicted and the measured audience and reduces the reliability of data collected in traditional sample-based methods (Napoli 2003: 140). It certainly increases the 'research ask', and complicates the carefully calibrated equations that produce the ratings from smaller panels. While mass audiences can still be assured for certain major events, often live international sports championships, audiences in general have dispersed. Content providers, advertisers and research organizations have had to track not only timeshifting and 'catch-up television', but also migration across platforms, and even beyond the home. Audience fragmentation has precipitated proliferations of data, methods, metrics and technologies that in turn have allowed samples of a few hundred in panels or diaries to multiply into surveys of millions of subscribers and produce competing currencies. Opportunities for advertisers to reach consumers through media and other touchpoints have proliferated, while advertisers' and content providers' desire for solid numbers and discontent with the prevailing currency and methods have opened spaces for research and analysis.

Expenditure on media advertising has been volatile around the world since the onset of the global financial crisis. And whereas in the past, changes in methods or technologies of audience measurement were often stimulated by advertisers, now advertisers like research agencies find themselves in a position of reacting and responding to a rapidly changing and uncertain audience marketplace. In an effort to provide the kind of holistic measurement that advertisers and media buyers demand, services combining media measurement databases have been developed, such as Nielsen's Anytime Anywhere Media Measurement or A2/M2 service in the United States, or the IPA's Touchpoints Inititative in the United Kingdom, modelled on the BBC's Daily Life Survey that has been conducted periodically since the 1930s.

For Touchpoints, 5,000 initial panellists, rising to 6,050 by the third survey, were given self-completion questionnaires and asked to complete an e-diary via PDA to document media use over seven days at half hourly intervals. The panellists (all adults, from across the United Kingdom) are paid a 'respondent incentive' of £20–£25. Touchpoints has to date conducted three six-month surveys, each by different research contractors, in April–November 2005, September 2007–February 2008 and September 2009–February 2010. With at least £300,000 in respondent incentives alone, this is clearly an enormously expensive exercise, and one that requires considerable cooperation and input from across the media industries. As efforts intensify to determine a new currency and new standards, Touchpoints-like initiatives are being rolled out in other countries, including the United States. The information the survey supplies supplements BARB's measurements drawn from its 5,100 panellists, and from the National Readership Survey for newspapers and magazines, the Joint Industry Committee for Regional Media Research (JICREG)'s interviews and website measurement for regional newspapers, RAJAR's diaries for radio, Poster Audience Research (Postar)'s estimates of out-of-home advertising, and Film Audience Measurement and Evaluation (FAME)'s cinema interviews.

In the United States, NBC Universal used the Summer Olympics of 2008 and Winter Olympics of 2010 to conduct large-scale research on online, mobile and television viewing and to track advertising recall across media. In NBC's case, the research push reflected dissatisfaction with Nielsen's ratings system's capacity to capture viewing and engagement patterns of newly dispersed audiences and concern about its shrinking share of the advertising market. NBC's research, and that of the BBC and other content providers, into mobile media use has significant implications for the future of programming, scheduling, online strategy and audience measurement. During the Beijing Olympic Games in August 2008, NBC worked with a variety of research companies measuring viewing on its subscription channels, its website and its service for mobile audiences. The ultimate product was the Total Audience Measurement Index (TAMI), a combination of data from different media and different panellists. Unique browsers, video streams, page views, and time spent online at NBCOlympics. com were measured by Quantcast. An online survey was conducted by Knowledge Networks of 500 different Olympics watchers per day who kept a media diary to record how they watched the Olympics, where, when and on what media. Integrated Media Measurement Inc. (IMMI) established a panel of 40 people with cell phones equipped to record sound bytes in programme signals that allow measurement of time spent watching or interacting with Olympics coverage on all platforms throughout the day. A further 80 people in two major markets formed the Olympics Qualitative Panel for interviews and focus groups, and in partnership with the IAG, NBC conducted surveys of consumers' recall of ads, brands, marketing intent and consumer behaviour across television, internet and mobile. Nielsen measured television ratings, Rentrak monitored video-on-demand usage, and viewing through personal video recorders was also counted. Over 17 days, NBC distributed 3,600 hours of video over broadcast and cable television, via the website, and over mobile telephone networks.

At the Vancouver Winter Olympics in February 2010, NBC added to this research effort by employing up to 15,000 respondents, including 2,000 equipped with Arbitron Portable People Meters (PPMs), and 40 with IMMI's mobile technology, both of which can report out-of-home and at-home viewing. Research company Keller Fay was hired to monitor social networking sites and viral communication. But despite a research budget in the 'mid six figures', NBC foreshadowed a loss on the Vancouver Olympics of US$250 million (Chozick 2010). Once again, the scale of the research, and the associated costs, make such ventures special rather than regular events, and it is difficult to see many individual media companies taking on such an exercise alone in the future.

Efforts to monitor audience behaviour anytime, anywhere, on any device, have been hampered by differences between media in the metrics, methods and terminology used to track audiences, as well as by the lack of broadly accepted standards in online viewing measurement. Broadcasters and traditional television providers have established online portals either independently or collaboratively through services like Hulu, or through dedicated 'channels' on YouTube to both provide for and try to profit from online video viewing. Initiatives like Time Warner's 'TV Anywhere' measurement of streams, average minutes and other user data taken from server logs can be combined with data from Nielsen's NetView panel or VideoCensus system, or comScore's Video Metrix to paint a picture of online viewing behaviour, but there are still many questions and discrepancies.

New metrics and analytical systems that have been developed to answer some of the questions raised by technological change also pose challenges to ratings providers about their capacity to deal with the explosion of raw and customized data on audience behaviour. The volume of information about audience and consumer behaviour that is available for aggregation and analysis has grown enormously, but with it has come a host of uncertainties about the direction and use of audience measurement, and of the ratings. Uncertainty has driven an extraordinary research effort, a flight to accountability, in which a proliferating number of information and research companies have tried to make sense of the accumulating data about media use, often with conflicting results. This was one of the reasons behind what Alan Wurtzel calls the 'crisis in measurement', although the wealth of data and the efforts being made to analyse it may mean that this period could be looked back on as a golden age if the industry's ideals of massive amounts of data that can be cross-tabulated and 'fused' with other data sets can be realized. This would potentially produce the advertising industry's holy grail: single source, or what the World Federation of Advertisers calls 'consumer-centric holistic measurement', although serious questions about privacy would also arise.

Despite the crisis, which is multifaceted, ratings data are still and will continue to be in demand because there will always be need and use for common currencies for buying and selling advertising and programme content. There will undoubtedly be changes in the practicalities of audience measurement, particularly given the challenges presented by the likely spread of broadband-enabled set-top boxes. Information gathered from individual set top boxes can inform the insertion of advertising tailored to viewers' interests (as determined by past preferences in programming and viewing of advertising) into programme streams. The expectation is that viewers will be more 'engaged' with tailored advertising that speaks to their interests than with the scatter-gun, un-targeted advertising typical of broadcast and pre-digital television. The emotionally engaged audience is valued extremely highly for the bond they form with a brand.

Neuroscience, Neuromarketing and New Technologies of Measurement

Cross-media ratings projects like Harris Interactive's work with MTV Networks on 'Multiscreen Engagement' have emphasized the need to study the emotional connections between audiences and content (Harris Interactive and MTV Networks 2008). The Multiscreen Engagement study surveyed 20,000 people to discern engagement with MTV programmes across media. The study found that multiplatform media campaigns are two to three times more 'effective' than single-platform campaigns, even though television is the most important medium for brand awareness. For audiences to seek out and proliferate content about a particular programme across media and devices, the study found that a strong emotional connection or level of engagement must be present. It also found that multiplatform media campaigns are two to three times more 'effective' as single-platform campaigns, even though television is the most important medium for brand awareness. Purchase intent, or consideration, was reported to have nearly doubled when brands' advertising was recognized across platforms.

In a paper presented at the Advertising Research Foundation's annual convention in 2007, British academic Robert Heath developed definitions of attention and engagement, and outlined the distinction between them:

> Active attention is primarily a rational construct, and level of attention is therefore defined as the amount of conscious 'thinking' going on when an advertisement is being processed. Engagement is a subconscious emotional construct, and level of engagement is therefore defined as the amount of 'feeling' going on when an advertisement is being processed. (Heath 2007)

Using recent research on emotions and cognition, Heath argues, following Antonio Damasio, that 'emotions and feelings are always formed pre-cognitively'. This approach turns on its head Lavidge and Steiner's influential thesis that argues that motivation is the sole influence on decision-making (Lavidge and Steiner 1961). Heath argues that emotional and subconscious processing form attitudes about decisions before conscious thought kicks in. Following from this is the finding that attitudes (towards brands, in this case) 'can be changed without active conscious processing' and so 'the level of engagement a consumer has with advertising is going to be entirely dictated by the amount of "feeling" that goes on at the start of the process'. If this is the case, then tapping into that feeling will be enormously profitable for advertisers. But how to access this subconscious feeling and trigger the elusive 'buy-button in the brain' (*Nature Neuroscience* 2004)?

Step forward neuromarketing, which has been described as 'the application of neuroscientific methods to analyse and understand human behaviour in relation to markets and marketing exchanges' (Lee, Broderick and Chamberlain 2006: 200). A variety of techniques and methods fall under this definition. First, electroencephalography or EEG, in which the viewer-subject wears a hat or helmet to which a number of sensors are attached. The sensors measure brain activity indicative of attention, emotional engagement and memory retention. Second, functional magnetic resonance (fMRI) measures brain activity by monitoring blood flows that accompany neural activity. Unlike an earlier method of generating images of brain activity, positron emission tomography or PET, fMRI is non-invasive (not requiring injection of radioactive isotopes as in PET) and quick to perform. The disadvantages of fMRI include its cost, and the requirement that viewer-subjects must be placed in an fMRI machine (although the machines are becoming smaller and more portable). Third, other physiological measures such as galvanic skin response and heart-rate monitoring which measure stress (or emotional response) can be combined with eye-tracking and facial expression monitoring to measure attention and engagement. These methods may then be followed up through interviews.

By directly measuring brain or other bodily responses, proponents argue that neuromarketing is able to circumvent the problem of subjects' stated responses to advertising not matching their buying behaviour. Neuromarketing purports to measure 'direct responses' to advertisements, so that responses can be collected while subjects are participating in the behaviour. Unlike studies of engagement which rely on self-reporting and which, as a result, may be prone to a variety of errors, neuromarketing claims insight into responses to advertising that are unmediated by conscious thought or reflection.

Interest in neuromarketing has been stoked by a number of recent developments. In February 2008, Nielsen made a strategic investment in NeuroFocus, a company based in Berkeley, California, that uses brainwave analysis, eye-tracking and skin conductance tests to measure the effectiveness of advertising, branding, packaging, pricing and product design. In partnership, the companies became exclusive providers of neuromarketing research to film studios and television networks. Nielsen announced its intent to install NeuroFocus technology at the CBS Television City Research Center in Las Vegas, and later in the year the service was launched in Japan. NeuroFocus subsequently bought UK neuromarketing firm Neuroco, whose clients included Sky Broadcasting. In May 2008, the Walt Disney Company announced that it would build a new neuromarketing research facility in Austin, Texas, to be run in conjunction with Professor Duane Varan of Murdoch University, Western Australia. It was reported that the lab would test a range of advertising methods including 'interactivity, split screens, brand integration, sponsorships, addressable advertising, broadband video and mobile devices on a diverse group of subjects, with the results transmitted to [Murdoch University] for analysis' (Collings 2008). Each year, Sands Research releases split-screen videos showing the EEG data of the brain activity of a panel of viewers watching commercials screened during the NFL Super Bowl, traditionally the highest rating programme of the year. The EEG analysis is used to rank the commercials according to their 'Neuro Engagement Factor' or NEF. In Figure 5.4, eye-gaze analysis has been added to show which parts of the video people are looking at.

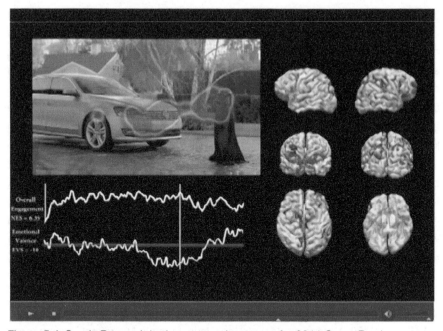

Figure 5.4 Sands Research brain maps and eye gaze for 2011 Super Bowl advertisement, 'VW Darth Vader'
Source: Used with permission, Sands Research, http://www.sandsresearch.com/2011SBMovies.aspx

In Australia, the Nine Network worked with Australian biometric measurement company Neuro-Insight using patented technology developed by Professor Richard Silberstein, founder of the Brain Science Institute at Swinburne University, to develop what it called the Program Engagement Power Index (PEPI). The PEPI uses a form of EEG analysis on viewers watching television programmes to gauge their popularity. Neuro-Insight is a rapidly growing company that has worked with major advertisers in Australia and from 2009 in Europe, following a deal with German media-buying agency Media Plus, who will provide neuromarketing research services under licence to advertisers and the media in Germany, Switzerland and Austria. Interestingly both Sands Research and Neuro-Insight's work has been used to argue the importance of story and narrative in producing successfully engaging content, which may be enough to ensure the survival of film and television drama.

The neuromarketing area illustrates the trends of convergence and proliferation that are shaping audience and consumer research. On one hand there is conglomeration, with Nielsen using its financial muscle to buy up competitors or start-ups it finds useful. On the other there is proliferation, as a growing number of firms are established, new metrics and technologies are developed, and existing ones modified. But neuromarketing is not an uncontested emerging technology for ranking and rating responses to content. There have been concerns raised about the commercialization of academic research in this field, with one prestigious neuroscience journal dismissing neuromarketing as little more than a new fad, exploited by scientists and marketing consultants to blind corporate clients with science (*Nature Neuroscience* 2004), and another raising concerns about the ethics of using brain imaging techniques for marketing and market-related purposes (*Lancet Neurology* 2004). Then there is the small matter of the complex and subjective nature of human emotional experience or the individual's life context, affecting results. Neuromarketing is also a costly form of research, which limits the number of participants. It is also often conducted outside the normal or familiar viewing environment, and participants often have to wear special equipment or be subjected to various tests which will be difficult to replicate across a larger population.

Timeshifting and Technologies of Counting

Timeshifting of viewing has been possible since the introduction of the home VCR, but it has become more of an issue since the introduction of digital video recorders (DVRs) as a new technology of counting. The integration of functions for receiving and facilitating programme (information) flow, recording and storing programmes, and returning information to a service provider in set-top boxes like Sky+, Foxtel iQ, or TiVo has intensified the question of how ratings instruments accommodate timeshifted viewing. In the United States, Nielsen began reporting 'Average Commercial Minute' data in May 2007. The measure provides an average rating for the commercial minutes in each television programme, covering live viewing; live viewing plus DVR playback on the same day; and live viewing plus DVR playback for one, two, three and seven days. At the time, according to Nielsen, less than 20 per cent of US households had DVRs. The Live + 3 days or 'C3' measure quickly replaced the live programme ratings as the currency for buying and selling commercial time. At the time of the introduction of the Average Commercial Minute measure, Nielsen reported that:

> Among households with DVRs, the average primetime broadcast program audience increases 40 per cent when including same day DVR playback and 73 per cent when including three days of playback. Audiences for commercial minutes within these broadcast programs increase 18 per cent and 32 per cent respectively. Both cable network and syndicated programs and commercials also show increases, although at lower rates. (Nielsen 2007)

In the United Kingdom, the Broadcasters' Audience Research Boards (BARB) introduced a service in 2010 which reports audiences for on-demand material that has not been broadcast live within the previous week. (At present, ratings are only provided initially for programmes viewed live and recorded on the same day of transmission, with consolidated figures for all viewers capturing timeshifted viewing only up to seven days after transmission.) The BBC will also soon begin to publish consolidated data which will include content viewed on DVRs and the BBC iPlayer, which is reported to have had 350 million programme requests since the end of 2007, with an average 500,000 users requesting more than 1.2 million streams per day. According to the *Guardian*:

> Timeshifting is booming ... Drama was by far the most popular timeshifted genre, with only 63 per cent of series and 68 per cent of soaps viewed live in the first two months of 2009, according to Sky's figures. The number of people who watched the first screening of the opening episode of the fifth series of Sky 1's *Lost* – 608,000 – was eclipsed by the 647,000 who chose to record it on Sky+. With repeats and on-demand included, its total audience reached 1.57 million. (Plunkett 2009)

The issue of measuring timeshifted viewing has historically been one of the main subjects of dispute between subscription television operators and OzTAM in Australia. Eventually the operators' frustrations would lead to a split, with Foxtel, Austar and MCn announcing in March 2008 that they would commission a new audience measurement system to begin reporting on 1 July 2009. There had been a row between subscription television operators and OzTAM in 2004 after the findings of a commissioned research report conflicted with data provided by OzTAM about viewing of the 'catch-up' channels (rebroadcasts of particular channels usually on a two-hour delay) (Sinclair 2004). Foxtel launched the iQ box which incorporated a DVR in February 2005, and in the same month OzTAM changed its methodology for measuring subscription television audiences, weighting data from this panel separately from the regional and metropolitan free-to-air broadcasting panels to better reflect age and demographic spreads and larger average household size of subscribers. The change in methodology was anticipated to result in an increase in ratings for subscription services (Sinclair 2005). By November 2005, more than one million digital set-top boxes were reported to have been installed in Australian homes, but according to research by OzTAM and Eureka Strategy for the Australian Communications and Media Authority, only 10 per cent were being used to pick up enhanced digital services (Douglas 2005).

In March 2006, ASTRA called for tenders for its audience measurement contract, which was due to expire at the end of 2007. ASTRA wanted the successful tenderer to deliver data on use of interactive services, timeshifted viewing and non-broadcast use of the television set, perhaps indicating dissatisfaction with the OzTAM/Eureka

Strategy findings (Schulze 2006). By December 2006, ASTRA was reported to be contemplating commissioning Taylor Nelson Sofres (TNS) to set up a new ratings system that would include out-of-home, timeshifted viewing, mobile television measurement and data on non-broadcast uses of the television set (Sinclair 2007). When in April 2007 OzTAM signed a new seven-year contract with AGB Nielsen Media Research to provide ratings data from January 2008, ASTRA declined to commit, citing concerns about OzTAM's failure to address concerns about measurement of new digital services and timeshifted viewing. Figures from the United Kingdom at this time showed over 90 per cent of Sky+ households (the equivalent of households with Foxtel iQ box) timeshifted viewing. At the time of the signing of the new deal between OzTAM and AGB Nielsen, OzTAM chair Doug Peiffer said OzTAM 'hoped' to start reporting timeshifted viewing in 2008 (Canning 2007; McIntyre 2007). Later in April 2007, the discontent between subscription television operators and OzTAM became public again when David Dale revealed in the *Sydney Morning Herald* that OzTAM was using different methods to report ratings of shows on free-to-air and subscription television that were screened more than once during the week, to the detriment of the STV programme (Dale 2007). In the same month, media buyers were reported to be pressuring OzTAM to measure and report on non-broadcast use (which includes timeshifted viewing) of television sets.

In December 2007, OzTAM announced that it would begin reporting timeshifted viewing from February 2010 following trials of a new measurement system, Unitam. Just before Christmas 2007, agreement was finally reached between ASTRA and OzTAM for an extension of the agreement over audience measurement for the period 2008–14. Despite the new agreement with OzTAM, in March 2008, Foxtel, Austar and MCn announced that they would fund a new digital television audience measurement system with a panel size of 10,000. The system was to be created by TNS and based on a similar service already operating in the United Kingdom and the United States. The system measures timeshifted viewing, and responses to interactive advertising. It was reported at the time of the announcement that the system would cost approximately US$3 million, or 1 per cent of projected revenue of subscription television operators in 2009. The system was intended to begin reporting in July 2009 (Sinclair 2008). The current service covers: Live – viewing of television broadcast content at the actual time of broadcast (live broadcast); As Live – viewing of recorded television broadcast content that occurs within the same research day as broadcast, but at a different time to the original live broadcast time (a research day is 2 a.m. to 2 a.m.); Time Shift – viewing of recorded television broadcast content up to seven days after the live broadcast time; and, Playback – As Live + Time Shift viewing.

Ian Garland noted that the move by the television companies was necessary because media agencies had their own similar tools, and there was a need for transparency and accountability as to who is watching what, and when.

> Advertisers want information not just on 30-second and linear ads, but also value-added components, such as sponsorship campaigns ... The new system provides us with a competitive advantage, not just with advertisers, but because we understand our viewers better. Seven, with their TiVo device, could do something similar to us, but it's just one small portion of the market – our business model is just very different to theirs. (Garland 2008)

Channel Seven network director of sales, James Warburton, claimed his company was 'not that far behind', and acknowledged that measurement of timeshifted viewing is a critical feature: 'Timeshift is the vital element – 70 per cent of viewing is done live, with 10–15 per cent of recorded shows shown that night. PVR (personal video recorder) users watch two hours more of television than other users, so this notion that they are avoiding ads is wrong – they are seeing more impacts than ever before' (Milman 2008).

The Increasing Technical Complexity of Audience Measurement

As the discussion above shows the challenges to audience measurement services are multiplying. Advertisers and media buyers are seeking and requesting ever more detailed and granulated data about audiences and audience behaviour. Market fragmentation and the expansion of entertainment options have further increased the difficulties for interested parties to gain a full picture of audience behaviour. As a result of these issues and developments, there has been significant growth in the number and variety of research services and technologies of counting offered around the world. Increasing technological sophistication has allowed data to be collected from significantly larger sample groups and from a variety of databases to be integrated and analysed together. The growth in sample sizes and the development of new services has been described as the 'flight to accountability' in measurement services. Some evidence of this is provided by the host of new services announced in recent years.

January 2007: TiVo's StopllWatch service, claimed by the company to be 'the first national, syndicated measurement of program and commercial-spot television viewership by digital recording households in the United States', is launched. It was the first service to provide live and timeshifted viewing data on a second-by-second basis.

February 2007: Nielsen in the United States announces DigitalPlus service to measure digital set-top box data.

July 2007: TNS Media Research develops CommercialView service, combining second-by-second data from 300,000 Charter Communications cable subscribers in Los Angeles with ad occurrence data.

September 2007: Rentrak unveils Television Essentials service. By March 2009, the service is claimed to process data from seven million set-top boxes, analysing audience flow, audience retention, day-part analysis for linear and on-demand television.

December 2007: OzTAM/AGB Nielsen announce their new Unitam service in Australia due to report on timeshifted viewing from January 2010.

January 2008: TNS Media Research launches DirectView service, using second-by-second set-top box data from 100,000 DirecTV subscribers around the United States. Nielsen launches the Nielsen On Demand Reporting & Analytics (NORA) service to aggregate and report on video on demand usage collected from set-top boxes of Comcast cable subscribers.

February 2008: Nielsen launches VideoCensus online video measurement service. In the same month Nielsen acquires Audience Analytics, provider of Audience Watch service, and makes strategic investment in NeuroFocus, a Californian neuromarketing company.

March 2008: Optimedia launches Content Power Ratings report, a quarterly index ranking reach of top 100 programmes based on number and quality of viewers across traditional and digital media. Content Power Ratings combines proprietary research, Nielsen Media Research's NTI database, comScore's Media Metrix, E-Poll's FastTrack, Keller Fay Group's TalkTrack, and Factiva.

April 2008: Nielsen buys IAG Research, a New York-based firm specializing in measuring consumer engagement with television programmes, national commercials and product placements.

May 2008: Disney-ABC launch Advertising Value Index (AVI). AVI 'allows advertisers to choose from more than 15 criteria, including factors such as income level, education, employment status, how long viewers tune in to commercials or how engaged they are with the program' (Kang and Vranica 2008). Irish firm Openet announces phase one of Advanced Advertising Solutions service. Targeted at cable television providers, it 'enables the correlation of real-time subscriber activity such as television viewing behavior and broadband mobile service usage with demographic and psychographic profiling information'.

June 2008: TNS Media Research's Return Path Data (RPD) service is launched. The service extracts data from set-top boxes to track viewing patterns and service use. The service is trialled in South Africa and in the United States through TNS's partnership with Comcast. The service claimed to 'give broadcasters and advertisers the chance to target viewers with bespoke commercials' (Shepherd 2008). TRA and TiVo announce a deal, in which TRA will access anonymous viewing data from TiVo's 1.7 million set-top boxes across United States. TRA matches viewing data with purchase data from more than 70 million frequent-shopper cards. Partnership merges TRAnalytics service with TiVo's StopIIWatch ratings service.

November 2008: TRA's announces 370,000-household, nationwide, anonymous single-source database which overlays television viewing data from 1.5 million cable and TiVo households, consumer package goods purchase data from more than 55 million households, and anonymous demographic data from more than 100 million households.

Calls for Harmonization

In the face of the proliferation of services outlined above, media buyers and advertisers have issued calls for harmonization of metrics and terminology to allow meaningful comparisons to be made across media. Back in 2005, bodies representing television, radio, magazine and newspaper owners met to devise common definitions of age and economic affluence of Australian consumers as a first step towards harmonization of demographics across all media (Lee 2005). Problems with the measurement of online audiences have also intensified calls for a unified approach. In February 2008 at a meeting of the Interactive Advertising Bureau, attendees urged internet publishers (e.g. Ninemsn, News Digital Media, Fairfax and Yahoo!7) to spend up to US$10 million to fund a new online ratings system to allow advertisers to compare online audiences with those for television, radio and other media. This followed concerns over slowing general internet ad growth (up 21 per cent in 2007 compared with 56 per cent in 2006), and feedback that ambiguity and inconsistency among audience metrics was hindering high-quality online brand advertising. In 2007, the Interactive Advertising Bureau (IAB) tried to establish ground rules and in August the organization issued a research document and invitation to companies to tender for the development of an online audience measurement system, but media agencies expressed dissatisfaction with IAB's November 2007 announcement that it favoured panel methodology rather than tagging sites.

The agencies wanted a hybrid system that takes site-centric data and uses it to calibrate panel data for accuracy. In early 2008, media agencies were reported to be working with Nielsen to develop a hybrid system called Data Integration, although there were concerns that Nielsen's NetView panel size would need to be doubled to provide more accurate data and capture traffic to niche websites. In February 2009, it was reported that Nielsen was likely to be the only provider of the online measurement system. Roy Morgan Research, comScore and Amethon Solutions/Aimstats had also responded to the 2007 brief, but only Nielsen was prepared to let an independent auditor review its online research system. Nielsen appeared to be on track to launch an expanded panel of 5,000 by June 2009 to track internet use at home and at work (the current panel of 3,770 only tracks home use). Paul Fisher, Chief Executive of IAB, says its aims are 'to fix the panel, create numbers based on people – not unique browsers – and give advertisers and media buyers audience-reach figures that will enable them to compare the Internet with other media' (Shoebridge 2009).

In the United States, Nielsen has a panel of 30,000 for its NetView product. Web activity is tracked through interviews and meters. But some analysts argue that panels undercount online audiences by between one third and one half. Research companies like Nielsen and comScore like panels because they provide demographic data and give information about what people do when they have seen an online advertisement. Quantcast's service uses panel-like data or 'reference samples' provided by third parties including market research firms, internet service providers and toolbar companies. Quantcast uses server logs, adjusted for multiple computers, spiders and bots, and cookie deleters, and combines the 'reference samples' with these logs using a 'mass inference algorithm' developed in conjunction with Stanford University. The company claims 85,000 'publishers' including Disney-ABC, NBC, CBS, MTV, Fox and BusinessWeek use its service. Criticism of Quantcast centres on its low take-up; it won't become a new currency until more publishers elect to be counted (Pontin 2009).

Measurement of online video use presents a variety of problems, but the measures appear to be becoming more robust. Most broadcasters and traditional television providers in the United States now either have their own web portals or use the Hulu player. The BBC iPlayer has been a huge success in the United Kingdom, while ABC's iView in Australia has had limited but still impressive success. Measurement of streams, average minutes and other user data taken from the broadcaster/providers' servers combined with data from the leading audience measurement services (Nielsen's VideoCensus and comScore's Video Metrix) are showing some interesting trends, although YouTube continues to dominate the field. In data on (US) online video usage in February, Nielsen reported that YouTube is by far and away the largest online video provider, with over 5 billion videos streamed from its site by over 88 million unique viewers. Hulu is the second largest provider, with just over 300 million streams in February. And yet YouTube still struggles to attract advertising, while Hulu is attracting major brands to its service. Forrester Research's prediction that 187 billion videos would be streamed over the internet by 2009 was close to the mark.

Summary

The world is made up of countries at different levels of diffusion of audience ratings technology as well as different levels of development of media technologies. Panel technology for audience ratings is well established and each year more countries come within the syndicated fold.

As we have seen, there is now a range of different technologies competing for the measurement pie. Measuring the motivation of the audience has always been a part of audience ratings research, whether driven by Freudian theory or by some other approach. However, modern techniques provide a new dimension where eye gaze can be studied, heartbeat recorded, brains scanned and galvanic skin responses obtained. The aim with these techniques is to gain predictive advantage and to understand what audiences want now and what drives their needs into the future. As noted at the beginning of the chapter, though, there is no industry agreement on what is going to happen with biometrics or other techniques as a stable currency.

Measurement of this kind, of course, raises the problem of intrusion into people's lives, not only in terms of privacy but also, as we witnessed in the Chapter 3 on panels and surveys, issues of intrusion into the technology itself. These will be explored further in Chapter 9. The role of the ratings provider in this complex mix is what the authors will now turn to.

6 The Ratings Provider

> Most sampling frames in China are based on very outdated census figures which, even then, take account only of demographic and geographic factors, and not information on set ownership or viewing behaviour ... [The] most serious problem is one peculiar to China. It is standard practice to offer gifts and incentives to panellists taking part in the ratings surveys. Many of these gifts come complete with TV station logos. For whatever reasons, it is highly probable that many panellists feel they should return the favour by recording high viewing to the sponsoring channel. Many may feel, especially with Party control of the media, that it is their 'duty' to watch certain programmes such as the news. Andrew Green (Green 1996)

Andrew Green of Saatchi & Saatchi is here bemoaning the fact that there were in 1996 political and market difficulties in setting up ratings in China, not least the lack of a proper census from which to create an establishment survey, but of course also distortion. As we will see, his company was not passive on this issue but put proposals to China for change and these proposals have for the most part come to fruition. Green was concerned that because of the absence of a ratings provider as the point of coordination there had as a result been a massive duplication and multiplication of measurement services, all going their own way. As a stakeholder in China, Saatchi & Saatchi was not going to rely on many measurements that provided no basis for genuine currency. This might sound ironic, given the authors' last chapter where a ratings provider, like Nielsen, is incumbent, but everyone has still gone their own way. Green's argument, though, is sound from the point of view of ratings as a convention.

For all of the seeming apparent attention given to the ratings provider in news stories and industry debate over the ratings, surprisingly little attention has been given to the ratings provider, whether as an independent owner or in joint-industry collaboration, as the key coordinator of the ratings convention. The ratings provider fits into the convention as the nodal point around which knowledge accrues and the survey operates tactically. The provider is the knowledge broker – it is the intermediary which makes the ratings as a coordination rule a reality. The companies do the data collection and they provide information from this collection; they are the entity being evaluated by formal and informal auditing. This ensures that they are a ready target for criticism. In this chapter we want to shift the focus on to the ratings provider and the kinds of politics, knowledge, behaviours, tactics and strategies appropriate to their carriage of the ratings.

The Official Truth

Saatchi & Saatchi, one of the biggest spenders in the Chinese advertising market in 1996, had a problem. It did not trust audience research in China or its evolving ratings system. Television in China is organized around the five complex political layers of the Chinese bureaucratic system: the national level (*zhongyang*); 30 provinces (*sheng*); 2,148 counties (*xian*); 622 cities (*shi*); and 'work units' or *danwei*. Each level has a Communist Party and a separate government structure. There were in 1996 estimated to be 330 million households of which 83.4 per cent had television reception. The Propaganda Department of the Chinese Communist Party (CCP) controls what is shown. The Ministry of Radio, Film and Television is represented at national, provincial and city levels. China, for Saatchi & Saatchi, was complex in political and market terms and its concerns about hypoing were matched by its concerns about a proper establishment survey to represent television and radio households.

As a result, Saatchi & Saatchi, on behalf of the Hong Kong Association of Accredited Advertising Agencies (4As), presented to all the major TV stations in China carrying out their own surveys five major recommendations on reforming China's ratings system:

1 The service should be national, covering all major provinces and cities. Each survey currently in existence involves different companies in different cities using different techniques;

2 The service should be continuous. All the current advertising agency surveys suffer from the weakness that they measure only one point in time that is not representative of other periods of the year;

3 The service should be led by research buyers rather than research sellers, with the television stations as the primary partners and founders, as in most western markets;

4 There should be only one ratings system in China. The alternative, as has been seen, is a mess;

5 The service should be reliable, independent and transparent in its operation.

What we can see in China mirrors, as the authors have tried to show, the early history of audience ratings in the West. In those countries which established commercial broadcasting media early, such as Australia, the United States and Canada, audience measurement started with customized research undertakings of advertising agencies and stations. Fan mail is a good example of this type of customized research. It could be used to assess the popularity of programmes. The trajectory from customized to syndicated research occurred because a collective understanding of audiences in a growing broadcast market was needed. Without it no systematic trade was possible. A ratings service – the convention of standardized measurement – *cannot be imposed*. The need for it has to grow out of the experience, needs, understandings and interests of the various media players, and out of their common recognition that consensus on a convention provides stability and certainty in the market. As a corollary, a sufficiently developed, competitive and differentiated media market must be in place to require competitors to become collaborators for the purpose of supporting an independent media broking service.

The idea of an independent, industry-wide audience measurement service took some time to emerge in the United States and elsewhere, and it developed at different speeds. The United Kingdom could have adopted ratings for radio but decided against it and only did so when the market became competitive. Because audience measurement began as customized research by advertising agencies and radio stations this research was often limited by the interests of the commissioning service. Customized audience research was currency, as it still is in markets without a convention, and advertising agencies in these circumstances are well placed to function as 'brokers' and coordinators of a fragmented market place. In these circumstances customized research is '*the* only way for advertisers to learn about the audiences for media outlets' (Miller 1994: 63). This is the case for African countries and, indeed, in advanced industrial states where the panel sizes for ratings may be too low. As a result, advertising agencies and the individual station face a credibility problem with advertisers and media outlets. Each has a vested interest in the research. Advertising agencies have a potential conflict of interest as media buyers and planners while stations have a vested interest in promoting research favourable to themselves. In the history of the United States, these custom studies inevitably 'created a cacophony of incomparable audience claims' (Miller 1994: 63).

As the authors have argued, and as China as a modern exemplar demonstrates, there needs to be a different approach if ratings are adopted, one that can arbitrate competing claims and be accepted by all as a fair and representative measure. For this to happen the several interests involved with competing media outlets, advertisers and advertising agencies have to come together to help construct and accept a standard measure and the convention that goes with it. Syndicated audience research was born out of this necessity to construct 'a common template for assessing the audience' so as to permit the orderly development of an advertising and media market. Writing of the US experience Miller argues that advertisers sought a trade-off in survey design. More outlets could be measured with less detail, but to the detriment of rich data which is more costly. An underlying demand for rich demand, though, remained (Miller 1994: 63).

Ratings research is a large-scale research undertaking. Both costs and logistics ensure that ratings research is syndicated because its costs are borne by the various media players although, as we heard from Gale Metzger, in the United States the broadcasters themselves usually ended up footing the larger part of the bill. These outlets have an interest in coming together despite the often intense competition among them. In the United States they had 'something important in common – the same market to sell' (Barnathan 1964: 172). In the case of China, Green is pointing out that Chinese stations need to understand this as they already saw themselves in competition. To this end it makes sense for the different Chinese television stations to support the provision of regular, comparable, 'longitudinal information about audiences that can be used to sell advertising space and time' (Miller 1994: 63). China, in fact, recognized that television and radio have a common interest in ensuring that the ratings data is taken up by advertisers and media sales people. To ensure the credibility of the ratings system among the several groups who rely on it, the organization providing the syndicated research must be structurally separate from both media businesses and advertisers. Ratings providers must function and be seen to function as independent brokers. The Chinese government partnered with TNS in its initial incarnation. It has been and will be up to the players in the market to see whether the agreements to the convention are kept. What ratings providers seek is to establish an 'official truth': an agreement for the description of audiences for a number of media products which can be offered for sale to a number of clients. As Miller perceptively puts it:

> A service's case for becoming a convention is heightened to the extent that it can claim to capture all of those viewing, reading, or listening – every audience member for every program or articles, at all times. This criterion is particularly important to media clients who will pay the most toward the service's existence. The service's bid to offer the official reality will also benefit from a demonstration that its method detects only real viewing, reading, or listening and not false or misleading impressions. This criterion is particularly important to advertisers on whom the media clients rely for income. (Miller 1994: 67)

Persuading the full range of media players from the competing media companies that a particular technology or service for collecting and analysing audience data is suitable is no small achievement. Most importantly, the need for these services to prove themselves is continuous, especially when new systems or new players win ratings services. The early use of ratings was, for the most part, a check on performance of individual radio stations and their programmes, much like an internal audit on performance as well as a currency for trade. Indeed, there was no expectation that audience ratings *should* be made public on a routine basis, but that would come later. As a consequence discrepancies in data were a largely intra-mural matter for the broadcasting industry. Early ratings surveys were also not conducted on as regular basis as today. In Perth in Australia, for example, there was for many years only one sweep a year over a few weeks. Diary and personal interview data were necessarily limited. With no computational power the data analytics were narrow as was the 'window' to the audience. Agencies and stations could only ask so much of the data, and ratings research could only collect and analyse so much data from the audience.

The Silent Revolution

Australia is a good example of the impact of peoplemeters and the expansion on the window to the audience. In 1980 McNair-Anderson in Australia was partially acquired by the UK-based Audits of Great Britain (AGB) ratings research group. AGB were investing heavily in meter and other related technologies. The cost involved in developing meter technologies was outside the scope of the Australian company. This had been the case even in the early days of ratings in the United States where Nielsen took a massive personal risk in his investment in the Audimeter. AGB McNair lost the metropolitan TV television ratings tender to Nielsen for start-up in 1990. Both tenders were for peoplemeters – 'an electronic push-button way of recording the presence of individual viewers, with periodic prompts and the meter itself automatically recording which channel is on at the time' (Barwise and Ehrenberg 1988: 176).

The trial of peoplemeters was in 1989 for rollout in 1990. The longstanding use of diaries in the television market stopped in December 1990, although the diary method is still used today for remote regional areas, including Darwin. After Robert Maxwell died in 1991 AGB worldwide went into a management buyout including the Australian and New Zealand operations, and ACNielsen (as the Nielsen company was known) then purchased the Australian interests from the management buyout team in 1994. ACNielsen as a result became the main provider of Australian radio and television ratings. It held this position until AGB Italia won the metropolitan TV ratings contract in 1999.

The peoplemeter trial was run alongside the diary method over several months and showed as much as a 20 per cent increase in viewing time reported by the peoplemeters, especially at non-peak times. Peoplemeters, it was argued, are better at picking up single-person viewing. Single viewers tend to under-report their viewing in diaries. This under-reporting was widely known within ratings agencies prior to the introduction of the peoplemeter. Single viewers often under-reported for privacy reasons such as not wanting other members of the household to know and because they were less likely to remember to fill in the diary when unaccompanied.

By registering continuous viewing, peoplemeters pick up more audience movement within programmes. The peoplemeter permits the 'assessment of all televised offerings that can be received by the sets; it does not tire no matter how long the sets are on; and it counts reception time continuously' (Miller 1994: 68). Pushing buttons on a remote that sends messages to a set-top box on the computer seemed to remove the problem of fatigue in filling out diaries and truthfulness. For all of the importance of the turn to peoplemeters, the most significant 'revolution' in ratings after 1970 was not the replacement of diaries by peoplemeters but the quiet revolution associated with the coupling of ratings with computational power. In this context peoplemeters and computers permitted a greater detail and range of operations, better interrogation of data and additional manipulations of ratings data in analysis routines.

Computer-related programmes started to become a feature of syndicated audience measurement from the early 1970s in Australia. In this period the computers were all mainframes requiring specialist programmers within ratings agencies to run them. Over the 1970s a range of different types of services were explored or set up, including combined media-monitor products. McNair in 1970 had its single source Prime Prospect Profiles. From 1971 AGB also provided marketing information for products and services from a single-source data collection called Consumer Market Profiles. AGB McNair installed the first online ratings data delivery service to all the main advertising agencies in 1981. AGB Australia introduced the world's first electronic diary consumer panel in 1986. The computer concept provided for use of in home, online portable computer terminals recording purchases of all barcoded products to map grocery buying. The peoplemeters were established in 1990 with a Sydney, Melbourne, Brisbane, Adelaide and Perth panel of 2,400 people replacing the Sydney and Melbourne panel of 1,200. Peoplemeters permitted the ratings results to move towards becoming an overnight service as results from the previous day were 'uploaded' to the ratings' agency computers via the telephone line for processing overnight. This 'overnight' phenomenon had initially emerged as a premium ratings service in the United States in the early 1970s for large markets such as New York and Los Angeles. It was becoming a feature of the basic service in Australia. Large-scale and immediate data collection also brought with it greater demand for publication of ratings results, unknown in the early history of ratings. People today can look in a magazine and see the programme and station ratings.

The advent of peoplemeters coincided with the PC revolution which had not only distributed to the individual desktop computational power previously the preserve of mainframes but had also encouraged the development of software programs designed to carry out data analysis routines previously the preserve of programmers. This combination ensured that a greater range and variety of data manipulation of ratings results was able to become routinely available and delivered to the burgeoning workstations of advertisers, television and radio personnel and the like.

Ratings operations also moved from the back room of ratings agencies to the front room of media businesses, advertisers, agencies, media planners and media buyers. What were previously more incidental, ad hoc and expensive research undertakings on the part of ratings agencies for selected clients, requiring a programmer with advanced programming skills, now became more frequent, routine queries on the part of dispersed users of ratings. The databases were now available on their desktops and delivered through software programmes without the need for specialist programmers. The ratings book was being replaced by the ratings database.

For example, ACNielsen's 'Media Advisor' was integral to its provision of ratings services over the 1990s. This personal computer software package was designed to run under Microsoft Windows and allow the user to examine audience trends over time. The database program used statistics such as ratings, share, reach, frequency, hours and minutes viewed, audience profile and the number of people watching as its base. It contained a variety of software modules designed to cover all aspects of analysis and planning for programmers, media business sales departments, schedulers, advertising agencies and advertisers. Media Advisor included modules for dealing with smaller periods of time (quarter hour periods), with larger day-parts, and for tracking the performance of a programme over time. Over the decade additional features were added: tools to enable the user to analyse a television advertising campaign after the fact, to display the ratings according to a person's viewing patterns, to analyse audience 'loyalty' for programmes and stations, and to build media schedules 'based on TARP or budget objectives'. Software was also developed to better handle reports generated by Media Advisor and these included modules for 'viewing and formatting' and 'managing' reports. The official ratings provider from 2001 for metropolitan television markets, OzTAM, provides a similar facility as Media Advisor with its AGB WorkStation. It has a similar audience database that promises individual by individual, minute-by-minute data delivered overnight, 365 days of the year. The development of these ratings software/databases ensured that the ratings became available to a larger variety of ratings clients who now had available to them a greater variety of pathways into the ratings data previously the preserve of the agencies and their largest clients. Advertising agencies and media companies alike were now conducting their own analysis of the ratings data. With this move to a ratings database came a corresponding increase in the complexity of data collection and analysis, and the complexity of intermediate decisions on the audience and its relative value to advertisers and stations. Media planners emerged as intermediaries in the buying and selling of advertising based on the ratings and consumer profiles research. Other intermediaries emerged capable of interpreting ratings data and linking ratings data either to other datasets or customized qualitative and quantitative survey instruments. The 'window' to the data was clearly changing to respond to new circumstances including advertiser needs. In the 1930s soap manufacturers were the largest advertisers and their judgements were based on information on a simple categorization of the audiences as 'housewife'. By 2000 there are thousands of advertisers with judgements based on hundreds of different classifications of audience.

There is no doubt that the need to know about what audiences and consumers do has increased in complexity and computers have provided one means of drilling down to provide this information. Slowly and imperceptibly a paradigm shift was occurring in ratings research with the move from the ratings book to the online, disk and CD-based ratings computer database. At one level not much had changed: the databases provided the same basic information as the ratings books did and peoplemeters were still the basis for this information. But the presentation of the information had changed. It had moved from being pre-structured to cover the most common analyses of the data in a book based delivery system to a more open-ended resource capable of offering diverse users a variety of manipulations of constantly updated data based on their individual needs. With the ratings book the end user had very limited means of handling, responding and interpreting data – they were inevitably constrained by the costs of data manipulation. With the ratings database it was now the users who were doing the manipulations. The ratings agencies were now concerned to facilitate their users in their use of the software/database, to ensure that the analytical tools met client needs and to develop tools to allow additional queries to be made using the software. 'Knowing their audience' was now the business of ratings agency clients in a new way: the programme-makers, the schedulers, the space sellers and buyers, the media campaign managers/ creators and so on were now 'constructing several pictures' themselves from these databases. If the ratings have always had an 'end user' focus, this embodiment in a ratings database placed special onus upon the users of the data to manipulate, extract, evaluate and generally make meaningful the ratings information.

The ratings database also placed a different onus on the ratings agencies. They now needed to provide users with a sophisticated understanding of the nature and character of the audience and of the database. Ratings agencies were having to cooperate with their clients not only to facilitate the generation of information but also to illustrate, train or otherwise inform an increasingly larger range of clients in how to use the system and carefully explain its limits. Because the focus was now on the client generating meaningful data from the system, ratings providers had a significant and ongoing information management and software training problem. Products like Media Advisor required people who could use the software in sophisticated ways and who knew the limitations of the database and had developed appropriate research techniques.

Like any software and database there were significant risks for users and providers alike. Clients were being presented with a mountain of information and a variety of pathways through this information. And this carried a risk in that too much information can complicate rather than simplify the decision-making of users. Another risk is that the end users might have an imperfect understanding of the meaning of ratings and ratings methodologies – leading to poor decisions on media placements, media vehicles, presentation to clients and so on. Consequently training needs increasingly occupied personnel in ratings agencies that were looking for ways to disseminate information and develop capacity for handling media database product on the part of those already in or likely to go into advertising agency and media positions. For clients to use the ratings efficiently and effectively they need to understand both the potential and limits of the data. With the increasing range of manipulations able to be done the tolerances and uncertainties in the ratings instrument are becoming more visible and less a specialized understanding.

With the move to PC-based information, ratings services around the world discovered new clients were emerging for these services. As the principal costs for ratings measurement are 'first copy' costs – the costs associated with the measurement process and producing the database – once the database is set up the service can be sold to additional clients at minimal expense. These new clients placed further training pressures on ratings providers. The rapidly developing PC market also made it possible for additional services to be developed which sought to develop more comprehensive understandings of audiences in relation to different media and not just in relation to different outlets within a particular medium. From one side organizations such as Roy Morgan developed Roy Morgan Single Source based on a large interview sample (50,000) with questions related to lifestyle, attitudes, media consumption (TV, radio, pay-TV, cinema, newspapers and magazines, catalogues and the internet), brand and product usage, retail visitations, purchase intentions, service provider preferences, financial information and leisure activities. From the other side ratings providers like Nielsen started to bring together its range of previously separate software/database products.

Nielsen's 'Panorama' is one such syndicated multi-media marketing database that integrates consumer demographics, product usage and media consumption. Here the aim is to add value by fusing together its various products. In mid-2001 Panorama was drawing on Nielsen's TV and radio ratings data, its readership surveys, and specifically designed product and service usage questionnaires with plans to 'incorporate consumer goods purchasing information from the ACNielsen Homescan consumer panel'. This fusion product promised media planners and sellers the capacity to 'go beyond demographics when analysing media consumption patterns'. It was sold as enabling media strategists to 'conduct detailed analyses of viewers by demographics, print and television media, and product usage'; brand managers to 'define target markets and profile consumers by demographics, lifestyle habits, product usage and media consumption'; and media sales persons people to 'learn about your target's buyergraphics and doergraphics' and profile programme audiences against category and major brand users to demonstrate to advertisers the niche audience efficiencies of lower rating off peak programmes.

'Superior Technology': ATR-OzTAM and ACNielsen Controversy in Australia

The trend towards more tailored ratings, customized at the individual level, 'micro-audiences' and the shift of audiences to diverse media has had a similar effect on television as it had on radio. These different considerations no doubt weighed heavily on the minds of the technical experts and executives from the networks when they met to write the specifications for the tender for metropolitan television ratings in Australia in 1999 and to evaluate the rival tenders. The ratings debate of late 1999 and the first half of 2001 was both like and unlike previous debates. Like the first peoplemeter contract, it was over a change of provider as the incumbent: ACNielsen lost the lucrative metropolitan television ratings contract to newcomer AGB Italia's Advanced Television Research (ATR) – which provided OzTAM with its data. Unlike previous controversies, which were between different research technologies and methodologies, the OzTAM/ACNielsen controversy was over different results using the same peoplemeter technology. This similarity undoubtedly made the reported discrepancies both surprising and disturbing.

There were two parts to this debate. The first part, in late 1999, was in the aftermath of the announcement of a change in ratings provider. It centred on the networks' motives for dumping the incumbent in favour of a comparatively unknown newcomer. The second part of the controversy occurred in the first half of 2001 as discrepancies between the two systems became evident and set the stage for public dissension over just 'whose' figures were accurate. Any change in the provider of ratings conventions is bound to excite controversy. The incumbent has all the advantages of incumbency: it is a known quantity, with experience and a reputation as a known agency for providing reliable and comprehensive measurement for a variety of media outlets and related syndicated services. In Australia ACNielsen had been providing the 'convention' for several years and in its provision of several syndicated services was well placed to provide ratings services for converging media environments. Furthermore this was an incumbent that not only traced its history back to the beginning of ratings research in Australia but also carried the Nielsen name – a global name in ratings technology and the major supplier of ratings services within comparable English language markets.

By contrast the new provider had to establish its credibility with both prospective users, particularly those not involved in making the decision to select the new provider, and with the broader public. In this case ATR was a 'new player' unknown inside English language television markets. Its reputation for ratings services came from Latin America and continental Europe. Rather than setting its credibility against that of the incumbent, ATR/OzTAM promoted its service as an innovation – a technically superior service. Additionally, it attempted to secure the services of credible figures drawn from within the Australian ratings industry in the period leading up to and immediately after being awarded the contract. Ian Muir, a prominent figure in audience measurement in Australia for several decades, became OzTAM's chief executive officer and was joined later by other former ACNielsen personnel. (Interestingly, Muir had led the losing AGB McNair bid for the peoplemeter contract a decade earlier; his 'crossing to the other side' was critical to the local standing of the AGB Italia bid.) ATR also relocated one of its European experts to Australia for the critical start-up period (Wilmoth 2001).

Further complicating the credibility problem facing the new provider was the move on the part of the television networks to 'own' the data previously owned by the provider. ATR is supervised by OzTAM, a company established and financed by the three commercial networks. While ATR does the work, OzTAM owns the results and sells them to subscribers. This structure raised important and legitimate concerns as to the potential for conflicts of interest in the provision of ratings data. While it is not uncommon for media outlets to 'own the data' internationally, this was not the Australian practice. This move raised several concerns about just how independent, rigorous and believable the OzTAM data were likely to be. Just how much control over information was being demanded by those who paid for it and relinquished by the ratings provider? These integrity concerns were a real issue for those users not involved in the decision to change ratings providers, such as advertisers and media buyers. They were also a major concern for network television's competitors such as pay-TV television providers. In a local climate where free-to-air television networks are widely perceived both locally and internationally as having inhibited pay-TV television and other new kinds of television development, the ATR decision was going to be inevitably read as another move by the networks to protect their patch at the expense of others. Certainly, pay-TV television providers had less reason to cooperate with OzTAM – the provider of only free-to-air ratings – than with ACNielsen, an independent company, who provided ratings for several media services.

As Miller notes, persuading the full range of media players that a particular technology for collecting and analysing data for their audiences provides 'the basis for their costly transactions' involves the research firms in 'an elaborate ritual of testing and "validating" the new measurement system' (Miller 1994: 66). ATR/OzTAM had to 'prove' itself particularly in the crossover period between the two systems. With the television networks initially claiming that their choice of ATR was based on its 'superior technology', they undoubtedly expected the new system to provide very little in the way of surprises. It would be more a tweaking of the system to reveal greater levels of detail on exposure to programmes and advertising, and to prepare for the circumstances of television environments as much as seven years hence. What they got in the initial set-up period of the ATR panels in early 2001 was something quite different.

In the first weeks of the new rating period of 2001 there were considerable differences between the OzTAM and ACNielsen results. In the week beginning 11 February, OzTAM figures for Melbourne as a 30.5 per cent audience share for channel Nine; 29.5 per cent for channel Seven; and 19.3 per cent for channel Ten. ACNielsen figures had Nine on 33.4 per cent, Seven on 26.7 per cent and Ten at 21.4 per cent. The OzTAM figures stunned the industry, giving rise to concerns that it might be seriously flawed. While the discrepancies between the old and new results narrowed over the year as the OzTAM panel was 'fine-tuned', by May it was clear that the OzTAM ratings system had resulted in a consistently improved outlook for Seven (Balnaves, O'Regan and Sternberg 2002). Nine may have won seven of the twelve ratings weeks up to that point but it was only narrowly beating Seven with a 30.5 per cent share compared to Seven's 30 per cent. Seven had narrowed Nine's lead considerably – a circumstance which encouraged projections by analysts such as Credit Suisse First Boston of increased earnings for Seven and diminishing earnings for Nine over coming. SBS's ratings also went up (SBS thought this was because of better coverage of non-English-speaking households on the part of OzTAM); ABC's went down; and the results for the Ten Network were mixed though improving over the year (Balnaves et al. 2002).

At the same time the ratings results were also indicating trends towards less overall television viewing. This was predicted to translate into pressure on advertising revenues as media buyers reassessed the value of free-to-air television. It also showed that audiences were moving into and out of programmes in ways which considerably complicated understandings of programme popularity. David Keig of Keig and Co had used OzTAM's facility to 'take a snapshot of who is watching every minute' to 'track the way a viewer flicks from network to network' (Dale 2001). Based on Keig's analysis of the average prime-time programme in March 2001, only '36 per cent of those who dipped ended up watching the whole show, while 51 per cent of the supposed audience watched less than a third' (Dale 2001). For Keig, 'Most programs now are like revolving doors, with people coming in and out all the time'. These audience behaviours would need to be factored into media buying and advertising placement.

A damaging controversy ensued. The controversy was not initially centred on the difficult methodological issues surrounding the construction and implementation of ratings systems, particularly its panels. Quite the contrary, it began as a controversy with a far simpler narrative. This was a 'war' among the commercial interests of the various parties: Nine supporting the ACNielsen results because it conferred upon them an unambiguous no.1 spot; Seven and later Ten supporting OzTAM as its figures gave them their best chance in years to whittle away Nine's lead. There were allegations of 'greed' on the part of those reluctant to accept the 'umpire's verdict' – with Nine being seen as reneging on its own earlier ringing endorsement for the new official convention holder, OzTAM. Indeed, the Nine Network's CEO, David Leckie, was widely reported as having pushed the hardest for the AGB Italia bid. (In a curious ways this helped the 'standing' of the OzTAM system among non-television station users of the system as it indicated the 'independence' of the system in that it could provide bad news for those who paid for it.)

The consensus underpinning the ratings system seemed to be falling apart. As none of the vested interests involved could settle the matter in their favour, queries about both systems intensified. Was there some circumstance polluting what ought to have been an objective, empirical project of determining the ratings? There was a crisis in confidence in the system. Journalists reported warnings from media buyers that their clients were holding back from buying television advertising as the controversy continued. With advertiser media-buying decisions starting to be affected a growing consensus from advertising agencies, media planners and media buyers was that the damaging controversy needed speedy resolution. Intermediaries drawn from advertising such as the Media Federation (representing 'most media specialist agencies') emerged seeking to 'broker a truce between warring factions'. From their point of view the issue would not be resolved by maintaining two parallel rating systems – that would only 'continue to show that they were different'. The central issue for the Media Federation was in its President Peter Cornelius's words, 'why they are different?' Because of the prima facie similarity between the two systems, the methodology – how ratings panels and data collection techniques are constructed – became the issue around which the conflict could be resolved. Was one of the panels flawed? Was it ACNielsen's panel or OzTAM's? Or both? Or neither?

With such a damaging stand-off undermining the credibility of the convention and with two panels causing consternation in circumstances where advertisers had become accustomed to one agreed standard, an independent audit became necessary. Professor Peter Danaher, a New Zealand expert on sampling, was brought in to 'adjudicate' the dispute – that is to explain the differences between the systems. Central to his brief was to assess the representativeness of the two panels. In making his assessment, census data on the makeup and character of the Australian population would be central. While the report is confidential, the absence of commentary would seem to indicate that Danaher's report contained few surprises. It is almost as if his appointment as auditor itself brought the controversy to an end.

When Danaher reported his results the differences between OzTAM and ACNielsen results were narrowing, there was a growing consensus that the differences between them had been exaggerated, and that there were not serious enough flaws in the OzTAM panels to warrant revisiting the ratings contract.

As Julius Barnathan noted in the context of public discussion of ratings in an earlier period in the United States, discrepancies between ratings systems are not issues to do with the rigging or fixing of ratings by broadcasters, but turn on the 'operational flaws in the techniques used by each rating service' (Barnathan 1964: 172). Typically, these flaws are 'known to the sophisticated researcher but unknown to the layman'. The problem the layperson encounters in these public controversies is the uncertainties of the ratings – the fact that they are 'estimates' not 'hardfact yardsticks' (Barnathan 1964: 173). While the discrepancies between the two systems may be unsurprising to an insider and be may well be within acceptable bounds, to an outsider these same discrepancies point to flaws which undermine confidence in the ratings and therefore the decisions flowing from these.

All concerned had been educated in the 'the problem' facing contemporary ratings technologies. Panels by their nature are 'samples'. They are liable to error, as the media players know. OzTAM's website foregrounds the fact that 'like any survey, a sample will never be as accurate as surveying the entire population', so 'results obtained can and do fluctuate'. Anyone running an analysis using OzTAM's data will therefore need to 'always consider the size of the sample from which you are drawing your results from' (OzTAM 2001b). Samples are part of the trade-off for ratings research. No two samples are going to be exactly the same. It is difficult even with larger panels to be representative in a fragmenting media environment increasingly characterized by niche audiences and a culturally diverse society. It is therefore likely that both OzTAM and ACNielsen figures were both right.

The concerns that the OzTAM and ACNielsen debate has generated about the representativeness of panels, their size and therefore the accuracy of modern audience ratings techniques will not disappear. The increasing individualization and sheer quantity of data create greater uncertainty and will put pressure on panel size. The problem existing panels pose for broadcasters such as SBS, according to Ken Sievers is that the current sample sizes have been 'relatively efficient in measuring the mass audiences of the commercial stations who achieve quite high levels of ratings' but present difficulties when dealing with smaller, niche audiences (Sievers 2000). OzTAM and ACNielsen were competing in the tender to become the 'official' reality for audience measurement, but when their results conflicted the debate was not resolved among the players themselves but in the public domain, with the protagonists being the very owners and users of the ratings. The issue of 'truth' was not simply methodology but the process of coordination and agreement among the different players who define and agree on the social convention. Public trust is also a part of the agreement. The OzTAM and ACNielsen debate brought in all the media players because they all have a stake in how ratings, as currency, are defined and accepted.

'Superior Technology': Nielsen versus Hooper, Nielsen versus Arbitron

> Some months ago, the rating people were vigorously assailed by a distinguished committee of the National Association of Broadcasters for producing 'what appears to be conflicting testimony' on the standing of shows. Last December, they were attacked by Sponsor, a trade publication for radio and TV advertisers, in a report headed What's Wrong with the Rating Services? Among other criticisms, the Sponsor article voiced suspicion regarding relations between some rating services and certain of their customers. Said the report: 'Stations, agencies, all bring pressure to bear to keep ratings high. Sponsor has seen letters from stations to rating services promising to buy the service "when you can show us on top".' Currently, a second important group of broadcasters is investigating the whole ratings industry.
> B. Davidson (Davidson 1954)

Sautet has an interesting thesis about modern firms in competitive environments. Firms have visions of what the future could be like (Sautet 2002: 83). The successful ones are 'alert' to opportunities and the discovery of not yet perceived or used knowledge.

The US audience ratings history is a story of entrepreneurial action and success by Nielsen in the face of powerful competitors and defence against continuous attacks on credibility from a range of players. At some points in its history Nielsen was an innovator and at other points it was an incumbent wielding its power and taking advantage of innovations created elsewhere. In the Australian system, after a period of entrepreneurial competition, the ratings contract became the mechanism that framed the actions and bids by particular entrepreneurial firms. In the contemporary moment, there are in US audience measurement many competitive rivals in different fields but the last great rival to Nielsen in the United States was the American Research Bureau (ARB). The ARB changed its name to Arbitron in 1973 because of concerns that a name like the American Research Bureau sounded governmental.

Nielsen has been able to obtain remarkable longevity as a firm. It has operated in an 'open market' and has not had the 'contracts' to hide behind. As Penrose wrote:

> A firm specializing in given products can maintain its position with respect to these products only if it is able to develop an *expertise in technology* and *marketing* sufficient to enable it to keep up with and to participate in the introduction of innovation affecting its products. (Penrose 1995; Sautet 2002: 135)

This would suggest that a firm has to maintain its advantages through continuous developments in technology and in their expertise in marketing. Both fronts seem important. Marketing here should be interpreted broadly as Nielsen aggressively used and uses the courts, congress and various other venues to support its strategy or defence. This becomes particularly important when we consider the very idea of 'superior technology'. C.E. Hooper mobilized Hans Zeisel to support him in the critique of CAB's techniques, claiming superiority of technology in audience ratings. The broadcasters also never forgave CAB for denying them access to and formal participation in its work until 1936.

But Hooper was soon to find himself under an even more aggressive attack from Arthur Nielsen. He launched a public and academic campaign against Hooper, his diary method and, not least, sampling. Moreover, Nielsen was determined to have the Audimeter and automatic recording accepted as the 'superior technology'. In this, Nielsen was brilliant. His established and close links with strategic partners paid off. The Advertising Research Foundation (ARF) conducted the first major critique and recommendation for audience ratings standards, completed in 1954. It examined the conditions under which a study was made, questionnaire design, interviewing procedures, sampling, executive execution of survey, editing, coding tabulation and interpretation of results. This process involved over 100 meetings and conferences, not including consultation and written feedback from the seven ratings services. The study covered all the major methods of the time:

1 diary

2 recorder

3 personal coincidental

4 personal roster recall

5 personal unaided recall

6 telephone coincidental

7 telephone recall

8 combination telephone coincidental and telephone recall

9 combination telephone coincidental and diary

10 combination telephone coincidental and personal roster recall

While the report did not name specific ratings services, it favoured Nielsen's recorder method. By 1950, Nielsen's Audimeter was in 1,500 homes providing data on:

1 homes using radio

2 programme ratings

3 station coverage

4 homes per dollar

5 total audience

6 audience flow

7 commercial effectiveness

8 talent popularity

9 programme preferences

10 product sales related to programme ratings

11 network audience

12 unaffiliated stations audience

13 commercial audience

14 minute-by-minute audience

15 cumulative audience

16 audience turnover

17 frequency of listening

18 audience for spots

19 non-network programme audience

20 network sustaining programme audience

21 station area data

22 Pacific network ratings

In 1950 Hooper and Nielsen brokered a deal where Hooper would have local radio measurement and Nielsen national radio measurement. Hooper introduced a TV measurement service in 1952, but he was killed in a boating accident in 1954. Television was in 83 per cent of American homes by 1958; however, Hooper's city TV ratings services were sold to ARB in 1959 with Hooper's company retaining local radio, which had expanded to 200 markets. By 1955 Nielsen had spent US$12 million on the Audimeter and his anxiousness for its success was not surprising. He was also head of the largest market research organization in the world, with 3,500 full-time employees in 17 offices in 11 countries and an annual gross of US$24 million, of which 22 per cent was from his broadcast division.

What is very interesting is that Nielsen, like Hooper, was quite happy to aggressively argue, with statistics appended, on the weakness of competitive audience ratings technologies, but then to adopt them himself if needs be, just as Hooper had done with recall. Nielsen dropped the Audimeter for the TV markets and substituted it with diaries until the 1970s when the Storage Instantaneous Audimeter (SIA) was deployed. This meter collected data from television sets in homes and sent the data back to Nielsen. Twice a day Nielsen would retrieve data from each of the 1,200 SIA homes. The SIA cost network subscribers US$300,000 per year. The Nielsen Television Index (NTI) provided continuing estimates of TV viewing and national sponsored network programme audiences, including national ratings 52 weeks a year. It measured TV station audiences in over 200 local markets. An 800,000 diary sweep verified the accuracy of Nielsen's 1,200-home panel. By 1977 Nielsen's US TV services cost its 3,000 clients over US$26 million. Of Nielsen's overall revenues of US$270 million, the TV division represented 10 per cent.

Arbitron at the same time ran into difficulties with its meter, having contracted a company called E-Systems to provide a device that was supposedly 96 per cent accurate. However, on delivery 91 per cent of the meters failed within four weeks of operation. The court case against E-Systems was won, but took six years between 1973 and 1979 to come to a US$3million judgment. Arbitron never caught up with Nielsen in the television market as it went through management and takeover difficulties that delayed or affected the speed by which plans went ahead. With the evolution of computers, however, Arbitron provided innovative services like its Audience on Demand (AoD) service that offered clients the ability to use data in their own computer calculations, including reach and frequency. By 1974, Nielsen and Arbitron each produced 170 reports providing more data than the industry could possibly handle. This proliferation of data also created another form of distortion, where companies would do calculations on the data, even if the sampling tolerances did not allow it. Companies would, with no sense of shame, charge *extra* to distort results, in some cases charging up to US$8,000 (Banks 1981).

It is not necessarily superior technology, therefore, that wins the day. The ratings provider has to be proficient at dealing with all the politics of the ratings field and be able to negotiate with all the players successfully. This includes, not least, ensuring that within its own methodology, execution of methods and analysis of results that distortion is rigorously controlled, or if coming through hypoing, aggressively pursued. The best example of this is in 1966 when Nielsen discovered that 6 per cent of its Multinetwork Audience sample had received questionnaires asking them to watch particular commercials on a certain day. Nielsen found out that 5 per cent of the National Audimeter sample had also received the same letters. On further investigation Nielsen discovered that Rex Sparger, one of the former investigators of the Congressional committee on ratings, had stolen the names of the Nielsen sample from Nielsen's rubbish. Sparger did not deny this and also said that he planned to write a book revealing hypoing, but Nielsen found that Sparger himself was involved in the practice. Sparger had a contract with Charles Lowe, the producer of the Carol Channing special that went to air at the same time as his hypoing spree. Sparger was alleged to have been paid US$4,000 to rig the show's ratings. Nielsen sued for US$1.5 million for illegally obtaining trade secrets, but the matter was settled out of court. Nielsen, the company, knew that hypoing was not just a technical issue for the methodologist but a hot political issue that can embroil government committees and the public. In this case, given the quick actions of Nielsen, the federal government did not order a probe.

There can be little doubt that Arthur Nielsen's strategic nous was extraordinary and his personal experience became embedded in his company's strategic actions generally. What Nielsen learnt, like his competitor Hooper, was that the debates over innovation in audience ratings methodology and technology were primarily about the disposition at any one time of the broadcasters, the advertisers, governments, technical expert committees, research institutes and not least the public. This did not mean that innovation did not happen, but it did mean that Nielsen as the central entrepreneurial firm in audience ratings was able to deploy knowledge – not yet used or not yet perceived knowledge – in dramatically effective ways that often wrong-footed his competitive opponents. His harnessing of professionalism, discussed in the next chapter, is another example of this.

Summary

Syndicated audience research such as ratings is necessarily contentious. Some of this contention is structural because the reporting of syndicated research in ratings comparisons can never drill down to the levels of specificity required by the various players. Standardization produces tension. In this sense the ratings will always 'fail' to satisfy the need for a more detailed picture of the audience. By definition ratings systems only know the audience in certain capacities. The various interested industry parties – broadcasters, programme producers, advertisers, regulators, media planners, ad agencies – need to supplement ratings with customized research. The 'problem with the ratings' is not so much a problem with methodology and sampling, as is commonly claimed, but with the ways various players perceive the ratings system and its limits. In circumstances where the ratings are seen as delivering 'the perfect' picture of the audience the structural imperfections of syndicated research – arrived at as they are by negotiations among several parties and interests – are ignored. Customized research is necessarily able to give a more in-depth picture of audience behaviours. It is not constrained by syndicated research's need to establish aggregate measures and agreement among dispersed stakeholders.

Research firms who supply customized research routinely comment on the imperfections and blunt character of ratings research, pointing to the need for alternative (additional) knowledge and research on audiences. In much the same way, public and academic commentary on the ratings system routinely draws attention to the conventional, constructed character of the ratings, their closure to social differentiation, their hegemonic construction as arbiters of programme value and decision-making within the industry in comparison, for example, to the fickleness and changeability of audiences themselves (Ang 1991: 171–94). These several constructions of the ratings persist, alternatively overly inflating and diminishing the value and purpose of the ratings. This public 'sound and fury' over the ratings can sometimes obscure the often precise understanding of the limits and therefore value of the ratings on the part of the various actors and the complementary character of customized and syndicated research.

It is important to acknowledge the public character of ratings research as syndicated research. This aspect of ratings research is sometimes ignored when the ratings are considered as industry-imposed orderings of diverse audience behaviours and pleasures. From the perspective of the ratings provider, the ratings system is at base an auditing and therefore accountability measure. Those involved in delivering ratings systems understand themselves as providing a public service. They necessarily operate 'above' the interested stakeholders who nonetheless support this auditing service and make it possible. With the move towards ratings databases and the interlinking of several databases the function and character of syndicated and customized research alike is changing. It is becoming increasingly common for syndicated research instruments such as ratings databases to form one basis for customized research activities which draw on other databases and qualitative research methodologies. In this way 'ratings research' databases are becoming an integral part of customized research. The 'service' character of the ratings instrument is being extended in ways analogous to the 'data mining' undertaken by private corporations on Australian Bureau of Statistics census data. Does this distract from the core task of providing independent, reliable and benchmarked data? Probably not, as any compromising of independence and of the ratings standard setting function would diminish the market value of the research base for diverse users. But it certainly does mean that the ratings instrument is becoming less embodied in a separate system with quasi-firewalls between it and customized research activities, and becoming more a function capable of being rigorously separated out from other uses of the datasets.

There has been an historical trend evident in broadcast and media markets around the world for broadcast markets with multiple ratings providers to be replaced by markets with single ratings providers. Ever since Nielsen took over the local television market ratings and had these alongside its longstanding national market ratings in the United States, it has been not only the main game but the only game. There have been rumblings over its monopoly provider status and criticisms that it acts as a law unto itself; and significant controversy has surrounded its operations. In different ways similar concerns have been expressed about single ratings providers in Australia, the United Kingdom and continental Europe. Indeed, in the contemporary period ratings provision is often characterized by quasi-monopolies and multinational companies. While there have been considerable controversies surrounding those firms and agencies that provide these single ratings measures, much of this attention focuses on the ratings monopoly rather than on why a monopoly became necessary. Trends towards 'single measures' within ratings provision connect up with the increasing demands made upon ratings providers to develop a single coordination rule, to construct and operate increasingly larger panels, and to provide more frequent and timely ratings results. They are also connected to the scale of the technological apparatus that needs to be increasingly brought into play. It is clear that in the computer era deep pockets are necessary to conduct ratings operations and to undertake the innovations essential to the continuing relevance of the ratings convention.

At the same time ratings providers, no matter the conditions under which they operate, need to negotiate common expectations of performance and behaviour that are largely taken for granted. This includes expectations of integrity, structural separation and transparency; trade-offs required of ratings providers in managing internal expectations of research performance and innovation on the one hand, and broadcaster and advertiser willingness-to-pay on the other; and not least managing their dual identity as a provider of a quasi-public service in undertaking syndicated research and as a market research provider critical to the operation of commercial markets. The US experience confirms the existence of these expectations, even if the way they play out may be different, country by country.

7 The Networks (and Other Media Providers)

Dear Cecil

I don't understand TV scheduling. I would assume that since a greater number of the Teeming Millions is awake from 9 to 10 p.m. than from 10 to 11 p.m., more of them are ogling the idiot box during the earlier hour. This means that during the last hour of prime time (10–11 p.m. in New York, 9–10 p.m. in Chicago), many more people are watching in the Central zone than in the Eastern zone, allowing a far great number of Buttoneers, Popeil Pocket Fishermen, and tubes of Tickle Deodorant to be sold in the Midwest than on the East Coast. Accepting this, which any sensitive and thoughtful individual would, why on earth does West Coast TV operate under the East Coast schedule?

As an addendum, Cecil, if you are called upon to destroy my assumptions, please be merciful and don't employ your laserlike wit to grind me into pulp.

Allan S., Evanston, Illinois

The media providers – the networks, other broadcasters, later joined by the subscription television services, and now online portals and channels – have become the fulcrum of the ratings convention. The ratings were integral to radio displacing print as the main medium for advertising, and then television displacing radio as the main medium for advertising, to broadcasters becoming vendors of audiences, to their winning control of their schedules from advertisers in the early 1960s, to the development of in-programme advertising by a variety of advertisers, to allowing networks to schedule better and therefore make better offers to advertisers, and to the development of a stable currency permitting systematic strategic planning. But the vehicle that got them to the top is the same one that is taking them down. Pay-TV, internet protocol television (IPTV) and online providers are attempting to dislodge the dominance of traditional syndicated ratings and are setting up alternative ways of measuring.

In this chapter the authors chart the trajectory of ratings from the perspective of media providers. Although media providers – particularly larger and more dominant broadcasters – benefited significantly from systematic audience measurement their initial response to the ratings was mixed. We will explore how the ratings entered into the calculation of broadcasters and other media providers and how they used the ratings to 'sell audiences', to construct flow through schedules, and to analyse, develop, anticipate and chart the programming cycle. In particular, we will show how the ratings became critical to the advertising offers of media providers and their corporate and competitive market strategies. The chapter will also explore international differences in the evolution of audience ratings. In the United Kingdom public service management actively resisted the development of systematic ratings, preferring self-selecting listener panels. In the end, however, audience ratings became central to all broadcasters – commercial, public service providers and later pay television networks.

TV Economics

In the contemporary moment, we have a situation where measurement has become more, not less, important; where there is a proliferation of measures and channels; and where people are using media more, not less. The broadcast television networks in the United States – ABC, CBS, NBC – had their peak in 1978 when they claimed 93 per cent of the viewing audience in prime-time evening slots. By 1996 this had dropped to 53 per cent. With the introduction of new networks, such as Fox, Warner Brothers (WB) and United Paramount Network (UPN), and the spread of cable channels, the networks invested in pay television, changed its traditional financial arrangement with affiliates to cut costs, and fought a legal battle to change consent orders that restricted them in their ability to make and show. For 25 years ABC, CBS and NBC were forbidden to syndicate their shows and each network was required to purchase performance rights for many of the prime-time shows they showed from the programme producers. Figure 7.1 shows the money arrow. ABC, for example, did not own *Roseanne* and leased its episodes from Carsey-Werner

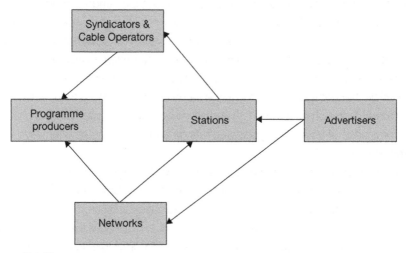

Figure 7.1 The money arrow

Company. In the resulting court case Hollywood studios argued that a half-hour show cost around US$500,000 and the money they received from the networks did not even cover the cost of production – a TV series needed to run for at least five years in order to provide a reasonable return. The US Court of Appeals, however, allowed the consent order to lapse, allowing the networks to hold financial interests in syndicated television programming and to syndicate their own programmes.

Free-to-air, advertiser-supported television networks had four major benefits:

1   Networks reduce transaction costs by creating efficiencies in procurement of programme and advertising time.

2   Networks offer advertisers an efficient way to distribute advertising budget risk.

3   Networks provide efficiencies in programming schedules.

4   Networks reduce transmission costs by transmitting programmes simultaneously to all affiliates within a time zone.
   (Owen and Wildman 1992: 53–4)

Ratings in this context are essential because they demonstrate the existence of large audiences. However, a decline in audience viewing brings the whole profit process undone. Subscription (cable) television by contrast does not have the same economics. Indeed, early subscription television in the United States was able to make a profit even when its audience economics were not necessarily healthy. The success of a subscription television business lies in the relationship between profit per subscriber, churn (the number of people who come and go) and subscriber acquisition costs. US subscription television was booming up until the 1970s. Cable systems did not fail because the value of the service kept rising. Cable television services generated income from installation charges, US$100 to US$300 a customer, and monthly service fees of US$5 to US$20:

> Most of the money was ploughed back into the companies, with hardly anything going to pay dividends to shareholders. This high cash flow could service an immense amount of debt, which was used to buy more systems. So the actual value of the acquired systems was always growing. Moreover, the companies paid hardly any tax because of the high depreciation of the equipment. The average cable system enjoyed a profit margin of 57 per cent, far fatter than most businesses. (Robichaux 2002: 14–15)

Cable television, of course, has to plan for provision of programming to audiences, or subscribers, in the same way as networks – understanding demand and who its audience is. The global mediascape give a sense of what the future holds, or at least what major media strategists say the future holds. Australian incumbent free-to-air operators likewise have created additional digital channels, with the blessings of the Australian federal government. The Australian market, like the Western European and United States markets, share the same anxiety about what is happening to audience share as pay-TV and new entrants fracture the market. This shift in audience share has led to changes in the revenue pie from television, with cable television for the first

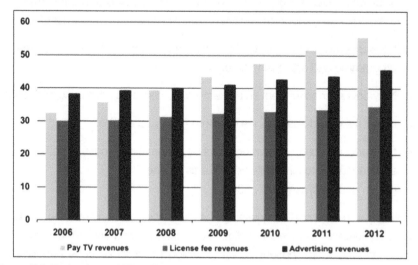

Figure 7.2 Projections of West European cable television versus advertising revenues, 2006–2012
Source: Screen Digest

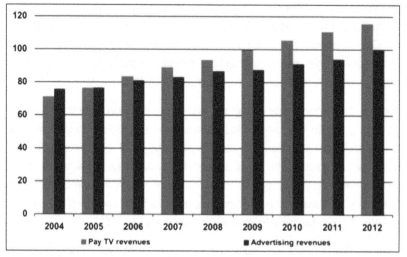

Figure 7.3 Projections of United States cable television versus advertising revenues, 2006–2012
Source: Screen Digest

time overtaking traditional advertising revenues from broadcasting. Figures 7.2 and 7.3 provide an overview of these changes, together with projections to 2012.

Within this complex media mix, there are revenue streams by content (a growing demand for specialized and paid content), advertising shifting to the internet and interactive transactions on television. You can see clearly, however, why there is debate over what is going to happen next. There is a range of possibilities:

1 There is the possibility that television may become the super-premium service for advertising because it will be the only medium able to get access to large audiences in spectaculars like the Super Bowl, the Olympics and the World Cup.

2 There is also the possibility of converged media delivery to television, computer and mobile where a person subscribes to a single converged service and gets a single bill – a world of subscribers. Buyer graphics linked to subscriber services would then be the main marketing research tool, with proprietary media research within each media vehicle.

3 Traditional audience ratings will as a consequence only be used for calibration of other media offerings and their associated research and super-premium advertising.

All this assumes, of course, that the audience concept has no public interest component and that media trade requires no intervention, and has had none, from the public or governments. This, as the authors have argued, is far from the case. Federal Communications Commission (FCC) consent orders in the United States had effects on ratings agencies and media providers after the Congressional hearings on ratings. Anti-monopoly laws attempt to ensure diversification. Minority groups have been vocal in expressing their concerns about representation in ratings in courts and public hearings. Moreover, as we have seen, setting up audience ratings is a very expensive business and advertisers have not been the majority funders of this type of enterprise. And, as we witnessed with Saatchi & Saatchi in the case of China, the demand for transparency remains fundamental in media markets.

Standardization

When advertisers set up the Cooperative Analysis of Broadcasting (CAB) ratings they excluded the radio broadcasters from the distribution of the results. The radio broadcasters bootlegged the CAB results up until 1936 when CAB relented and added them to the syndicate list. Television broadcasting never had this problem and Arthur C. Nielsen developed an intimate relationship with advertisers and broadcasters in radio and television. Looking back now, the whole process for organizing audience research and audience ratings might look linear and the innovations and organizational structures obvious. However, this was far from the case. Many audiences and media were not measured at all and there were many measurement companies competing for media business. As we found in Chapters 2 and 3, there was confusion about how to decide which method of counting was superior in or across the different audience markets until the Advertising Research Foundation in 1954 settled on Nielsen's technology as the best. There was also confusion, however, about accountability for the dollar spend. Even when television emerged in the market there was still significant advertising money directed to unmeasured media and accountability was often by virtue of personal acquaintance rather than metrics (Hurwitz 1983).

There was another problem that emerged in the 1950s mediascape. Television's rise in the market had unanticipated effects on radio management and retention of its strategic expertise. Between 1948 and 1958 television stations increased in number from 15 to 520 and television homes from 200,000 to 42 million. The average television set use was between five and six hours per day. Between 1946 and 1950 1,800 new radio stations had opened for business, raising problems of fragmentation of the radio audience and the audience market generally. The experts who might have addressed this problem for radio had been sent by networks to television. Radio's income and the expenditures put into its development declined (Hurwitz 1983). These former radio executives, however, had learnt that audience ratings provided an insight into how to get an overall picture of the audience and how audience habits could be tracked across time. They also recognized that appropriate metrics could assist in accountability of the dollar spend.

To create, order and schedule programmes, network executives drew on their radio experience and audience knowledge that they had learned in radio and adapted radio block-programming strategies to television as a fast way to build audiences and sell time to advertisers. Blocks included westerns for children, soap operas for mothers, sports for men, and situation comedies and variety specials built around stars for the whole family. With the TV networks assuming the costs and risks of programming, advertisers were put in the position of buying audiences ready-made rather than building them for themselves. For the networks, unsold minutes became an unaffordable vice. Measurement needs became paramount.

By the beginning of the 1950s in the United States there were twenty-two research organizations dedicated to television research. The call from network executives was to 'centralize, standardize, validate' as figures for set-ownership, coverage, ratings and sales effectives of the new medium became paramount. Television had massive start-up costs and the limited amount of channel space available made it a high-risk endeavour. Programming, sales and promotion were interdependent and required a planned approached. Broadcasters were looking for programmes that would sell receivers and by extension expand the audience. Expanded audiences would at the same time increase advertiser interest. There were high potential returns to networks if they took back control of shows from advertisers. Good standardized research metrics promised to reduce the risk posed by high programming costs by providing a clear picture of audiences over time and the success of the programming.

Arthur C. Nielsen was well aware of the television network executives' push to centralize, standardize and validate audience research in the management and economics of modern television. Measuring the entire audience throughout the full broadcast schedule brought with it the opportunity to show more clearly return on investment (ROI). But Nielsen, in his dealings with both broadcasters and advertisers, also recognized another, important, element in the standardization mix – the role of professionalism. Nielsen argued that television and advertising managers were scientific business specialists. Nielsen himself purposefully created an aura of technical expertise and professionalism in his own behaviour. Market research, in particular, provided the foundations for this professional status. The effect of this process of professionalization and reliance on metrics was that personal acquaintance was slowly displaced as a means of demonstrating ROI. The advertising executive could no longer simply say to a client at an expensive lunch, 'Everything is going well,' without actual justification.

> The use of meters provided them with an authoritative research audit possessing the apparent thoroughness and accuracy of twenty-four hour, minute-by-minute information that was detailed, recorded, and projectable. The cost of mechanization was controlled by the use of a small, continuing sample yielding voluminous data, and by the syndication of results. Together, the meters and panels definitively secured the primacy of listeners and viewers above programs or stations. The adoption of households as the unit of measurement served to stabilize findings to allow broadcasting to be more conveniently compared with print media. The information supplied allowed for the diagnosis and prescription of both programming and advertising plans. Nielsen's advice and his precise, schematic writing helped to make his procedures appear understandable, and his success freed him to devote his efforts to increasing the speed with which he could deliver. (Hurwitz 1983: 196–7)

It was not only the senior management ranks that got increased status by linking themselves to the aura of scientific market research and the black-box technology of Nielsen. Time-buyers in television now embodied the efficiency expert and sought recognition for their work.

> Though purchase of spot time may not require as much creative strategy as campaign planning or as much executive ability as campaign management, it demands more technical knowledge than either and as much judgement ... Media buying has become a big, complicated maze of innumerable possibilities. It has become, more than ever, a job for professionals. (Hull cited in Hurwitz 1983: 169)

Following the lead of Proctor & Gamble and Lever Brothers, advertisers started to pay closer attention to the components of the whole economics of the media buying and planning process and to costs, rather than continuing to simply aggregate homes in order to maximize coverage. Broadcast time-buyers had to be familiar with a range of markets, audiences, programmes, stations and talent.

> On the one hand, what this required was large, projectable research numbers, the production of which involved time buyers ever more deeply in interpretive social science. On the other hand, it called forth a new group of management-oriented media specialists who could fit all the pieces together into media 'strategies' and then explain them to agency and advertiser alike. (Hurwitz 1983: 179)

The changes in programme control altered the cycle of the business of broadcasting. James Aubrey president of CBS during the early 60s said that: 'With the elimination of "individual advertiser" program association, pure circulation becomes the only criterion for the purchase of network television time ... and those programs which give diversity and balance while delivering smaller or more qualitative circulation would inevitably ... be forced out of the networks schedules' (Hurwtiz 1983: 87).

As audience tastes became known they were rapidly transformed into habits via rationalized programming procedures. Scheduling of television programmes was refined to take account of an ever more imposing edifice of audience constituents. The television networks are, therefore, central to the audience-ratings convention as the party that brought, with Nielsen as collaborator, standardization to ratings as selling and buying currency and forged a professional media class with improved social status. This enhanced status included advertisers who could now not only be 'salesman', and they were men at that time, but manager-scientists, familiar with the black arts of audience and media economics.

Television network dominance of the mediascape was possible by virtue of its social status, regulation and the nature of network affiliation. CBS-TV was established in 1951 and dominated the audience market with a half-hour television format and an increased number of sponsors. NBC-TV was given its own president and company standing equal to that of radio. ABC was formed in 1943 when the US Supreme Court upheld the FCC's chain broadcasting rules and forced NBC to divest itself of its Blue Network. ABC was late on the radio scene and struck a deal with Paramount Pictures for a transfusion of funds and programmes and a pipeline to Hollywood talent, but did not become viable in the television market until the 1970s.

In the United States, there are rules governing how many stations a single business organization is allowed to own. Prior to 1985 the FCC permitted one corporation to own a maximum of seven AM and seven FM radio stations and a maximum of five VHF (Very High Frequency) television stations, plus two UHFs (Ultra High Frequency). Deregulation lifted the limit to 12 stations each, as long as the total audience did not exceed 25 per cent of the national TV audience. Newspaper and cable concerns are forbidden to buy television and radio stations in the same area; a single company is prohibited from holding two broadcast properties in a market. Television networks, like radio networks before them, attracted independently owned affiliates to carry regularly scheduled series, news, drama sports and other programming produced by the network itself. Each of the three networks had about 200 affiliates in 1985.

Advertising in the television network system is also not a simple animal. There is a difference between national network advertisements, national spot advertisements and local advertisements. Large brand-name companies with national distribution often find that purchases of national network time through agencies are the most efficient means of communicating with potential customers. However, for some nationally distributed products a particular local audience can often be reached more effectively through national spot purchases on local outlets, as arranged with station representatives (reps). Reps know the various rate cards and demographics and are conduits for time sales for their own broadcasting companies for groups of other stations. In 1984, commissionable spot billings for the 15 national TV rep firms were over US$4 billion, or more than 90 per cent of all spot time sales. At an average commission rate of 7 to 8 per cent, estimated rep firm revenues approached US$350 million in that year.

The television network ratings leader can command higher prices because advertising campaign managers, who buy upfront large quantities of time well in advance of use, bid aggressively to gain optimum spots. The remaining spots are sold on a scatter basis and are normally lower priced, primarily because they are sold closer to broadcast time and may not provide advertisers with optimal reach or frequency. A network ratings leader may also, of course, attract new affiliates and these new affiliates in turn boost the audience size. There is big money riding on even one ratings point. In network television a prime-time ratings point won or lost was worth at least US$50 million in pretax profits in 1985: 'To place that in perspective, according to estimates by Television Digest, in 1984 the ABC network had billings of US$2.64 billion, and pretax profit of US$260 million. Comparable billings and profits for DBS were $2.24 billion and $280 million, and for NBC $1.93 billion and $55 million' (Vogel 1986: 171).

Broadcast networks use ratings in a variety of other ways. Given that they provide an assessment of the makeup of the audience on the basis of gender, age, income, cultural background and location, they can be used as a public accountability tool. Ratings are routinely used by public service broadcasters to demonstrate their social reach, to justify their public funding, and to meet various governmental equity and other initiatives. If they are a public service broadcaster wholly or mostly reliant upon public funding they are also interested in the ratings as a way of being publicly accountable to the whole of society and to particular groups within it. They use ratings as a way of demonstrating their public remit.

Broadcasters also use the ratings to develop their schedule, paying particular attention to the makeup of the schedules, the flow of programmes, and variations in television usage in summer and winter (which in the 1960s was an hour's difference). They not only use the ratings to construct a schedule that would optimize audience flow over a week's programming but they also use it as a tool to identify weaknesses which would permit counterprogramming against their competitors. They use the ratings to schedule a line-up and to win evening segments.

Like individual programme producers they also use the ratings to analyse and develop programmes, as Ehrenberg and Twyman put it, 'to help program originators to gauge public response to their programs and to plan accordingly' (Ehrenberg and Twyman 1967: 1). They use it as a way to monitor the progress of a programme – and use it iteratively to help them renovate a programme by working with producers to 'keep a programme' alive. They also use the ratings to identify areas of weakness in a programme line-up to construct and inform the selection and development of the individual programmes they will screen. Independent programme producers likewise use the ratings in a complementary way to identify and pitch aspects of their proposed programme's appeal to broadcasting networks as meeting their objectives and interests in reaching particular audiences they might be weak or strong on.

Finally, as public companies broadcasters have an interest in the ratings as a proxy for the company's share price, its return on investment and overall financial health. In this case the ratings are part of financial accountabilities and part of the very business reporting of commercial broadcasters. They are integral to shareholder accountabilities and company forecasting. Senior management are therefore a crucial audience for the ratings and the literature we have on senior management points strongly to their desire for favourable portrayals of ratings performance often being an important factor shaping their ratings reporting.

Broadcast networks have an interconnected but nonetheless distinct set of interests in 'guiding general and social programming policies' and in facilitating 'the increasingly sophisticated usage by the advertising industry' (Ehrenberg and Twyman 1967: 35). Ratings are therefore a decision tool which is integral to: the audience market for the buying and selling of audiences; the operation of the broadcast schedule; the content market for the commissioning, continuation and cancellation of programmes in the programme production market; the performance of accountability of public service broadcasters; and shareholder value of media properties.

Small Audiences and Set-top Boxes

So, in the real nitty gritty world of, can we produce a product that is viable and unproblematic from the standpoint of all the consumers who are spending billions of dollars in advertising? It's not a slam dunk, so it might be that TNS or Nielsen or some other company with a brand name who has a reputation for providing a currency and perhaps has a probability sample that it can use to marry to digital set top box data, can offer a currency that takes advantage of some of the good attributes of that potential way of harvesting data. And I know Nielsen, and this is no secret, Neilson is trying to figure out exactly how to do that. James Webster, 2008

As Leo Bogart once put it, 'The bigger the media vehicle, the more economical its rates are apt to be in terms of impressions or exposures delivered' (Bogart 1967: 93). The television network system had other advantages in that it was able to generate 'huge audiences at the same moment in time'; it came 'closest to the intensity of interpersonal confrontation'; and it permitted 'the advertiser to encounter the consumer in a relaxed frame of mind, ready for whatever light entertainment the magic box will bring him, eyes and ears simultaneously engaged' (Bogart 1967: 99).

The same phenomenon that shored up traditional network revenue, primacy in providing massive audiences, also works against the networks, of course, if the audience ratings figures go down, as they have done so continuously in the United States since 1978. The opening up of the US mediascape to new networks and the rise of pay-TV and cable provided the television viewer with far more choices.

This meant that there emerged a 'long tail' of medium and smaller channels of different kinds that delivered much smaller audiences.

'At a time of rapid technological change in the television industry' is a common phrase in the contemporary moment, although the same phrase could be found in Crossley's time and Nielsen's time. It is one of those rhetorical statements that are taken for granted, but signal that something is going wrong. In this case, the television networks as space provider for advertising and content provider for audiences were losing audience share. Their effect in the audience-ratings convention had been to standardize the role of audience ratings within the mediascape, providing an orderly infrastructure for the delivery of programme schedules, a professional workforce for analysis of audience ratings, and a system for forecasting and planning. The rise of cable and pay-TV services fractured the market much in the same way that the expansion of radio fractured the market at the time of the rise of television. The difference between the 1940s and today, however, is that all media are measured and there is an expectation that all audiences will be covered. Advertisers are unwilling to commit precious dollars to anything unmeasured, unlike in earlier history where they had little choice. Television networks are still part of the audience-ratings convention, but its relative disposition in the market has changed.

Television programmes broadcast by Fox were hard hit in test runs of local peoplemeters in New York City. Rupert Murdoch's News Corporation spent nearly US$7 million stirring public opinion against Nielsen's local peoplemeters. Nielsen spent the same on defending its technology:

> Each media faction that stood to lose ground relative to its competitors would likely be encouraged to engage in public relations efforts to influence the accreditation outcome, or at least to slow down acceptance of the new method. Delaying the process of accreditation could produce substantial economic gains for certain businesses. (Furchtgott-Roth *et al.* 2006: 29)

Television ratings methods, in this context, are not being questioned. They remain gilt-edged, gold standard means for delivery of a reliable currency. The issue with fractured media and measurement using traditional ratings is one of cost-benefit in increasing the size of the sample or panel to cope with measurement of smaller groups. It is worthwhile reading at length the industry debate recorded at the 1996 Advertising Research Foundation (ARF)/European Society for Opinion and Marketing Research (ESOMAR) conference on broadcast research, held in San Francisco. The key themes of single source and fusion continue. As Sue Elms (Elms 1996) pointed out, Gesellschaft für Konsumforschung (GfK, the German 'Society for Consumer Research') *gave single source a thumbs down* as the future of television panels, due to the knock-on effects of trying to measure both sales and television viewing from the same homes. GfK, in an expensive and robust test, found that only 50 per cent of the television meter panel could be expected to convert, and that the mortality rate of the panel goes up by 10 per cent. The experimental panel no longer exists and GfK did not plan to use single source in its panel.

Roger Godbeer from Colgate Palmolive said at this 1996 conference that fusion is the only hope in the future for a primary source of information:

AGB UK proposed an alternative to today's 4,300 'regional' meter panel as a model for future research set-ups – the objective being to measure ratings as accurately as we do today with the added necessity of stable data (i.e. minimise fluctuations caused by design). Obviously the ideal solution is to increase the panel size, but this is too expensive, so the challenge is to find ways of affordably maximising sample sizes. AGB has conducted numerous analyses that lead it to believe that a region's viewing can be accurately predicted by (a) homes ratings from set meters, and (b) an audience profile factor derived from a national panel of peoplemeters. If it concentrated its resources on getting good household ratings it could provide (at the same cost as today) 3,000 households reporting in the same way as now, but on a network basis, and a further 7,000 set meters recording homes ratings. The audience were quick to raise issues such as the need for higher sample sizes to get accurate profiles for channels too. However, we must face the awful truth that tomorrow's world will demand 'less than perfect' solutions. (Elms 1996)

The ratings providers have been active therefore in addressing the expansion of channels and their measurement. This continues. Nielsen in 2007 established a multi-year, strategic relationship with Google's TV Ads advertising platform to combine Nielsen demographic data with aggregated set-top box data. Google could then, it is argued, provide advertisers and agencies with comprehensive information to help them create better advertisements for viewers and maximize the return on their advertising spending. Google TV Ads is an online platform for buying, selling, measuring and delivering television advertisements. Its advertising inventory includes hundreds of channels and all day-parts. Data derived from Nielsen's representative television ratings panels are intended to provide Google TV Ads advertisers with the demographic composition of the audience.

In 2008 Nielsen struck a deal with Charter Communications to analyse set-top box data from 330,000 homes in the Los Angeles area. Nielsen has similar agreements with other cable Multiple System Operators (MSOs) but the Charter deal goes a step further because it licenses the ratings company to create ratings reports from the data that it can then sell to clients. Charter struck a similar deal in November 2006 with Nielsen competitor TNS Media Research, which sells reports based on the Charter set-top box data to clients via a syndicated package it calls TotalView. Publicis Groupe's Starcom was the first media agency to sign up and other buyers and sellers of television time have signed up since then.

One shortcoming of the set-top box data is that it does not provide the demographic data that the Nielsen ratings provide, although various companies including TNS, TiVo, Google and Nielsen itself are looking at developing algorithms and other techniques that could apply demographic estimates to the set-top numbers. The set-top box data has raised issues, taken up in court in the United States:

> Let me sketch out what are some of the limitations of the digital set top box in the current environment. Number 1, many sets are not connected to digital boxes. Many households do not have, even if they've got cable, don't necessarily have digital set-top boxes capable of downloading the software that can record and report back upstream the kind of information or intelligence you need in order to pull off audience measurement. You don't know who in the household is watching, although there are certainly ways you could impute that. You've got, because not all sets and not all households are hooked up to digital set-top boxes, you've got another analogous problem to non-response. So are the people who have got digital set top boxes systematically different from those who don't? And the answer is, yeah, it looks like they are. They're more affluent, they're probably better educated, there are a number of things so the question is, can you infer from that group what the other group is doing. So, as I said it's an analogous non-response to the problem of non-response. You've got a problem of being able to figure out what's on the television set, which is not inconsequential. So, with current peoplemeter technology you've got active passive measurement that at the point of the set can capture information about what's actually being displayed and sometimes it's not even linear television, sometimes it's a video game. Well, our digital set-top box is going to be programmed with sufficient power to make that kind of discrimination so how do you figure out what's actually on the screen when you've identified that person is watching that screen? Or that household is watching that screen.
>
> In a nutshell my argument was the system that ErinMedia had described would fall far short of what would be expected of any company offering a full fledged alternative to what Nielsen now offers. And some of that's inherent problems with digital set-top boxes and some of it was the way ErinMedia was proposing to solve problems or problems that they hadn't even really given any serious thought to. (Webster 2008)

The media providers are a critical strut of the ratings convention. In this chapter we look at the ratings from their point of view. The ratings enter into the calculation of broadcasters and other media providers in diverse ways. They are part and parcel of the armoury of information to be used strategically to 'sell audiences'; to analyse and develop the broadcast schedule and individual programs; to perform public accountability; and to report media outlet profitability to shareholders. They are not the only information and data source for doing these things. But the ratings have proven to be important to the performance of these diverse tasks. And a great deal of knowledge in and facility with the ratings has typically resided in the broadcast television networks. There is probably no other user of the ratings which routinely performs such a range of tasks with them. Nor has there been any other party to the convention beside the ratings provider itself with such an interest in the performance of the ratings and the ratings providers.

These diverse uses and therefore purposes behind the broadcast networks working with and working through ratings data means that the ratings are best considered not as one thing but several different things depending upon the purposes and uses being made of them. The information ratings provide is certainly substitutable by other information sources and data; and broadcasters would immediately cease to rely on the ratings if the information they provided was not relevant to their operations and if less costly alternative data were available to collect the same information. But historically the ratings have been and continue to be resilient information sources for broadcasters and their clients in the audience and content markets in which they operate, and in scheduling and programming. Ratings also have the advantage of a single information source which allows broadcasters to make a variety of calculations touching several areas of their operation. The ratings data is also an effective proxy for other information such as engagement. And it has all the advantages of incumbency over other alternative measures in that people are used to working with it, they understand its operations and set-up, appreciate its checks and balances, and know its weaknesses.

There is certainly evidence of such a proliferation of measures happening for television. There is a certain way in which the ratings as they currently stand can be seen as primarily serving the interests of free-to-air, advertiser-supported television. There is a certain path dependency in the ratings here as they evolved primarily as an instrument for coverage in depth and detail of free-to-air television. In this context the new extension of ratings to cover and analyse timeshifted viewing through 'fetch TV' and TiVo is simply a means of extending the ratings as an effective measure for advertiser-supported television. The ratings are here continuing to provide large-audience media outlets with lots of useful data in developing and analysing their schedules. They are in the business of constructing flow through schedules, analysing, developing, anticipating and charting the programming cycle. Broadcast networks want information from ratings in a form which promotes the value of the sale of commercial time for their programmes. They in turn want to promote their value proposition: network TV as a mass medium still able to command significant audiences, to provide viewers and able to be described by robust audience data which is not as readily available for programming with smaller audiences. This recognizes that the ratings are still able to provide the most authoritative source of such information.

At the same time, because of the proliferation of subscription television and its 'long tail' of channels only ever registering small ratings, and sometimes with ratings that are not even reported publicly, the ratings system is a congenitally failing operation. Its sample sizes are simply not big enough to capture data on small audiences: to do so the samples would have to be so extensive as to put the ratings beyond the scope of the media system and small providers to pay for it. With the ratings not being good for the 'long tail', and therefore the lower ends of the market, these media providers do not have the same interest as free-to-air broadcasters in the ratings as a preferred instrument. Unlike free-to-air broadcasters operating almost wholly in an audience market (that is, depending on advertising revenue), these broadcasters are reliant upon subscriptions and are consequently more sensitive to factors affecting churn of subscribers. Thus, for broadcasters reliant upon subscription the ratings can be less important to the selling proposition on individual channels – their audiences are so small that ratings data are not able to provide the kind of demographic rich data, with lower sample errors, that are available for large audiences. In practice this has meant that these media providers have become interested in alternative audience measures capable of generating large samples and more information on their particular broadcasting universe. The contemporary interest in set-top box data as an alternative source of audience measurement information is a case in point.

United Kingdom

The introduction of competition into the British television market with the commencement of the ITV service in London on 22 September 1955 posed a number of questions about audience research methods and uses. Because the Independent Television Authority (ITA)'s and the ITV programme contractors' purposes in knowing and measuring audiences were different from the BBC's purposes, and because the BBC research under Robert Silvey did not provide all the information or detail the independents needed, a new market for audience research was created. The competition between ratings providers particularly in the period before the contracting of Television Audience Measurement (TAM) as preferred supplier in January 1957, produced a range of new information about the availability and reception of ITV across the United Kingdom. The competition between companies like Gallup, TAM, ACNielsen and Pulse to provide research services, and especially that between TAM and Nielsen to supply the industry service, highlighted and hinged on differences in methodology and reporting. Broadcasters, and especially the ITA, used comparisons between different services – including Silvey's work for the BBC – to inform themselves about the total number of sets and households able to receive ITV, the share of overall viewing versus the BBC, patterns of national use and top-rating programmes. In the first years of commercial television, the ITA was also embroiled in a controversy about the designation of service boundaries, with ITA, TAM, Nielsen and the BBC all differing in their definitions of particular service areas, with implications for the calculation of the audience universe and for the reach of advertising and programmes.

The creation of the ITA in 1954 stimulated the development of audience research in the United Kingdom. Up to this time, the BBC's studies of its own audiences were the only television audience research. In the run-up to the launch of ITV in September 1955, several companies entered the field of television audience research in the UK. The costly competition between these firms for the attention of the ITA, the ITV programme companies and advertisers in the period before the awarding of the industry contract to TAM in 1957 has much to tell us about methodology, process and approach in the design and development of ratings services. It is also revealing of the ways in which broadcasters (and broadcasting authorities) use ratings and audience research in different ways than other subscribers.

The prospect of commercial television in Britain was raised in a white paper on broadcasting policy in May 1952 and, after vigorous political debate, the Bill to create the Independent Television Authority was introduced into Parliament in March 1954, becoming law on 30 July. The Television Act of 1954 established the ITA for a period of ten years, empowering it to build and operate transmitters and contract with programme companies to provide programmes. Although the ITA was not officially created until after the Act passed into law at the end of July, with great foresight Arthur C. Nielsen met with Sir Robert Fraser, the first Director General of the ITA, in April 1954, and gave him a memorandum entitled 'Present and Future Position of the ITA with Respect to TV Audience Research'. In September, Nielsen sent ITA a series of reports that his company had conducted in the United States to give an indication of what could be done in Britain, and the following February, Nielsen produced a detailed booklet, 'Television Audience Research for Great Britain', which was sent to ITA Chairman, Sir Kenneth Clark. In particular, the Nielsen company took it upon itself to promote the benefits of television advertising and audience measurement to advertising agencies and large firms. A rival British company, Television Audience Measurement (TAM), was set up in April 1955. Both TAM and Nielsen used meters to measure audiences, with both having small panels in place in London in time to begin reporting as soon as ITV broadcasting began in September 1955.

Once the meter system had been accepted by the programme companies and advertisers as the most appropriate for regular, ongoing audience research, TAM and Nielsen were left as the only competitors for the first industry contract. Despite a vigorous campaign by Nielsen, TAM was awarded the first five-year contract by Television Audience Research Advisory Council (TARAC) in January 1956. The following month, Arthur C. Nielsen wrote a long letter to Sir Robert Fraser criticizing the committee's decision and labelling the original specifications 'little short of ridiculous'; the committee had initially specified a panel of 100 homes in the London area, and 100 for the whole of the rest of the country. Nielsen felt that TAM had been given preferential treatment, including being given the opportunity to submit a revised bid, and sought to convince Fraser to pressure the ITV programme companies to reject the 'Committee service' and sign up with Nielsen, thus killing off the TAM service. Fraser politely declined.

Nielsen continued to operate a competing meter service in parallel with TAM's until the two companies merged in June 1959.

But ratings was only one of the sets of data produced by Gallup, TAM and Nielsen, and bought by the ITV companies and the ITA, which also subscribed to BBC research for a short period after the launch of ITV. Calculations of the number of homes able to receive ITV and the overall split of viewing between ITV Broadcasters' Audience Research Board and the BBC were most important in the very early period. The ITA also initiated assessments of programme quality and public attitudes to television in 1957; following the Pilkington Committee's inquiry into broadcasting, the 1964 Television Act made the conduct of such surveys a statutory duty of the ITA.

From the first public BBC television broadcast in 1932 until 1955 in London and later in other parts of the country, viewers could only receive one station: the BBC. Many of the televisions sold in the United Kingdom until the mid-1950s were only capable of being tuned to VHF Band I, the frequency used by the BBC, so when ITV commenced broadcasting on the higher frequency Band III, viewers needed a new aerial and set-top converter, or a new television set, in order to receive the new service. For many years, a critical measurement for ITA was the proportion of total sets able to receive an ITV service as it was progressively rolled out across the country. Gallup, TAM, Nielsen and the BBC all researched these figures, but from even before the launch of ITV there were many discrepancies between the data produced by the competing services. These discrepancies were due in part to methodology; they opened the space for comparison and contest both between aided recall (favoured by Gallup and the BBC) and meters (used by TAM and Nielsen), as well as between the two competing meter systems. But they also had implications for a variety of calculations and definitions: the ITA's concern with the placement of transmitters and the definition of 'acceptable reception', the contours and boundaries of service areas, the construction of a regional advertising campaign, the constitution of a panel and programme ratings.

In August 1955, the British arm of Gallup published the first provisional results of what was intended to be a regular survey entitled 'The Potential ITA Audience'. The survey of 1,000 households was conducted in the London region, where Gallup estimated there were 1.5 million sets in use and 2.1 million non-television homes. At that point, a month before the launch of ITV, Gallup found that only 22 per cent of homes with television contained sets that were fitted with a station selector switch, and therefore were ready to receive ITV. While the survey also found that a further 48 per cent of households with television were planning either to adapt their existing set or buy a new one, 30 per cent of households with television were either reluctant to change or stated firmly that they did not want commercial television. Only 8 per cent of households without television were expecting to buy a television within the next six months, meaning that out of 3.6 million households, the potential ITV audience amounted to only slightly more than 1 million households, or just under 3 million people out of a total potential population of around 10 million. In the seventeen days after the first broadcast in London by Associated Rediffusion on 22 September 1955, Gallup conducted over 20,000 interviews on patterns of viewing and attitudes to commercial television. The company continued to monitor the total number of ITV homes on a regular basis through interviews drawn from a random sample of households.

In the first months of the London ITV service, the ITA received contradictory data from the BBC Audience Research unit, Gallup, Nielsen and TAM about the total number of homes with television, the numbers able to receive ITV and the share of viewing with the BBC. The correspondence of the Director General of the ITA, Sir Robert Fraser, in November 1955, two months after the commencement of the London service, charts the issue of comparing audience estimates. On 15 November, Fraser wrote to Mark Abrams, chairman of Research Services Ltd:

> We are now almost a fortnight past the middle day of the week of this Silvey [BBC] measurement, so that it would look as if the number of ITA homes, on his figures, must now be of the order of 600,000. The Nielsen figure for a mean date of Oct 8th – that is to say, over 5 weeks ago, was 346,000. Dowson

[of ACNielsen] told me, about a fortnight ago, that he thought the figure had risen by then to rather more than 450,000, and that the rate of growth was somewhere between 25,000 and 50,000 homes a week. I know that the early Nielsen figs were underestimates, because they had not allowed for the quite frequent reception of ITA programmes in homes without Band II aerials. On the lowest basis, the Nielsen figure, for today, could not be less than 500k. I think Silvey is our best bet, for he codes it every day and his returns are so steady. I suppose the margin of error in the 12.5 figure might be one per cent, but even so ... (Fraser to Abrams, 15 November 1955, ITA Archive)

On 17 November, Fraser wrote to Graham Dowson, the Director of Nielsen TV Index, highlighting his concerns about the discrepancies between BBC and Nielsen figures:

As you know, the BBC carries out fairly large scale daily interviews in the course of which those questioned are asked whether they live in homes in which the ITA programmes can be seen. The percentage of those interviewed claiming to live in ITA homes is monthly and steadily rising, and in the week which ended on Nov 5th the percentage was 12.5%. The BBC interviews are a random sample of 14,980,000 people, so that in the week mentioned, and if the sample was accurate, 1,870,000 people must be assumed as the population of the ITA homes. The average number of people per home in the area covered by the BBC research is 3.3, so giving us a figure of no less than 565,000 ITA homes. A fortnight has passed since the mean date of the week to which the figure of 12.5% relates, so that the number of ITA homes today, on any calculation, should exceed 600,000. Surely there is something very wrong indeed somewhere – but where is it? (Fraser to Dowson, 17 November 1955, ITA Archive)

Three weeks later, Dowson replied with new data that differed again from earlier estimates:

A new estimate of ITA homes in the London area. This estimate is based upon a survey, the mean date of which was Nov 17th, which showed the ITA universe at that date to be 449,000 homes. The evidence we obtained from this survey has also enabled us to provide an estimate of the rate of increase in ITA homes. In fact, that rate of increase we estimate as being 26,000 ITA homes each week. We have, therefore, applied this rate of increase to the period since the mean date of our latest survey, and have arrived a figure of 501,000 homes relating to a mean date of Dec 1. (Dowson to Fraser, 8 December 1955, ITA Archive)

In reply, Fraser questioned Silvey's measurement of total viewers and failure to break this down to the household level, ITV's (and the meter operators') preferred category. Fraser also noted that Silvey was counting viewers beyond the 'secondary service area', or the area of acceptable transmission strength, thus potentially skewing the results. Dowson agreed:

> I would be inclined to believe that you have hit the nail on the head when you mention the difference in the size of ITA homes and the fact that in any event people tend to give misleading information when asked for interviews. On the basis of the information we have on this subject, ITA households tend to be somewhat larger than ordinary BBC households. In fact we are using privately a figure of 3.9 persons per ITA home. Thus it would seem quite likely that any interview method which disclosed figures which were then divided by the lower estimates of persons in TV households would certainly give you a very much larger 'apparent' number of ITA homes. (Dowson to Fraser, 14 December 1955, ITA Archive)

In a booklet published on 1 January 1956 comparing the Nielsen Television Index and the aided recall methods used by the BBC, Nielsen confirmed the issue of service/research areas as a factor in differences in estimates (and as a reason why the mechanized service was more efficient than aided recall). The booklet noted:

> The London area as defined by BBC for its research is considerably larger than the London area as defined by ITA and measured by Nielsen. If there could be absolute assurance that the latter covered 100% of the homes capable of receiving ITA broadcasts, no material difference would result from this factor ... However it is known that certain persons living beyond the Nielsen London area can receive ITA broadcasts to some extent and under certain conditions, but in some of these cases the reception may be so poor that the ITA share of audience in such homes will be abnormally low, causing the BBC research to report lower shares for ITA than would be true if BBC confined its research to the area used by Nielsen. (ACNielsen, 'A Comparison of Television Audience Measurements: Nielsen Television Index (a wholly mechanized audience research system) versus Aided Recall (personal interviews, prompted by programme logs), as conducted by the BBC', Oxford, 1 January 1956)

The issue would arise again at various times before the awarding of the industry contract to TAM in early 1957. For example, Sir Robert Fraser wrote to Major George Harrison of the London Press exchange in November 1956 about significant discrepancies between TAM and Nielsen figures for Band III homes (i.e. those able to receive ITV) for the first week of November 1956. Where Nielsen calculated the total number of homes receiving ITV as 1,907,000, TAM put the figure at almost 500,000 higher. Fraser wrote:

> Differences of this magnitude bring TV research into disrepute, and that is in no one's interest. It seems to me that some authoritative body should call on the 2 agencies for an explanation of their own figures and for their comment on the differences, and might then see whether, perhaps in discussion with the 2 agencies, it could not bring about a closer approximation, not of course by suggesting the suppression of figures in which either of them believes, but by examining whether the inconsistencies may not be due to the collection of the figures at different times, or from areas that do not exactly coincide, or by the use of different criteria about what constitutes a Band III home. I cannot think of anybody so proper or so competent as the Steering committee to look into the matter, and I therefore write in the hope that you may feel able to pursue it. (Fraser to Harrison, 9 November 1956, ITA Archive)

As ITV became available in other regions – the Midlands and North 1956, Central Scotland in 1957, Wales and West, and Southern in 1958, North East, East and Ulster in 1959, South-West, the Borders and North-east Scotland in 1961, the Channel Islands in 1962 – disputes continued over the size of the universe, and the lack of coincidence between areas mapped by the ratings providers and the ITA's broadcast transmission maps. Discrepancies in mapping of this kind had commercial consequences in the problems created for advertisers and buyers in calculating CPM (cost per mille [thousand]). They also had implications for the representativeness of the panel, and subsequently for the ratings. In 1958, the Television Audience Research Advisory Council asked TAM to approach the ITA about publishing maps that would coincide with TAM areas in order to end the confusion, but the ITA was concerned that it would be supplying misleading information if it issued maps that might suggest that there was adequate ITV reception in an area when ITA's own surveys show that substantially less than 50 per cent of homes would be able to receive the ITV signal with a normal set and aerial. The ITA published three maps showing the field strength of its transmitters, which defined the ITV service area. The first map showed the 'primary area' of service, that within the 2,000 microvolts per metre contour, within which almost 100 per cent of homes would be capable of receiving a satisfactory signal if they had a Band III set and a normal aerial. The second map showed the 500 microvolts per meter contour, within which less than 75 per cent of homes could receive a satisfactory signal ('the secondary area'), and the third map showed the 250 microvolts per meter contour, within which less than 50 per cent of homes would be receive a satisfactory signal ('the fringe area'). TAM undertook boundary surveys in order to establish the limits of the effective marketing area covered by particular ITA transmitters, but these were wider than the ITA fringe areas, and so well beyond the ITA's limit of adequate reception. TAM's inclusion of the fringe area within its boundary meant that areas where only 10–15 per cent of houses were able to receive the signal became part of its calculation; TAM was reluctant to discount these (potential) viewers because this would mean that a substantial number of homes that could receive television advertising would not be accounted for. An internal ITA memo dated 29 April 1958 explained the issues at hand and the concerns of the industry:

> The present TAM areas are very different from ours … An increase in the TAM estimates is going to make more and more people damn our figures as conservative, or alternatively doubt the TAM estimates because they are so optimistic. Nielsen for their part, have been extremely worried about this problem for a considerable time as it presents them with a choice between professional honesty on the one hand and satisfaction for their clients, the advertising agencies and the programme companies, on the other. Naturally the programme companies want to be able to claim the 'biggest circulation' they can and agencies are particularly interested in the cost per thousand. One can, of course, extend ones [sic] survey at will (and produce arguments to justify the boundaries taken) but to give an accurate picture of viewing habits one must place meters in homes which will give a representative picture of the area as a whole including of course those people who are in the extremes of the survey area. Such a distribution of meters can, however, add considerably to the cost of operation of an audience research service and can also slow down the collection of tapes each week. There is, therefore, a tendency to centralise meters and if this is done large numbers of viewers with poor reception are not represented in the sample. However, most people in the companies and the agencies are happy as (a) the 'circulation areas' are large, (b) there is a small cost per thousand and (c) there is also a comparatively high percentage of ITA viewing to BBC … there seems to be a strong feeling in certain quarters that the ITA should do something to establish a service area boundary which will be acceptable to all … We can, of course, easily argue that this problem has nothing to do with us but on the other hand there is a danger that the research methods used by the two companies on whose figures we rely may be thrown into disrepute. (J. Cuthbert to Director General, 29 April 1958, ITA Archive)

Boundary or establishment surveys are still routinely and regularly carried out to ensure the representativeness of the panel. TAM carried out establishment surveys in the United Kingdom to support its service from the mid-1950s. When TAM's contract was extended for a year in 1967, the provider committed to survey 25,000 randomly selected households from around the country in six surveys to determine the number and size of households, and the number of sets receiving ITV. From these surveys, the following panels would be established:

Table 7.1 Television Audience Measurement (TAM) panels

Area	September 1967 survey	January 1968 survey	February– March survey	May 1968 survey	Proposed panel size and method
London	Yes	Yes		Yes	350 TAMMETER (Weekly)
Midlands	Yes	Yes		Yes	240 TAMMETER (Weekly)
North	Yes	Yes		Yes	350 TAMMETER (Weekly)
Central Scotland	Yes		Yes		140 TAMMETER (Weekly)
Wales and West of England	Yes		Yes		160 TAMMETER (Weekly)
South of England	Yes	Yes		Yes	160 TAMMETER (Weekly)
North-East England	Yes		Yes		140 TAMMETER (Weekly)
East of England	Yes	Yes	Yes	Yes	180 TAMMETER (Weekly)
South-West England	Yes				100 RECORDIMETER (Monthly)
Northern Ireland	Yes				100 RECORDIMETER (Monthly)
Borders and Isle of Man	Yes				100 RECORDIMETER (Monthly)
North-East Scotland	Yes				100 RECORDIMETER (Monthly)

Today, the Broadcasters' Audience Research Board (BARB) Establishment Survey is carried out continuously, with 53,000 interviews conducted each year.

The issue of the number of households able to receive ITV gradually declined in importance as the ITA's national coverage and the number of new or converted sets rose, although the issue of the share of total audience between the BBC and ITV continued to be contested, with the BBC Audience Research unit regularly recording higher shares for BBC than those recorded by Nielsen and TAM. The appointment in 1960 of a committee of inquiry into broadcasting under Lord Pilkington turned the question of share of viewing into a political issue. Unlike the BBC, which regularly made viewing figures public, the only data published regularly by TAM (which by that time held the industry contract for ratings research) was a weekly 'Top Ten' programmes. Figures on audience composition and share of audience were only published when they were newsworthy rather than as a matter of routine, although such figures were a regular part of the weekly National Tamratings Report that was issued to subscribers. Concern within the ITA over discrepancies between the BBC's published figures for share of audiences and the private figures recorded by TAM welled up in 1962. Mike Hallett, the ITA's Information Officer, wrote to Charles D. Harris of TAM in April requesting that the company make some data public:

> The BBC figures, naturally I suppose, favour the BBC and it is, from our point of view, unfortunate that the BBC should get this favourable publicity easily and regularly. The only way to counteract it is to arrange for the regular publication of TAM statistics comparable to those of the BBC. A form of words could be devised that would show the different bases of the two sets of figures, for instance that TAM figures are based on two-channel sets whereas the BBC figures include single channel sets. This would avoid the appearance of a head-on contradiction of the BBC figures. Would you take this up and see if TAM can be persuaded to issue regular statements? The position may be strengthened by the report of the Pilkington Committee. It considered TAM and may well, it seems to me, make some favourable comments in its report that could judiciously be quoted, thereby reinforcing TAM's position. (Hallett to Harris, 25 April 1962, ITA Archive)

Ever quick to seek a return for TAM's research, Harris wrote back that while the company felt that the issuing of regular press releases 'would be incompatible with our position as an independent research organisation' (something that had never troubled Nielsen or Gallup), they would 'co-operate by providing, at cost price' the information that the ITA would need to issue its own press releases (Harris to Hallett, 2 May 1962, ITA Archive). Hallett replied immediately, stating that the ITA could not publish TAM figures 'unless it [the ITA] were prepared to guarantee the statistics, which it could only do if their production was under its own control. It is not that we doubt TAM results'. Hallett continued, somewhat disingenuously since TAM's results had been repeatedly questioned over the years by ITA staff, 'it is simply that they are yours and not ours' (Hallett to Harris 3 May 1962, ITA Archive). The ITA suspected that TAM's reluctance to publicize its figures stemmed from a fear that when TAM results disagreed with BBC results, the latter would be believed thus damaging TAM's image. TAM eventually agreed to publish monthly share of audience figures for each area and for the ITV network, and a 'Quarterly Account of Viewing', beginning in July 1962, which would list the network share figures for each month in the quarter compared with the previous year and include a special study of audiences for 'serious' programmes. This last study was a response to the Pilkington Committee's concern with the balance of 'light' and 'serious' programmes on ITV and BBC, and to the perception – reinforced by data released by the BBC – that the ITV companies' schedules were weighted too heavily towards 'light' programmes (Briggs 1995: 280–1).

Concerns about the quality of programmes on ITV had been voiced by politicians and other commentators since the beginning of the service, prompting another research path. Following the recommendations of the Pilkington Report, the 1964 Television Act made it a statutory duty of the ITA to conduct audience research into public opinion on programmes and advertisements, and to encourage the public to make suggestions and comments, although in practice the ITA, along with several private companies, had already begun similar programmes of research. Before the requirement in the 1964 Act was imposed, the ITA had commissioned a series of general surveys and special inquiries to gauge audience attitudes, including parents' attitudes to children's television (July 1958), attitudes to advertising (October 1960) and attitudes to religious programmes (July 1961). Once the requirement was announced, the ITA received proposals from five companies to supply appreciation data: TAM, which had secured the rights to use the American TvQ system of AGB Research Ltd, the company that would win the industry contract from TAM in 1968, proposed 'a continuous research operation collecting data on all widely networked programmes' in order to record audience appreciation; Schwerin Research Corporation proposed to conduct studies into the effects of violence on television, and tests of the 'communicative power of programmes and advertisements'; Social Surveys (Gallup Poll) proposed a 'Television Quality Index'; and Research Services Ltd, the supplier of many of the ITA-commissioned reports on attitudes to programming, offered to continue its work.

At this time the ITA had already committed to funding the work of the Television Research Committee (known as the Noble Committee) into the use of television as a means of fostering 'moral concepts and attitudes' for a period of five years at an annual cost of £50,000, £7,000 more than its entire annual Audience Research Programme budget. In December 1964, the ITA subscribed to the TAM TvQ service despite the Independent Television Companies Association (ITCA)'s Research Liaison Committee counselling against such a move on the grounds that the formula used to determine the appreciation of programmes was unreliable. The ITCA's committee was also concerned that other subscribers to the TvQ service included advertising agencies, and within a year had put forward an alternative scheme. The ITA rejected the alternative and maintained its subscription to TvQ principally on the grounds of cost, although the service was discontinued later in the 1960s. These surveys were the precursors of contemporary research on engagement, which we discuss elsewhere in this book.

Summary

Ratings have been so core to broadcast network operations that they have since the 1940s provided the bulk of the funding for ratings services. The networks and ratings providers set the scene for the standardization of audience ratings and the professionalization of those involved in key components of its operation. This reflects the networks own interests in audience measurement as a market organization tool and their commitment to a single coordination rule which allows the systematic examination on an ongoing basis of both their and rival networks' audiences establishing relative standing among competing media outlets. It also marks out the terrain of their often testy engagement with the ratings and ratings providers, and their vital interest in the conduct of audience measurement by ratings providers.

Audience ratings still provide television networks with the most robust data with the best systems of overview and checks and balances. This extends to every level from the smallest component – how things are installed in the home, how people are recruited, organization of the sample, viewing areas and so on. It also provides as near as possible a total picture of media outlets in television and radio. It is the only available research for which a systematic comparison of media alternatives for buying and selling is possible. The competitor audience measurements based on set-top box subscription television lists provide only partial overviews of the total television media market but they also represent, like ITV's contest with BBC, fascinating insights into how coordination of different measurements is occurring.

Converged media delivery raises the possibility of new business models for delivery of content to audiences and for its payment, bringing together different technology and media platforms. However, these models will still have to deliver what television networks have long recognized – publicly acceptable ways of measuring audiences and strong auditing regimes.

8 Advertisers and Media Planners

Advertising is a craft executed by people who aspire to be artists, but assessed by those who aspire to be scientists. Advertising executive John Ward (Mayer 1991)

With media advertising revenue either static or even declining and below-the-line advertising – trade shows, promotions – increasing there is now considerable ferment within the advertising-marketing-promotions field about the best strategies for reaching consumers and the best methods for interacting with them. Advertisers have built analytical techniques and vocabularies to manage audience ratings. These techniques are used to place advertising within media and to evaluate their success. What is striking about the advertiser side of the ratings convention is that the limits of advertiser-supported media were apparent from its inception, suggesting ways in which the attachment to advertiser-supported media and spot advertising has always been much more provisional than it appears. As we have seen, advertisers were major contributors to research in the early years of the media industry and were responsible for the development of the first ratings surveys. Later they became more detached from research as ratings were increasingly paid for by the media providers themselves; today, this research focus within advertising is returning and there is considerable debate over the nature of the settlement and its intellectual basis coupled with active explorations of alternatives.

The Dual Persona of the Advertiser

One of the first surprises to confront the advertiser when he gets serious about the possibilities of radio advertising is the dual personality back of this radio business. He finds right from the start two radically different viewpoints that of the advertiser and that of the showman. To an advertising manager experienced in all the intricacies of visual media, a failure to adjust himself to this dual personality may spell ruin. Inability to see both viewpoints has probably accounted for many of the failures of the air – the sponsored programs that are not handing the advertiser a profit on his investment. Warren B. Dygert (Dygert 1939: 13)

This advice, dating from 1939, is from Warren B. Dygert, Associate Professor of Marketing, New York University; Secretary and Account Executive, F.J. Low

Advertising Agency; Member of University Radio Committee, New York University. Dygert himself was in the advertiser role with F.J. Low, but he was more than this, as you can see, with a post in marketing at New York University.

Peter Coleman later provided a less flattering, tongue-in-cheek description of the 'advertising man' as:

a sort of mixture of con-man and artist manqué, an unreliable, sentimental, cynical huckster with bags of sympathy for mankind when he was not contemptuous of it, a man who drank too much, lived on his nerves, grew ulcers, seemed to thrive on scandals which never affected his business, and who ended-up in the fundamental corruption of believing the rhetoric his trade taught him to think. (Coleman 1969: 677–8)

There is something very important in both Dygert's and Coleman's descriptions of the advertising persona. Advertisers, from the beginning, had a show role, having to come up with appropriate narratives and performances for clients to sell their expertise and advice, and a marketer's role, to decide on a range of sources of information about audiences, markets, goods, consumer attitudes and so on. The advertiser had to decide on all these sources of information in order to construct a narrative that was convincing to the client. The choice among sources of information, however, was not arbitrary. Indeed, in Dygert's *Radio as an Advertising Medium* he is clear that in 1939 the evidence suggested that radio should be thought of as a secondary medium, a 'good will' medium, that should be used in conjunction with other media:

But there seems no doubt that radio is at its best as a secondary medium as a good-will medium to back up the strong sales talk in newspapers and magazines. Survey after survey shows that advertising, as such, is less popular with listeners than with readers. One seldom hears these days of magazine readers tearing out the advertisements in rage but one does hear often enough of a listener tuning out the advertising message, particularly if it is a long one. The big advertiser will probably accomplish more by leaning toward good will in his radio program and using other media to pound the public into prospects. The small advertiser, however, who cannot afford this effective plan, must and can do his selling over the air. The caution is: Do not overdo it. (Dygert 1939: 216)

From an advertising standpoint, radio's greatest misfortune, for Dygert, is that it had played up this potential circulation too much. According to Dygert, the Joint Committee on Radio Research, sponsored by the American Association of Advertising Agencies, the Association of National Advertisers and the National

Association of Broadcasters, estimated in 1938 the number of families owning radio sets in the United States was 26,666,500. There were at the time approximately 32,641,000 families in the United States. 'This is a national coverage then of 82 per cent. But the advertiser should not take this too seriously. If broadcasting stations could offer this stupendous coverage to the radio advertiser on the same basis that an ABC publication can offer its specified coverage, then radio rates should be boosted many times' (Dygert 1939: 216). Dygert argued that the empirical evidence, surveys and other sources, had demonstrated that many people did not turn on their radio sets and many did not even listen when they were on. This great radio circulation represents a potential 100 per cent audience, listeners which no advertiser, no president, nor hurricane could ever draw to the radio at a single given moment. Dygert's advice to the advertiser in the case of radio was to:

1 determine what class of the public has the biggest sales possibilities;

2 design a programme to interest this class;

3 select a time of day and week best suited to reach the greatest number in this class.

And then use newspapers, magazines, direct mail in combination to boost sales.

Print for Dygert was still at that time the most persuasive medium for the advertiser. His book provides detailed overviews of how radio ratings worked, how to decide among different kinds of surveys and what the empirical data said worked. In particular, Dygert was keen to ensure that the advertiser kept their eye on cross media and did not forget that radio was only one medium among others. His examples were intended to be instructive. WSM radio for example took a two-column advertisement in *Tide* to tell of a nursery in Osage, Iowa, that offered in a 15-minute weekly programme a complete assortment of plants, shrubs and seeds for US$1. The programme consisted of music and a friendly voice, the Master Gardener, who talked of seedtime and planting and invited the listeners to order. Orders received were:

26 January	$2,203
2 February	$1,676
9 February	$2,697
16 February	$2,663
23 February	$1,905

Radio for Dygert did therefore sell goods. Another example he gives readers was *Captain Tim's Adventures*, run three times a week on radio at 6.15 to 6.30 p.m. for Ivory Soap. From 1934 to 1936, the programme gathered 2,700,000 members into the Ivory Stamp Club. Some 800,000 stamp albums and over 400,000,000 stamps were mailed out to listeners, at cost to the listener. 'Two Ivory Soap wrappers were required for the album, and two for each packet of stamps, plus 5, 10, or 20 cents, according to the richness of the collector's appetite' (Dygert 1939). Dygert, of course, was writing before the world of frequency and reach calculations had ideas on how many messages were needed to reach a particular broadcasting audience over time. That said, he was genuine in his interest in careful application of social science research. He had all the characteristics of the modern advertiser interested in how audiences worked, how different media worked and how the creative execution led to successful sales or consumer awareness.

The dual personality of advertiser therefore was one of analysis of 'cold facts' and the capacity to organize a good 'show':

> Where the businessman is geared to run on cold reason-why facts, the showman's machine is driven by emotion and enthusiasm. There never was a good showman yet who did not believe his ideas simply could not fail who would not rather use a $5,000 star even when the sponsor's margin of profit on his product could allow only a $1,000 one. (Dygert 1939)

The advertisers life was a tough one and some of this tough life even comes out in early television comedies like *Bewitched* where the husband has to sell the agency's ideas as the best ideas, compared with competitors, in order to 'win the account'. The origins of the collection of media, market, and audience evidence, as Hurwitz (Hurwitz 1983) shows, are closely tied to those of the origins of advertising agencies themselves. 'Space salesmen', employed by the newspaper publishers to sell advertising space, were the precursors of the modern advertising agent. As the sales areas of manufacturers expanded and more and more goods became available to consumers, those space salesmen, and they were men, serviced 'space jobbers', who wholesaled space from a range of newspapers in a range of cities across the United States. The competition was cut-throat as jobbers became affiliated with space buyers and offered them additional services to gain the advertising dollar. The outcome from this process was the creation of independent agencies that provided services to national advertising campaigns and the preparation of copy.

This is the earliest example of advertising agencies seeking to be 'creative' forces on the one hand, preparing copy that helped sell goods and newspapers, and 'researchers' ensuring return on investment (ROI) for the space that they bought. National advertisers, as they grew, discovered quickly that a substantial amount of their budgets was related to space cost and they wanted to know that they got value for their money. This led to the creation of a range of 'advertising clubs' that worked together to establish standards for measuring circulation and auditing measurement. Counting audiences-readership was an obvious solution to the problem of ROI on space buying. Decently audited circulation figures would at the least give an indication of effectiveness of advertising, in the absence of individual audience readership figures. This might sound a simple matter, but publishers everywhere did not want to give out their *real* circulation figures. In the United Kingdom this led to court battles. In the United States what the advertisers did was to deny uncooperative publishers their business. Bureaus of circulation were an outcome of this pressure from advertisers and these bureaus continue today.

It was advertisers, therefore, that started the intense interest in the social geography of people and their habits, and their relationship with media, by virtue of wanting clear metrics for estimating the success of advertising. These two core sides of the role of advertising remain:

1 Understanding the audience; and

2 Advertising effectiveness.

Dygert's concern about radio as a secondary medium starts to make sense in this context. From his point of view, analysing the evidence of the time, it was not at all clear that radio provided the actual reach to audiences that was claimed by radio broadcasters. Indeed, it was well known that broadcasters would exaggerate their radio footprint, where their signals went, in order to claim larger listening audiences than they actually had (Dygert 1939). Radio signals could sometimes for various reasons travel further than their normal footprint. If a listener wrote in from outside a station's footprint and said that they had heard a broadcast, then those stations often claimed the increased footprint as normal, not accidental. Print, on the other hand, had established practices that were better audited and controlled, in Dygert's view. His conclusions are, in fact, right, based on the evidence he had in front of him. His questions were the same ones that have always been at the forefront of the advertiser mind: 'Has the relevant audience been successfully reached?' 'Has the advertising been effective?'

The advertiser role in the audience-ratings convention has been much as it was in the lead up to the creation of audit of circulation bureaus, the 'advertising clubs' acting as quasi-research authorities that conduct comparative studies of different methods and measures when controversies arise over which might be best for use in planning and when there are doubts about ROI. Advertising has also had an intense interest in motivational research and many other forms of approaches to evidence about attitudes, behaviour or habits that might assist in constructing advertisements, designing campaigns or selling their expertise. The whole development of knowledge around media planning and buying is one important aspect of this. The creative side of agency work could still flourish in the face of 'cold facts' about the audience. However, the creative outcomes would always in some way reflect the research that informed the agencies overall.

By the 1960s, in the United States and Australia, the role of television in advertising strategy was well established. Australia did not have the 'advertising clubs' of the United States, but it did have advertisers who worked to established rules of the game. For example, at the end of March 1962 there were 1,355,589 television licences in force in Australia, with Sydney, Melbourne, Brisbane, Adelaide and Perth accounting for 73.9 per cent of them. It is worthwhile citing in depth an address by A.S. Cowan, general manager of Federation of Australian Commercial Television Stations (FACTS) to advertising students. This address was in 1962 and was specifically designed by Cowan to show how the industry had become both professionalized and standardized:

> To avoid a clash of picture signals, it is necessary for a system of licensing stations, rather than for anybody to at will set up a television station … Those frequencies allocated in Australia for radio and television are allocated by the ABCB. There are 13 channels available for television, but cities in different states, or far apart can be allocated the same channel without risk of interference. For example channels 7 and 9 are operated on in Sydney, Melbourne, Brisbane, Adelaide … The maximum amount of advertising permitted is prescribed by the Board after consultation with the industry. There is a distinction between advertising in sponsored sessions and for programmes containing spot advertisements.
>
> In brief the weekday advertising standards provide for 2 minutes for a 15 minute programme, 3 for a half hour and 6 minutes in an hour programme. Spot advertising may be placed at the rate of 1 minute in each 5 minutes of programme time. No more than 3 consecutive advertisements should be telecast, but billboards indicating the name of the programme and of the sponsor are not treated as advertisements. On Sundays the amount of

advertising time is restricted, and there is a total prohibition on the advertising of liquor …

All commercial television stations are members of the Federation of Commercial Television Stations known by its key initials as FACTS. It is the 'spokesman' for the industry, enters into liaison with the Government and Control Board and the advertising associations, represents its members in arbitration proceedings, deals with the complicated industry copyright matters and the like. It is its connection with advertising however which I will briefly outline.

The Television Advertising Board (TAB) which in fact has had a longer existence than FACTS, is now a Division of that body, responsible for accreditation of advertising agencies and the formulation of television advertising rules and procedures. Before an agent is entitled to commission on television business it is necessary for him to receive TAB accreditation, based on his financial position, experience, accounts and office facilities … An industry association does not concern itself with domestic matters affecting a station such as the rate structure and programmes but there are certain matters where uniformity as to procedure and treatment is desirable, and in fact is requested by the advertising associations …

The use of back-to-back announcements has been regulated. These are advertising films divided into commercials for 2 distinct products (say a one minute film divided into 2 at 30 seconds). This is permitted if only for 2 products in sponsored sessions, but only permitted by permission of the station if used as a spot message … The Broadcasting Act provides that a station shall publish particulars of its advertising charges, and shall not without reasonable cause discriminate against any person applying for the use of the advertising service. All stations therefore publish rate cards of the conditions applicable to advertising placed over it … A guide to viewing habits is carried out by independent survey organizations, of which Anderson Analysis and the McNair Survey Company are the best known. Regular capital city surveys are conducted by these two organizations, on viewing each quarter hour during the period of the survey. From this basic information is estimated for each quarter hour:

1 Number of families viewing each station

2 Number of people

3 Number of men, women, and children

4 Percentage of television sets in use.

These surveys form a guide to the most popular programmes, and represent a useful tool of measurement. Survey results have indicated the tremendous attraction which commercial television has for the public ... But the greatest development last year was in the ever increasing popularity of daytime television. Time does not permit a detailed examination, but surveys indicated that the aggregate afternoon audience to regular television programmes in most instances topped the combined audience to radio programmes at the same time.

All advertising media has its separate advantages, but TV holds a special place in the minds of the public apart from its advantages shown in the film you have just seen. A study in November, 1961, conducted by Elms Roper & Associates to the question 'Suppose you could continue to have only one of the following – radio, television, newspapers or magazines – which one of the four would you most want to keep', showed:

Television 42%

Newspapers 28%

Radio 22%

Magazines 4%

Don't Know 4%

This was taken on the American scene, but with the rapid acceptance of TV in this country, would be a logical basis to assume its application here. (Cowan 1962)

A.S. Cowan's account is instructive because it shows the dominance of television in the thinking of the advertiser and also the rules and context that governed the relationship between networks and advertisers, together with the government regulatory bodies. This is the era of the beginning of the dominance of the main free to air networks over the Australian mediascape, something that the networks as incumbents have maintained for decades. However, the relationship between the television networks and the ratings providers, just as the relationship between the advertisers and the networks, were not passive ones. All had an eye on the ratings and any perceived mistakes were immediately acted on. The letter on the next page is from Stan Fildes, a manager of the Perth television station TVW7, to Sir James Cruthers, its managing director. In this case, McNair had misprinted the titles of television stations in its diaries. Stan Fildes had, as a result, gone through all the diaries. McNair had underestimated the reaction to the error.

TVW CHANNEL 7
May 15, 1969
Dear Jim,

I went to McNair's office this morning and spoke with Ian McNair and Jim Grant, their Office Manager, about the incorrect heading of STW7 and TVW9 on the diaries used for their television survey in Perth.

Ian McNair commenced the discussion with an apology for the error. He went on to say that while he thought the error was serious in itself, it would have no effect whatsoever on the results of the survey.

Other points made by McNair are contained in a letter due to be delivered to this office later today for inclusion in our airbag. I read the draft of this letter.

Comments I made to McNair include the following:

We view the error in a very serious light.

Regardless of the fact that the information was correct at the bottom of each page, people read from top to bottom, so the incorrect information at the top could very well mislead.

Despite the McNair opinion that people think of the figure and not the letters in a station's call sign, we have spent a good deal of time and money on getting Western Australian viewers to remember both so far as TVW7 is concerned.

If the error was discovered at a point during the checking stage, I couldn't follow why the incorrect information was not physically changed on at least those books still to be checked. Furthermore, I was surprised the error was not correct with the respondent at the stage the diaries were collected.

Grant brought in a number of diaries for me to inspect and McNair invited me to look through all 300 of them as they came to hand. One diary did have three of our programmes written in by the respondent but had TVW9 ticked; however this had been corrected in the McNair office. McNair and Grant claimed this was not uncommon kind of error and could not necessarily be attributed to the diary misprint. I indicated that I was surprised nevertheless the error had not been corrected at the collection stage.

My approach could be described as firm and unrelenting. Clearly McNair was disturbed by the apparent seriousness with which we regarded the matter. As I started to leave their boardroom McNair attempted to brighten up the proceedings a little by saying 'Well Stan, I hope you have a good result in the survey'. I replied 'Ian, it had better be good'.

This type of interaction between the players engaged with ratings was everyday and ongoing. If it was not a network provider querying results through technical sub-committees it might be an advertiser complaining about contradictory results.

The new knowledge intermediary that grew out of these interactions was the media planner.

The Media Planner

National advertising originates with manufacturers, retailers, corporations and governments, located in many cases outside a particular medium's circulation or viewing area. As we know, a national ad in a single newspaper is often only part of a much wider advertising campaign. It may be backed up by advertisements in major and minor papers, in radio and television and even echoed on railway billboards. Today, this kind of campaign is normally managed by an advertising agency that specializes in researching the client's needs, devising the advertisements and scheduling them for publication. Some agencies concentrate their business in a single city, some have branches around the country and some are transnational agencies or partnerships between national and transnational firms. Some agencies specialize in certain forms of advertising or in servicing relatively few advertisers. Others specialize in coordinating wide-ranging campaigns which may include not only advertisements in the mass media but also launches, promotions, mail drops, DVD distribution, T-shirts, caps, advertising balloons and so on. A glance at the classified advertisement sections in industry journals gives some idea of the range of media and promotions available to agencies. These agencies are highly competitive and the competition has increased.

Generally, the big agencies are called full-service firms. They liaise with the client, work out their requirements, help define the market and the product, propose a campaign, draw up a budget, recommend appropriate media, create the advertisements, book media space and time, and liaise with media advertising departments. Global competition in this area of buying space increased considerably in 1998 when the world's largest marketing group, WPP (originally Wire and Plastic Products), pooled the media-buying power of its main advertising divisions, the agencies J. Walter Thompson and Ogilvy & Mather. Under the name of MindShare, they planned to be free to compete for the business of other advertising agencies in buying space in television in all its terrestrial, orbital, analogue and digital forms, magazines, billboards, bus shelters, screen-savers, sky-writing and much more.

Buying space, as we have seen, goes back to the foundations of agencies. But these days advertising, like much of the media, has been globalized and international full-service firms aim to provide more than buying services. Some can supply a full range of skills from their own resources but where they lack those skills they can organize or buy-in associated promotions and public relations services. They usually employ campaign planners, media buyers, copywriters, artists, creative directors and art directors but may hire more for big campaigns. Big firms daily hire outside photographers and film-makers, specialist artists, printers, actors, models, celebrities, voice-over readers and special-effects people. They also hire props and properties for advertising shoots. Indeed, they make a substantial contribution to sustaining the film, acting and photographic industries.

There are many accounts of how particular advertising campaigns were put together. Many of those from within the industry are pervaded by an atmosphere of triumphalism – hype, after all, is the common currency of advertising. One in particular, *True Confessions* by John Singleton, adds a note of iconoclasm to its triumphalism. It begins:

> Most of the books written about advertising have little to do with Australian advertising; or advertising at all if it comes to that. Advertising books are mostly written by antique principals of US Agencies as a sort of desperate last fling for some new business. Or as a deathbed rationale for the boredom or predictability of their performance ... First, it's important *not* to have too good an education. I don't know anyone in advertising whose mind is cluttered with too many bullshit degrees. (Singleton 1979)

Singleton's breezy and irreverent book is a great read, but Michael Schudson's *Advertising, the Uneasy Persuasion: Its Dubious Impact on American Society* (Schudson 1984) still provides a serious scholarly critical and analytical perspective. As R.R. Walker said in his survey of the industry, 'Advertising is not art, it is not literature, it is not design, it is not entertainment. It is part of a communications process between people with things to sell and people with money to buy. It embraces everybody. In many respects it is a business looking for professional status' (Walker 1967: 1). He also noted that even though the media depend on advertising for most of their revenue, the media were markedly reluctant to talk about either the role or process of advertising or marketing. Newspapers, he said, were very diffident about doing so, even though they wanted to know everything they could about other people and other businesses (Walker 1967: 199–200). These remarks came from a man who worked for 26 years in Australia's largest advertising agency and for some years wrote that rare thing, a column on advertising for an Australian newspaper, the *Age*.

The rise of the professional status of advertising itself has a long history, with Art Nielsen promoting market research as a core discipline and including 'the advertiser' as manager-scientist. The rise of media planning added to the science feel of advertising. In the mid-1970s a new type of time-buying service emerged, attracting clients of larger agencies who thought they could get more personal service from a small organization like Zenith. These companies were in turn bought by large European 'buying centrals' that had flourished in a climate of loose controls. Large agencies set up or bought up buying services as a substitute for their own media departments and in the contemporary moment this has become general practice.

Buying services originally began with the premise that they were uniquely skilled at bargaining down rates, but their main selling point shifted to the claim that they selected media with high sophisticated skill. They developed 'optimization models' that stressed 'accountability' and performance rather than cost efficiency. Similar models had been used – and abandoned – by agencies thirty years earlier. (The simplest optimization model might be a table ranking different media options in terms of only two variables: the cost of an advertisement and the size of the audience each would deliver – or, putting the two together, the CPT gross ratings points or impressions a given investment would buy.) (Bogart 2003: 169)

By adding information about the composition of the audience the comparison could then be refined further to the cost of reaching people of a certain kind, say men aged 18 to 34, mothers of children under six, professionals and managers, to use Bogart's example. Computers can create alternative schedules and budgets for comparison. When comparing schedules that contain different media and repeated advertisements the modelling becomes more complicated because it adds reach and frequency over the life of a campaign. Such schedules could provide an 'optimum' frequency such as three exposures per person. 'The audience measurement services fed this development, by supplying lots and lots of numbers to crank into the models. As the analysis of media schedules grew more complex, the large agencies and buying services had a further advantage, because they could afford the necessary technology and talent' (Bogart 2003: 170). Figure 8.1 provides an overview of the relationship of the 'media planner' within the agency context.

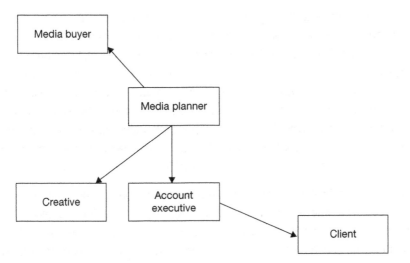

Figure 8.1 General model of the media planner

Media planning, therefore, has become a major part of the planning process because it provides optimum cost-efficiency plans for the delivery of advertisements across a range of media. The knowledge around media buying includes a range of formulae that have been developed over time, from frequency and reach through to understanding different patterns of delivery of advertisements and audience behaviour. It was worthwhile going backwards to the 1960s to see the advertiser view of these formulae before the advent of the personal computer.

Cost Efficiency and the Curve of Experience

The Australian Association of National Advertisers (AANA) held its annual conference in Perth, Western Australia, in 1966. One of the keynote speakers was Kevin Luscombe, head of advertising and marketing at Heinz. Luscombe told the AANA conference that Heinz had experience a massive loss in sales, with competition from both East and West Coast of the United States. 'The advertising you saw earlier talked about thicker, richer Heinz Ketchup, and from what we could see, to many consumers this seemed to be on target, but it lacked the demonstrable break-through that *convinced* people that ours *was* thicker, richer than the competition' (Luscombe 1966).

Heinz had noted in group interviews and quantitative home-use studies a connection between richness and thickness in its ketchup. Heinz appointed agency Doyle, Dane and Bernbach to look into the interview findings and how to use television as the main medium in a media plan:

> Then the answer to the creative problem was found, right in our own plant. During an Agency tour of the plant, they saw several tests being made, tests which clearly demonstrated that Heinz was richer and thicker, less 'runniness' than our competitors. Demonstration of this seemed to be the answer. Storyboards were pulled together with absolute singularity of purpose. Judgment on these boards came quickly and the commercials went into test markets in record time. Recall of communication tests quickly followed. We got a tremendous playback, almost verbatim playback from an agreeably large number of consumers. (Luscombe 1966)

Luscombe told the gathering that major media work closely with advertising agencies to provide a steady flow of cost-efficiency data and audience profile studies. Audience specifications, he said, can be very precise. 'I have a product for upper income families with children in the late teen bracket, in urban markets. They need to have a separate frozen food cabinet and entertain regularly.' A media plan with supporting facts can be selected to fit this need but in less specific markets, reach and frequency are the basic criteria:

In talking reach and frequency, I have run into some varying definitions. In this discussion, reach is a measurement of the number of different homes viewing a program (or programmes) in a given period. Frequency is the average number of times the average home that is reached saw that programme or those programmes. Reach and frequency data is most commonly based on 4 week data. (Luscombe 1966)

The following matrix highlights what Luscombe was talking about:

Table 8.1 Homes viewing matrix

	A	B	C	D	E	Total
Week 1		X		X		2
Week 2	X	X				2
Week 3		X		X		2
Week 4		X		X		2
Total Contacts	1	4	0	2	1	8

The determination of the reach with a combined buy using, for example, one programme spot and four night rotating spots is simply based on the laws of probability – the probability in this case of not seeing one of the television spots. For example, if this schedule of the programme calls for two telecasts of a show in the four-week period and that is seen by 29 per cent of households, 71 per cent of households did not see this show in a four-week period. In a similar manner it can be deduced that 30 per cent of households did not see one of the spot announcements in a four-week period. Therefore, accordingly to the laws of probability, 21 per cent of households saw neither the programme nor any of the spots: $71/100 \times 30/100 = 21/100$. This would mean that 79 per cent of households saw at least one announcement in the schedules.

Although estimates of reach and frequency give quantitative values on a particular media schedule, interpretation is still the judgement of the media planner. Decisions have to be made on such questions as:

- Should reach be more important than frequency?

- How is the frequency distributed? Are a relatively small number of homes getting heavy exposure at the expense of other homes?

The thing that makes reach and frequency information so critical in media selection is its role of supplying quantified evaluations of a broadcast media plan, for example, where combination buys are being used and a decision has to be made between several alternatives. Two plans, spending the same budget and delivering approximately the same total messages, can deliver markedly different reach and frequency results. This depends on the spread of day-parts involved and the type of programme that the majority of spots are clustered in. Reach and frequency numbers can be determined either by purchasing actual exposed tabulations from a ratings service (which will show a count of the number of different homes exposed to the schedule and the number of times each was exposed), or by making an estimate of the results of such tabulations.

Two years after Luscombe's presentation, case studies produced a number of reported case studies linking optimal exposure levels:

1968 3–5 exposures (du Pont)

1968 2–3 (GEC)

1968 3–4 (GEC)

1970 2 (du Pont)

In 1972 Herbert Krugman came up with a three-hit theory of advertising messages: on first exposure, the consumer's reaction is 'what is it?'; second exposure, this is the evaluative stage where the consumer moves from simply absorbing 'the message' to relating the message to its relevance; third exposure is where the person decides to act, assuming the message is relevant.

The three-hit theory is an attempt to reduce the 'scattergun' approach in a schedule, providing a heuristic measure giving some confidence that the target audience has been reached three times and, further, that a third exposure is inherently linked to motivation. Understanding reach and frequency, therefore, developed additional assumptions. Krugman's three-hit theory is one of those assumptions based on case studies. Studies on frequency distributions also provided the statistical modelling for the data, not least the work of Agostini, Metheringham and Leckenby, and Kishi.

A range of concepts are important in this context, including Unduplicated Audience (also known as exclusive or unique audience; it refers to that proportion of the audience of a combination of more than one media vehicle that is unique to one or other of these media vehicles), Audience Flow (the movement in audience in broadcast media from station to station at a given time), Average Frequency (the average number of times people or homes are potentially exposed to an advertiser schedule of advertisements), Cumulative Audience (or Reach; the number or proportion of different people or homes reached at least once by a medium as a whole or by specific media vehicle or number of advertisements), Gross Ratings Points (GRP, expressed as thousands rather than a percentage; it describes the total weight delivered by the schedule without regard to audience duplication), Opportunities to See (OTS, the number of potential impacts available to a given advertising message as expressed by an estimated audience), among others.

Reach is a measure of the unduplicated audience. If a placement in a television programme reaches 30 per cent of the target audience and a second placement has a reach of 28 per cent it is unlikely that the schedule reach will be as high as 58 per cent. Almost certainly some of the viewers of the first programme will also have seen the second programme. The reach may be in the region of 50 per cent (that is, 8 per cent of the target group will have viewed both programmes). Reach, frequency and gross ratings points are closely related:

GRP = Reach × Frequency

Luscombe, in his 1966 presentation to the AANA, made an important point about understanding frequency distribution and the role of mathematical modelling – it had to be used as part of what he called an *experience curve*. An advertiser needed to understand the limits of the statistics. For example, average frequency does not necessarily indicate how many people received how many exposures. A schedule analysed as having a reach of 75 per cent and an average frequency of 3.0 may seem to be quite reasonable, but the following frequency distribution which meets this 75 per cent/3.0 criterion shows up the difficulties:

Spots Seen	Target audience (per cent)
0	25
1	15
2	25
3	10
4	10
5	5
6	5
7	5

Here we have audience skew: 25 per cent of the target audience could be classified as having heavy exposure (more than 3), 40 per cent had light exposure (less than 3); and 10 per cent had the average level of exposure. If three exposures to the advertisements were necessary to get the message through, then this schedule would only have succeeded with 35 per cent of the target groups, not the apparent 75 per cent. Frequency criteria should be expressed in terms of minimum acceptable frequency or acceptable frequency range to avoid audience skew.

Barwise and Ehrenberg (Barwise and Ehrenberg 1988) also show why the experience curve is an important part of understanding the application of knowledge in this area. 'Double jeopardy' is a good example of this. The audience composition of most television programmes is much the same, although different individuals choose different programmes. But how regularly do people watch the successive episodes of a particular program? To what extent is it the same viewers each week? Most TV programmes appear as a series of episodes and if there are no big changes to channels, audience size ratings of a regular series tend to be steady from day to day. However, repeat viewing provides a double jeopardy effect for those programmes that get low ratings. Barwise and Ehrenberg's example in Table 8.2 exemplifies double jeopardy, listing contrasting shows that aired in the early, middle and late evening on four Wednesdays in New York.

Table 8.2 Audiences of four successive episodes (household ratings)

New York, November 1984	1	2	3	4
ABC World News 7.00 WABC	9	8	8	6
Wheel of Fortune 7.30 WCBS	14	15	17	14
Highway to Heaven 8.00 WNBC	13	11	12	11
Dynasty 9.00 WABC	25	26	24	24
St Elsewhere 10.00 WNBC	11	10	8	12
Channel 2 News at 11 11.00 WCBS	8	6	13	7

Source: Barwise and Ehrenberg 1988

These figures look like the audiences are stable. But in each case only about half or even fewer of those watching a programme in week 1 also watched it in week 2.

Repeat levels are even lower than they used to be, because there are more channels and thus lower ratings per program. In the US the average repeat percentage for prime time networks program is now down to 40 percent. Most series in the table averaged repeat rates of less than 30 percent. Popular soap series can have repeat levels 10 percent higher, averaging up to about 50 percent; but a relatively 'high' 50 or even 55 percent rate is not 90 percent that the popular mind might expect. (Barwise and Ehrenberg 1988: 380)

Nuanced understanding of what is happening with audiences is not a navel-gazing exercise. The consequences when translating figures into the market are startling. The figures below give some idea on the costs of a 30-second advertisement for high-rating programmes against a Nielsen rating.

Table 8.3 Nielsen ratings for 30-second advertisements in high-rating programmes

	30-second ad (US$)	Nielsen Rating
American Idol	$658,333	16.2
Survivor	$412,833	10.8
CSI Miami	$374,231	10.0
Everybody Loves Raymond	$315,850	9.8
Two and a Half Men	$249,017	9.6
Law and Order	$227,500	8.3

The language of quantity in any context requires caution. This does not mean that repeat viewing principles mean that a serial is not doing well or that people are not watching and involved, only that in presenting the statistics without understanding repeat levels skews the meaning of the results. Statistical modelling is now an established part of media planning practice and the language of quantity even more complex than the days of Art Nielsen's flip charts. The everyday media planner, the young woman or man sitting at the computer, does not necessarily need to know the mathematical modelling, but whether they have the experience curve mentioned by Luscombe is highly unlikely.

Modern campaigns combine different sources of information in their planning. For example, Caemmerer's report (Caemmerer 2009) on how Renault and Nordpol + Hamburg executed an integrated communication campaign is a contemporary example of how media and evaluation are used in tandem. The objective of the campaign was to increase consumer awareness of the safety of Renault cars with the message: 'Die sichersten Autos kommen aus Frankreich' ('The safest cars come from France'). The campaign used cinemas, the internet, television and print. Figure 8.2 shows the media campaign schedule:

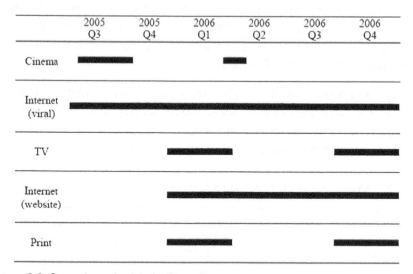

	2005 Q3	2005 Q4	2006 Q1	2006 Q2	2006 Q3	2006 Q4
Cinema	▬▬▬		▬			
Internet (viral)	▬▬▬▬▬▬▬▬▬▬▬▬▬▬▬▬▬▬▬▬▬▬▬▬					
TV		▬▬▬			▬▬▬	
Internet (website)		▬▬▬▬▬▬▬▬▬▬▬▬▬▬				
Print		▬▬▬			▬▬▬	

Figure 8.2 Campaign schedule for Renault
Source: Adapted from Balnaves 2010

TNS was employed to track changes in consumer attitudes and to evaluate the effectiveness of the campaign. The study showed an increase in awareness levels of the safety of Renault cars, from 44 to 52.2 per cent, and intentions to purchase a car from Renault. According to Caemmerer (Caemmerer 2009) an independent readership survey by the magazine *Auto, Motor und Sport* also showed that Renault had achieved a 7 per cent increase in consumer perception of safety. The Renault campaign is a good example of tactical use of media all focused on a single coherent message. The Director of Marketing at Renault held that cinema was a good venue for high quality film and advertisements. The combination of the media is assumed to enhance reach and frequency to the desired target demographics. What we do get by deploying the different media, however, is expansion of frequency and reach. What is most interesting is the viral marketing aspect of the campaign.

The media planner is faced by a range of different measures, rules of thumb and statistical principles in developing their media plans. Software packages are designed to provide access to the different sources of data and to provide the formulae automatically against the data. All major media, from television through to outdoor, attempt to provide frequency against demographics, but vary in how they do it. In cinema, reach and frequency are derived from the actual or projected campaign admissions overlaid with cinema-going demographics. In the case of Australia, this overlay is derived from Roy Morgan's single-source survey that fuses consumer questionnaires given to thousands of households against ratings and other data. As discussed in Chapter 2, the authors would not call this genuine single-source data, but Roy Morgan does attempt to fuse different types of data to give a picture of consumers or audiences. In the case of cinema, as the Val Morgan cinema network advertising says, a campaign aimed at a target audience is directed towards appropriate movies in each complex and booked each week. The total number of movies available each week against a particular demographic sets the optimum weight – the campaign weight required to reach all moviegoers in that demographic. Val Morgan's example of campaign achievements, in all-people admissions and reach against demographics for varying campaign weights, is outlined in Table 8.4.

What has emerged with this complexity is the problem of getting competent users of data, those who have an underlying understanding of the statistics as well as the 'experience curve'.

Table 8.4　Cinema admissions

14–24's Campaign Achievement						
	200 screens per week			400 screens per week		
	Admissions (all people)	%	f	Admissions (all people)	%	f
4 weeks	659,000	21.1%	1.0	1,318,000	34.5%	1.2
8 weeks	1,318,400	34.5%	1.2	2,636,800	50.6%	1.7
25–34's Campaign Achievement						
	200 screens per week			400 screens per week		
	Admissions (all people)	%	f	Admissions (all people)	%	f
4 weeks	659,200	12.5%	1	1,318,400	21.1%	1.2
8 weeks	1,318,400	21.1%	1.2	2,636,000	32.5%	1.5
18–49's Campaign Achievement						
	250 screens per week			450 screens per week		
	Admissions (all people)	%	f	Admissions (all people)	%	f
4 weeks	824,000	11.8%	1	1,483,200	18.9%	1.1
8 weeks	1,648,000	20.6%	1.1	2,636,800	30.7%	1.4

The Competent User

More research data and more complex ways of manipulating them on the computer made media buyers better informed but not more intelligent. Planners might switch from one yardstick, like cost per thousand, to another, like cost per reach point, but to make either the number of impressions or the number of people reached the sole criterion for evaluating media, or media schedules, was to fall into a fatal error. My studies taught me that in advertising there were simply no universal rules, no sure formulas for marketing success. There was, however, a formula for failure, and that was a reliance on formulas. I began to learn this lesson when I worked in the agency business.
Leo Bogart (Bogart 2003: 170)

The mathematical modelling of behaviour, as Bogart says, was once the exclusive domain of economists but it is now very much a part of marketing practice and of media research. Media buying now takes a growing share of advertising agency operating costs and inbuilt in its vocabulary are assumptions about audience attitudes and behaviour. Dygert's days are gone. Many of the overarching considerations in advertising remain, such as a principled understanding of diverse sources of evidence, and, above all, the dual personality of marketer and show performer. Not only do data need to be analysed, but, as in Luscombe's days, they needed to be convincingly sold. However, if Heinz's ketchup did not sell after an advertising campaign, then the agency employed by Heinz would most likely have been sacked.

There is now more computation than ever before. There is, though, an addition to this complex mix. The Advertisers Research Foundation (ARF) in 2007 created a more complex model of consumer behaviour and the advertising process. This included, not least, the addition of engagement as an important variable, above and beyond exposure. The figure opposite provides an overview of the model.

The contemporary advertising industry sees engagement as an alternative measure to exposure and a reflection of the changing nature of self and family in the online world. (Advertising Research Foundation 2009). Traditional media economics is now complemented by software packages that look into online activity and consumer generated media. Nielsen, for example, now has NetView, SiteCensus, VideoCensus, AdRelevance, BuzzMetrics, Custom Research – all related to online analysis and part of the push to treat advertising analysis as a 'conversation'. Figure 8.3 provides an overview of Nielsen online research analytics.

BuzzMetrics, represented in Figure 8.4, is designed to give business and organizations a sense of what is being talked about among audiences online. Computational semantics is a growing area providing algorithms for statistical analysis of language.

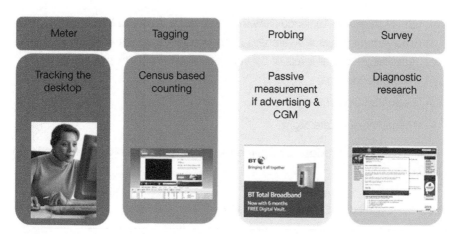

Figure 8.3 Nielsen Online Media Research Analytics

Volume	Number of comments Number of individuals talking	"Turns out the contaminated wheat gluten that
Sentiment	Overall tone, polarity to product, issue, brand, feature	has sickened and killed so many cats and dogs recently has ended up in quite a few brand names. I finally found a complete list of the affected brands here. I feed my cats — dry food, and fortunately the dry food was not on the list. The — wet is, though. Don't assume that your brand is safe. Check the list!"
Topics	Features and words associated with brand or issue	
Reach	Size of audience viewing CGM for brand or issue	
Dispersion	Number and types of communities where buzz exists	sfynes.blogspot.com, 04/05/07
Influence	Ability of individual to create buzz	

Figure 8.4 Nielsen BuzzMetrics

Optimedia's new Content Power Ratings (CPR 3.0) likewise attempt to estimate audience activity using composite measures. CPR 3.0 brings together:

- Optimedia's primary research
- Nielsen Media Research's NTI database
- Nielsen Online's VideoCensus
- Nielsen Mobile
- comScore's Media Metrix
- e-Poll's FastTrack Television
- Dow Jones Factiva
- Google Trends
- Facebook
- Nielsen BuzzMetrics

- CPR Measures: Audience Delivery – across TV, Web and Mobile platforms; Involvement – overall awareness of and loyalty to programme; and Advocacy – overall levels of conversation and PR activity, plus personal recommendations
- Evaluated Content
- Primetime and Late Night

Table 8.5 below, provided by Optimedia, shows its CPR ranking compared with Nielsen Ratings.

Table 8.5 Optimedia's Content Power Ratings

CPR 3.0 Rank	Nielsen Rating
1 AMERICAN IDOL FOX Reality/Contest	1
2 LOST ABC Sci-Fi	34
3 DANCING WITH THE STARS ABC Reality/Contest	2
4 GREY'S ANATOMY ABC Drama	26
5 HOUSE FOX Drama	28
6 FAMILY GUY FOX Comedy	63
7 THE OFFICE NBC Comedy	60
8 NCIS CBS Drama	4
9 GLEE FOX Musical	66
10 CSI CBS Drama	6
11 HEROES NBC Sci-Fi	65
12 THE BACHELOR ABC Reality/Contest	13
13 SURVIVOR CBS Reality/Contest	14
14 GOSSIP GIRL CW Drama	125
15 TWO AND A HALF MEN CBS Comedy	9
16 DESPERATE HOUSEWIVES ABC Drama	17
17 JAY LENO SHOW NBC Variety	55
18 TRUE BLOOD HBO Drama	131
19 SCRUBS ABC Comedy	81
20 BIGGEST LOSER NBC Reality/Contest	23
21 SO YOU THINK YOU CAN DANCE FOX Reality/Contest	50
22 HOW I MET YOUR MOTHER CBS Comedy	37
23 60 MINUTES CBS News	8
24 THE BIG BANG THEORY CBS Comedy	20
25 CHUCK NBC Drama	57

Like Roy Morgan with cinema, these are all attempts to give an overarching picture of what the consumer or audience is doing, something that goes back a long way in advertising history. Historically, also, there have been competing pictures of the audience and its behaviour and the role of these different measures sometimes come into conflict. Advertisers, however, as the voice in the market, are now bringing engagement into practice in a way that they were not able to do in the past because computing power gives them access to data in a way that was not possible before. The Advertising Research Foundation's 'On the road to a new effectiveness model: measuring emotional responses to television advertising' (Advertising Research Foundation 2009), like all ARF reports before it, puts engagement on the audience ratings agenda.

There is a real problem, however, of measurement experimentation speeding ahead of competent users of the data that are generated. The experience curve of Luscombe almost looks like it is being lost in computation of secondary data at the expense of competent judgement. The user is being given a desktop interface that is easy to use and translate requests into tabulations and decent graphs but, as is clear, understanding the intricacies of what is happening with audiences is a major exercise in itself.

Summary

Advertising is generally planned and evaluated in terms of campaigns rather than individual commercials. Advertisers have always been among the most sophisticated users and critics of the ratings. They have also been the group most likely to experiment with and embrace different sorts of research. They were the initial engine for the development of the audience market and for the ratings instrument itself (CAB/Crossley, Anderson, McNair). They established its basic vocabulary; they appear now as an important part of the engine transforming the ratings and interrogating its efficacy.

The American Association for Public Opinion Research (AAPOR) ethics research code has been revised to become more specific and demanding, but as Leo Bogart notes, there has also been 'ever greater abuse of survey research by companies and individuals outside AAPOR' (Bogart 2003: 112). The authors are not saying that any of the examples provided in the chapter are an abuse of statistics or of research. However, telemarketing, push polling and other market- or politics-driven methods have no doubt created confusion in people's minds about what counts as survey research. More importantly, this confusion leads to non-cooperation in surveys and diminishes the ethos of the modern survey.

The hunger for measurement has other downsides, not least providing a platform for people to enter the market, as in the days before the US Congressional hearings, to sell bogus methods or data:

> Then there was Norton Garfinkel, who satisfied the advertising business's inane appetite for a 'single source' of data on media and markets with his Brand Rating Index. The Index quickly rode to stellar success, and Garfinkel sold his company to the Arcata Corporation, a West Coast forest products company with dreams of becoming a giant conglomerate. BRI foundered after a presentation to the 1970 Advertising Research Foundation conference by William Simmons, whose company measured magazine readership as well as product consumption. Simmon's presentation demonstrated an uncanny resemblance between BRI's magazine figures and his own, as well as between BRI's television data and Nielsen's. In this case, too, the service went under, but Garfinkel remained on the party circuit. (Bogart 2003: 113)

The role of the advertiser in the audience-ratings convention is a complex one and it has changed over time. In its early days advertising clubs often conducted their own research, as did early advertising agencies. Today, research costs are most likely to be passed on to the client and pure research is not seen to be core business. There are exceptions, like Project Apollo, that attempt to create a single-source methodology that works. Accountability for the dollar spend, though, remains. Creating cost efficiencies in delivering advertising are core business. A special form of knowledge about how audiences work has built up around traditional broadcast ratings and exposure measures generally. That knowledge is complex and the 'experience curve' related to it involves not only knowledge of frequency distributions and mathematical modelling but the *actual limits of statistical knowledge*. In terms of the relative disposition of advertisers in the audience ratings decision-making, the advertiser brings to the table the voice of the market. They are voiced in terms of the currency of the ratings and also in terms of representing client interests. If a medium is seen not to be viable for the delivery of advertising, then advertisers will direct the client's money elsewhere. If the ratings do not deliver the size of audiences or the specific audiences that are required, then, likewise, they will redirect their dollars elsewhere. In the contemporary moment, however, modern broadcast ratings are still gilt-edged in terms of the robustness of their methods.

9 The Audience

The public is an audience, but it is also a market. It could not be a market unless it had given its consent to be an audience, and it could not remain an audience ... unless it had proved itself as a market.
David Potter (Potter 1967: 54)

In Chapter 8, we found that advertisers now 'enumerate' the audience in complex ways, many of which have inbuilt assumptions about who the audience is and in what audience behaviour consists. Advertisers are not only interested in a picture of the audience but in being able to predict what the audience will do. In this chapter we turn to the audience itself, an important but often unacknowledged partner to the audience-ratings convention. When Nielsen and Arbitron joined forces to set up the experimental Project Apollo in 2005 they expected to be able to capture all of the everyday behaviour of audiences, from reading papers through to using mobile phones and buying food. To their surprise they found that people did not want to participate. The more they were asked to do and to provide, the more they resisted and refused. This is just one of the ways in which the audience has a 'voice' in how audience ratings are developed and how the audience as informants and respondents actively sets limits to what information can be collected and how it can be collected.

Audience consent to research has been essential to the success of the ratings industry. The audience-ratings convention has been essential in balancing intrusion *and* demands for privacy. Part of this success has derived from the recognition of audience research participants that their data is being used in the public interest – that their own participation is in the democratic interest (literally and formally). Audiences also have a radical effect and limit on which technologies they are willing to allow in their household or to use to collect their data.

But there is another way in which audiences set limits to ratings. It is well encapsulated in the phrase the 'unknowable audience'. This is that audiences domesticate and use media in their own unpredictable ways. While the consumer electronics and computing industries marketed the additional radio sets, TV sets, VCR then DVD, mobile phones and games, and the media industry pushed catch-up TV, IPTV, cable, satellite and then digital versions, it was always the audience which domesticated this technology; it took it up at particular speeds and put it all together in particular ensembles. Marketing does its best to introduce some semblance of predictability into this uptake but audiences will always run ahead and run behind this marketing. They will configure media in ways that resist easy registration in ratings systems. The ongoing problems ratings agencies face are: determining what audiences are actually doing with their media receivers, monitors and recorders in a fast-developing media landscape; figuring out how what they are doing can be effectively tracked; and working out whether audiences would support this tracking. This was information the ratings could not provide.

This was a problem of knowledge at two levels: the ratings companies needed to develop ways of regularly assessing what was happening on the ground, in rooms within homes, and in other places in which media was being consumed and taken up; and they needed to find ways of working with audiences so that this use could be measured. The first was a problem of continually working to determine the effectiveness of the frame within which the ratings was being conducted. The second was of finding cost-effective, collection- and user-friendly ways of measuring this use. While this can be readily turned into a research problem which specialized companies such as Gale Metzger's SRI could help with, it is also an indicator of how audience behaviours and uses of technology powerfully shape ratings systems outside the control of these agencies themselves. Audiences, not media companies, put together media ensembles and associated viewing, searching, downloading and recording practices. Audiences shape the ratings convention in two ways: how they use media requires companies continually to update their understandings of how audiences are using media; and they set limits to what can be measured and how it can be measured.

This chapter will give an historical insight into how participants have been recruited into audience ratings studies and how issues of intrusion have been addressed. We will also discuss the implications of the decline of audience participation in research. New technologies that can draw data from households through, say, set-top boxes, do not solve the audience-participation problem. Indeed, the technologies have raised the problem of privacy of data, and thrown into question the 'public interest' component of audience consent to ratings research.

The Modern Audience

The patterns of modern audiences in advanced industrial countries tend to be relatively similar with media households marked by different mixes of media and media options. Canada and the United States are good examples exhibiting similar diffusion patterns but also some important differences with, for instance, the United States showing greater levels of personal video recorder (PVR) and multi-set households. Table 9.1 shows the massive differences in sizes of each media market but also similarities in media usage.

We know also, of course, that the patterns of media usage are diverse, with the computer and mobile media, including the internet, taking up an increasing amount of people's time. Table 9.2 shows how these patterns among young appear to be similar across different countries.

A major Australian study on family use of media provides a useful overview of overall activities among young people. It reveals the mix of activities within which ratings measures of, for instance, commercial and public service broadcasting takes place. Table 9.3 provides a breakdown by different types of activity. These are patterns that we can see in most industrialized countries.

Table 9.1 Comparison of Canada and US media households

	Canada	US
1. Population (2+ within TV households)	32,117,000	289,720,000
2. Households	13,139,000	114,890,000
3. BBM Markets, TV Markets – DMAs	40	210
4. TV Households	13,008,000	112,800,000
% TV Households	99%	99%
5. Cable + Satellite (% of TV Households)	89%	87%
6. Pay-TV (% of TV Households with digital capability)	58%	58%
7. PVR (% of TV Households)	9%	19%
8. Multi-set (% of TV Households)	67%	82%
9. Average Daily Viewing Per Household (Hours:Minutes)	N/A	8:14
10. Average Weekly Viewing (Hours:Minutes)		
Persons 2+	26:48	31:55
Men 18+	27:42	31:55
Women 18+	30:00	36:37
Teens (12–17)	18:30	23:21
Children (2–11)	18:06	23:51
11. Advertising Volume (2006) (US$)	13,673	256,826
12. TV Volume (2006) – millions (Canada CDN$/US US$)	3,240	59,928
13. TV Expenditure Per Capita (2006) (CDN$)	99	228
14. Number of TV Stations (Conventional + Specialty & Pay stations)	302	1,375

Source: 'TV Basics 2008–2009', Television Bureau of Canada (TVB)

Table 9.2 Average time young people spend per day on computer and video games (hours and minutes)

	10–14	15–19	20–24
Finland	1:51	1:35	1:20
Germany	1:42	1:55	1:46
Italy	1:17	1:18	1:23
Norway	1:35	2:02	2:36
Spain	1:30	1:35	1:41
Sweden		2:27	
UK	1:29	1:48	1:37

Source: *Cultural Statistics (2007)*, Luxembourg: Office for Official Publications of the European Communities

Table 9.3 Family use of media

	Total	Boys	Girls	8–11	12–14	15–17
General (non-media) activities	4:30	4:26	4:34	4:46	4:05	4:29
School	3:53	3:50	3:57	3:53	4:05	3:38
Homework	0:35	0:32	0:38	0:21	0:41	0:52
TV	1:54	1:58	1:50	1:54	1:55	1:55
DVDs	0:24	0:24	0:24	0:24	0:21	0:26
Mobile phone	0:19	0:13	0:23	0:03	0:19	0:43
Other phone	0:05	0:05	0:05	0:02	0:04	0:08
Music and radio	0:35	0:30	0:40	0:17	0:38	1:06
Video/computer games (includes online gaming against others)	0:39	0:55	0:24	0:38	0:39	0:42
Internet (e.g. messaging, email, music/ video content, visiting websites)	0:49	0:42	0:53	0:14	1:01	1:36
Other computer (not online or gaming)	0:04	0:04	0:05	0:04	0:03	0:07
Net electronic media/communications (excludes homework on computer internet)	4:49	4:51	4:44	3:36	5:00	6:43
Net screen time (homework on computer/internet + TV + DVDs + gaming + internet + other computer)	4:03	4:15	3:51	3:19	4:15	5:11

Source: *Media and Communications in Australian Families 2007*, Australian Communications and Media Authority (ACMA)

The future audience is computer, internet and mobile savvy, well rehearsed in moving from big screen to small screen, from one application to another. The picture of the modern audience also includes:

1 *Conduit multiplication and audience fragmentation:* With the advent of more television channels, more radio channels, thousands and if not millions of internet sites, mobiles phones, and so on, there is now an assumption of *fragmentation* of audiences. People have far more options available to them.

2 *Timeshifting:* People can use their *timeshifting technology*, like the personal video recorder (PVR) or TiVo to by-pass advertisements and make monitoring of their exposure difficult.

3 *New uses for television:* DVDs, game stations and other television-attached-media reduce attention to traditional broadcast television.

4 *Ambience:* Traditional broadcast television like radio is becoming a background medium with people doing other tasks while watching television.

5 *Shift to below-the-line advertising:* There is a trend towards a more accountable media spend because of conduit multiplication and fragmentation. Advertisers are demanding that there is evidence that their audiences are in fact exposed to advertising in a fractured media market.

Getting a 'picture of the audience' appears to be getting more difficult, or at least getting a more detailed picture that advertisers and others want is becoming more difficult.

The Average Household and the Representative Individual

Professor Elton Mayo was chair of Psychology and Ethics at Queensland University, Australia, when he gave the major address at the Second Advertising Men's Conference in 1920. Mayo went on to be internationally famous in the area of industrial psychology for the Hawthorne Experiments of the 1930s and 1940s. In his address he made an extraordinary statement that the advertising agencies' role is to 'educate in the broadest and highest sense of the term'. Their role is to identify the reasons for social disorder. Their role is to persuade in order to protect order. But Mayo goes further – 'you must think for the housewife'. While we can see Mayo as being paternalistic and condescending to women, Mayo is certainly not being derogatory. Housewives were not only the major advertising market of the time, such that the audience was typically conceptualized as a 'she' in this era and the most important business of advertising agencies was to collect data about housewives, but advertising agencies were seen to be entering into a particular kind of social contract with housewives. They were to be seen by the housewives themselves to be doing research: 'and if you do that for her and if she finds you are doing it, you will have her confidence' (Braverman 1974).

Mayo anticipated the complex role advertising and marketing plays in contemporary society. Advertising and marketing are not simply part of a merchandising and management cycle but are an essential part of a governance cycle in research. Research about audiences has to be seen to be legitimate and an accurate representation of the interests of the audiences concerned. Mayo believed that if 'thinking for' the audience became seen to be manipulation then it would not be seen to be legitimate. 'Satanism' and 'Bolshevism' in this context are not to be met by rage and hate. Scaremongering or unplanned campaigns against them must be accomplished by other means which seek out motivations and seek to enter into the same relation with audiences as Mayo prescribed for housewives.

At first glance, this might all sound a little contrived. It is important to remember, however, that Mayo was talking at a time when there was an intense interest by advertisers in the discipline of psychology and, of course, behaviourist psychology in particular. The interest in psychology came from a need to gain *predictive advantage* with advertising, to be able to anticipate what consumers would do. Classification or categorization of consumers was one step, but prediction was not possible if those categorizations did not represent possible motivations. Today, we talk about people-as-categories without second thought, labelling generations as Generation X, Generation Y, the Net Generation and so on, as though whole collectives had specific psychological characteristics that could predict behaviour.

Advertising agencies employed high-level academics in order to investigate the link between advertising, motivation and product purchase. J.B. Watson, for example, worked for J. Walter Thompson (JWT) while keeping his post at university, and investigated the link between advertising, consumer motivation and product purchase. In 1922 Watson was appointed vice president of advertising of JWT. One of JWT's major studies at this time was in Australia. As mentioned in Chapter 2, it employed two psychologists, A.H. Martin and Rudolph Simmat, to conduct research into the categorization of Australian consumers of advertising. In 1927 Martin established the Australian Institute of Industrial Psychology in Sydney with the support of University of Sydney's Psychology Department and the Chamber of Manufacturers. He used his own mental tests that he had created at Columbia University to measure consumer attitudes towards advertising. Simmat, his colleague, was research manager for JWT in Sydney and involved in the standardization of art production and research procedures in advertising. As discussed, Simmat and Martin divided Australian society into four market segments based on income and housewives, similar to those used by McNair and Anderson but with an additional interest in the psychology of the housewife. Classes A and B were high-income housewives. Classes C and D were average or below average income housewives. The categories, derived from interviews with over 30,000 women, were used to assist in creative production, helping JWT to fashion advertising for women within each of the classes. They were also used to make judgements about how to get information back from those classes, with recommendations from Simmat that interviewers avoid women in Class D and interview the husbands only (Simmat 1933).

Advertisers at this time were not only interested in enumeration – the number of people who looked at or listened to advertisements – but categorization – the *types* of people who looked or listened. This meant that the idea of making up 'representative' people became important in the whole advertising enterprise. The phrase 'the average housewife' is a description of a type of person that represents all other people within a collective. Moreover, these types could be counted. Categories of person could be linked to statistics and statistical decisions on what those types might do. When Crossley started audience ratings, therefore, it was not in order to just create a head count. Embedded in the ratings were the Classes. It is not surprising that CAB, the advertisers, wanted to keep its ratings secret. This was the first real linking of categorization to numbers. The broadcasters got the ratings on the black market up until 1936 when CAB gave in to industry pressure to give stations access.

It was not until later in the 1940s and 1950s, however, that the statistical representation of types of people in probability samples became commonplace. At that point, the 'average listener' could be found without having to interview 30,000 or more people; the average listener could be found from small samples and generalized to the whole of that statistical collective. Advertisers could talk about Class C being the average listener, for example, and the major user of radio. The categorizations of the audience, therefore, were definitely imposed and not 'bottom up', derived from interviews from the audience. Indeed, in order to find out whether someone was in A, B, C or D Classes for telephone interviews, research was done by rental classification in the geographic location where the telephone respondent lived – exchange and street address (Beville 1940). In the case of personal interviews it was left to the judgement of the interviewer to which class a person or household belonged. The social stratification of households in the early ratings radio surveys was: A, US$5,000 and over; B, US$3,000–$4,999; C, US$2,000–$2,999; and D, under US$2,000. But as Beville pointed out, none of these categorizations of individuals represented the typical, or the *normal*, listener (Beville 1940). The normal listener was a statistical construction based on the data.

Mayo's arguments about 'thinking for' the housewife assumed that the scientific derivation of categories of people, done properly, would be an accurate representation of the people concerned. There was, for Mayo, no manipulation of categories or subjective distortion when science was involved together with the proper application of psychological principles. With due respect to Mayo, of course, a simple translation of science to human society does not work and the influence of ideology is inevitable when constructing 'classes' of people for the purposes of analysis. Where Mayo is right, though, is that 'thinking for' people brings with it significant responsibilities, and his ethos for the role of the advertising agency remains a testament again to the strong democratic theme that existed among the early audience researchers and ratings intellectuals.

Early ratings data collection from samples, however, could involve very close contact with families. Gwen Nelson, field manager for McNair, as we found, knew all the families in the ratings samples. The categorizations A,B,C,D,E were chosen in McNair's procedure by the fieldworker's personal decision on which classification a household belonged to:

I went overseas in '55 to find out a little more about TV research. In 1956 we had the Olympic Games in Melbourne. I supervised the first TV survey ever done in Australia, and we combined it with our usual survey, checking what you were listening to or what you saw yesterday. And I remember very clearly, there were 3.2 per cent of Melbourne residents, according to us, that had a TV set. No one in the upper classes, around Richmond/Carlton area. The interviewer used to check if they found anyone who had a TV what they viewed yesterday, and how many people viewed. There was one house in Richmond, a very poor house, a very much an E, there was a huge group of people. And as the woman said, 'We're the lucky ones. We're the only one in the street that has a TV set. And we charge adults sixpence and children threepence and they all bring their own chairs to watch TV.' And that was the beginning of TV in 1956. (Nelson 2000)

The 'home' or 'household' was the first major unit of analysis for the purposes of categorization in ratings. Those units were then classified by Classes, the main target groups. Advertising and product planning revolved around the 'households' in Classes as the target groups. The unit of analysis then shifted to the 'individual' and a broader coverage of demographics and time use when mobile radios emerged and when peoplemeters came into operation. Today, this has been broadened again to the use of product purchase data, 'buyer graphics', rather than only general demographics to define target groups, with the calculation of achieved television ratings against buyer graphics (with a resulting optimization of the television schedules).

Ratings definitions of audiences are abstract definitions of the audience can in turn affect how the people see themselves. Ian Hacking makes this point in terms of the use of statistical language generally:

> We can think of average height as an abstract – the convenient result of an arithmetical operation – but we can also begin to think of it as a 'real' feature of a population. In 1988, it was noted that the longevity of Japanese has been increasing every year, to the point where the Japanese are now the most long-lived nation on earth. We find it hard not to think of this as being a real feature of Japanese life and culture, just as 'real' as the fact that Japanese corporate entities have among them the world's largest accumulation of disposable capital for investment. (Hacking 1990: 108)

Home Studies and the Public

It would be a serious error to assume that research into audience ratings and homes has only been about statistical estimation and not the in-depth investigation of the domestic lives of the people themselves. Historically, wherever the audience-ratings convention has held there have been significant and ongoing studies of the domestic environments of homes. This is perhaps not surprising. Everyday life has changed dramatically over the past century together with the technology that supports it. Ratings have always been recalibrated to changed circumstances. Mobility with the radio transistor created changes, computers created changes, as has the changing work and lifestyle habits; among many others. It is beyond the scope of this book to cover all the home studies in the United States, United Kingdom and Australia. However, the US Committee on Nationwide Television Audience Measurement (CONTAM) reports are an excellent example of the depth to which home studies go. *How People Use Television I* and *II* looked at television use in detail, how they interact with the medium, what they consider to be watching television (Committee on Nationwide Television Audience Measurement 1991; Committee on Nationwide Television Audience Measurement 1992). The studies found, for example, that: the average US person in the 1990s watched television five nights a week for two hours or more and primarily watched it for entertainment; 80 per cent of people knew in advance what they were going to watch on any given night; and half of women and 40 per cent of men did other things while watching television (reading, doing paperwork or chores, playing a game, eating a snack). The Systems for Measuring and Reporting Television (SMART) reports likewise covered in depth quantitative and qualitative aspects of households, including among others: 'Beyond ratings: what it means to be in the television audience'; 'A set of one's own: television sets in children's bedrooms'; 'Children's and teen's research workshop: progress on the hard to measure'; and 'Children's lifestyles study'.

It might be argued that citizens do not take much interest in the abstract categories created to describe them in the audience ratings. But this is far from the case. In the United States, as in Australia and the United Kingdom, fan mail operated on a massive scale. For example, NBC alone received 20,000 letters a day from radio listeners all over the country throughout the 1920s and 1930s. Letters, postcards, telephone calls and telegrams received in the course of a year as a result of national advertising on the air ran into the millions (Banks 1981). Hugh M. Beville, in his first job with NBC, recognized the advantages of fan mail and created regular ways of soliciting, collecting and interpreting the mail. The difficulties with fan mail, however, were that it was not collected in one place, with some of it going to a radio station, some of it to the networks, some to the personalities, some to the sponsor and, not least, some to government authorities. These letters often made it clear how listeners felt about ratings, about programmes and about personalities, among many other things. This fan-mail 'voice' of the audience declined over the 1920s as other ways of organizing voices emerged. By the 1960s active interest in how the media worked was represented in groups such as Accuracy in Media, Action for Better Community, Action for Children's Television, American Council for Better Broadcasts, American Medical Association, Federal Communications Bar Association, National Association for Better Broadcasting, National Audience Board, National Black Network, National Citizens Committee for Broadcasting, National Council of the Churches of Christ, National News Council, National Organization for Women, Parent Teachers Associations, Prime Time School Television, Spanish International Network and United Church of Christ. This is only a sample. There were 32 entries under the *Aspen Handbook on Media* called Media Action Groups.

The ratings provider did not directly need consent from these groups to run its audience ratings research. However, it did need consent from those participating directly in its panels or research for permission to enter into their households and their personal lives.

Audience Consent

The dynamics of recruitment into audience ratings research are complex and thorough, meeting the highest standards of any market research code of ethics, leaving aside problems of sampling bias for other reasons. The letter opposite from McNair Anderson from the early 1970s gives an insight into the appeals the ratings provider made for consent from the listener or viewer. The letter makes it clear that the participant's household is *representative* of families in their own area and that their cooperation is essential because they cannot be replaced by just any other household.

McNair Anderson

Marketing Reasearch
Advertising Research
Media Audience Measurement
Social Research
Nationwide Omnibus Surveys

40 Miller Street North Sydney
Australia 2060
Telephone 929 6122
Telex 26260
Cables:IPORES North Sydney

Also in Melbourne and Auckland

SURVEY OF RADIO LISTENING

Dear Household,

This brochure is to ask you to take part in a survey of Radio Listening in your area.

Naturally, the two questions which immediately come to mind are - "Why are we chosen" and "Why should we co-operate?"

These two questions can be answered very simply.

Firstly, there are a great many families living in the area covered by this study. Obviously, we cannot contact every one of these families, so we have scientifically selected a number of families in each of 100 different localities in such a way that the **Selected Families** will in total be truly representative of all the families in the area. Your family is one of these **SELECTED HOUSEHOLDS.**

Secondly, to ensure a high degree of accuracy in the results of the survey, a Household, once it has been selected, cannot in any circumstances, be replaced by another household. Therefore the co-operation of your **household is of vital importance.**

The object of this survey is to obtain basic facts to enable those concerned to keep abreast of rapidly changing conditions and to guide them in their programme planning to give continually improved programmes and service to Listeners.

Australia and New Zealand
representatives for
Starch/Inra/Hooper

Research facilities in over
60 countries.

Figure 9.1 McNair Anderson Survey of Radio Listening household appeal, 1970s

The appeal to *civic duty* was not accidental. People were surrendering their time and privacy to provide details to the ratings provider. The ratings provider, at the same time, understood the burdens that this might place on a household. Of course, a ratings panel, unlike a one-off survey, adds additionally to the participant burden because the data collection is continuous. The rationale of small samples representing big populations addressed important problems of intrusion. The whole nation did not have to be surveyed to obtain quality data. The participating household's sacrifice of its time to help researchers also limited intrusion to the minimum necessary.

Today, the high quality of recruitment techniques for panels remains. The environment in which Gwen Nelson at McNair's recruited her participants, however, has gone forever. As we saw in Chapter 2, there are special factors that appear to be affecting audience participation and consent for participation in ratings panels, not least the issue of intrusion into a household's technology for data collection. Non-response to surveys, though, is not just an audience-ratings issue. People are refusing to participate in surveys across a range of demographics and in many countries. We know that:

1 Non-response to surveys has been increasing, with steep declines after 1996.

2 The increase in non-response rates is happening for most types of surveys with telephone and personal interview highest.

3 Increases in non-response is a global phenomenon.

4 There does not appear to be a single explanation for the trends in non-response.

5 Long-term trend surveys provide the empirical evidence of changes in response and non-response.

Curtin, Presser and Singer, in their study on changes in telephone survey non-response over the past quarter of a century in the United States (Curtin, Presser and Singer 2005), demonstrate these trends dramatically. The University of Michigan's Survey of Consumer Attitudes (SCA) shows non-response is marked by three distinct periods, a gradual decline in 1979 to 1989, a plateau from 1989 to 1996, followed by a steep decline after 1996 towards figures as high as 40 per cent. This trend in non-response can be found in other studies and the US Census was proactive in 2000 in attempting to address non-response rates. To understand non-response we need to understand what is a response. The most common definition for response is 'sampling units completing a survey' divided by 'all sampled units'. But there are different types of refusal. There could be a direct refusal, non-contact (the householder never answers or sends survey back; the survey not delivered; the household could not be found), partial completion of the survey, or an inability to participate (literacy or language barrier, or legal status in the society).

The motivations for non-response in the modern context are many. Once civic and, in the American context, patriotic duty has left the mix as a motivation to join a survey, there are many motivational factors remaining to encourage non-response including: too many demands from survey researchers; respondents being too busy to meet the demands; concerns about misrepresentation and privacy; and, where the survey involves configuring home equipment, wiring, telephone and internet settings, concerns about the integrity of a home's media environment.

The survey researcher is, at the same time, faced with a range of access issues, such as answering machines, caller ID, mobile phones, multiple phone numbers, unlisted numbers, gated communities and limited access apartments, among others. Keep in mind that non-response from all these factors does not always equal non-response bias. However, if a survey researcher meets the point where the 'vitally important' type of household cannot be recruited in sufficient numbers to meet sampling needs, then sampling bias becomes a problem. Interviewing techniques and other factors, of course, can affect bias. But recruitment is key to having a sample and without that there is no participant to interview or household's media use to monitor.

Demand for more information from audiences or consumers is being matched by non-response from those audiences or consumers. Just as there has always been a trade-off between Case Rich and Data Rich designs, there have been trade-offs with participants on limits of intrusion. An understanding of these trade-offs has been integral to the audience-ratings convention historically and into the future. Equally integral to the convention is the longstanding ambition to marry ratings data with other data to create comprehensive systems of data measurement. These two tensions came together in Project Apollo. The desire for more information from people at all times led parties of the audience ratings to come together to try to create a single method for capturing all behavioural data.

Project Apollo started to take shape in 2004 as different parties to the audience-ratings and retail-panel conventions came together to try to use the same households to measure different things. Data was to be collected from 30,000 US households and involved close cooperation between ACNielsen, providing product-purchase data from its HomeScan panel, and Arbitron, providing media exposure information from its passive, Portable People Meter (PPM) technology. This was scaled down to 5,000 households. The aim of Project Apollo was to establish the ultimate single-source design, with purchase data linked to exposure, indoor and outdoor. The PPM system works by inserting an inaudible code into a broadcast transmission at the radio station. The small pager-type device, which is worn by the respondent throughout the day, uses a microphone to capture the codes and subsequently download them to a central computer. While technically feasible, participants in the Project Apollo study did not like the demands made upon them, demonstrating the limits of intrusion. The costs of getting the information, at the same time, were perceived to be beyond those who demanded it.

Over US$100 million was spent on the development of this project with Proctor & Gamble a key sponsor, and Kraft Foods, Pepsi, Pfizer, SC Johnson and Wal-Mart on the project's steering committee. Various reasons were advanced for the scaling back of Project Apollo to a pilot study and then cancellation. Arbitron said that there were not enough marketers willing to make the long-term commitment, and Proctor & Gamble said that Nielsen and Arbitron did not have the patience or money to invest in order to work through the challenges. There were spin-offs from the study, including the Touchpoints product. But audience resistance to intimate and extensive data collection was also a factor. This is not only a matter for traditional media or single-source experiments as audiences have voiced similar concerns in internet, cable TV and personal video recorder environments as well.

Some companies are using professional survey takers (PSTs) to ensure that they get usable survey results for targeted demographics. At one stage, comScore's behavioural tracking panel showed that some major panels had 30 per cent of their surveys being taken by less than 1 per cent of their panellists (Bortner 2008). Audiences in a broadcast ratings panel are not bought, although incentives might be provided as reward for participation. The ratings has relied on its identity as a pro-social service and relied on its volunteers as a source of its integrity. The PST phènomenon, however, raises a broader issue about voluntary labour in the audience-research industry and whether audiences should have a stake in the valuable data that they provide. In the case of TiVo, it is voluntary audience labour that produces the data that TiVo packages and sells on. The audience is not paid for this 'work' nor does it receive a dividend from the sale of its data. The PSTs have clearly recognized their value in the market and no doubt it will not be long until the issue becomes a more generalized, society-wide one. While it is doubtful whether ratings sampling needs will permit using PSTs, ratings provision operates within environments where being paid for participation is increasingly common.

The Knowledge Aggregators

Knowledge Aggregators typically use the capacity of interactive systems such as the internet and set-top boxes and personal video recorders (PVRs) routinely to register and record activity from users and viewers. The creation and maintenance of large datasets is intrinsic to the very design of these media – the internet, cable TV and PVRs. Having created these datasets and functions it is a seemingly small step to try to monetize them, turning the search engine company, the pay-TV provider and the PVR facility into a knowledge aggregator. But unlike the traditional forms of audience measurement which needed to be built on top of TV sets and devices retroactively fitted to sets with the active consent of participants, in these media the datasets, the information, are inbuilt whether as billing information or the registration of sites visited. Audience surveys are being built through the ordinary transactions and activities of people rather than through the active involvement of respondents. If the problem in the traditional ratings world was getting consent for participation, the problem in the knowledge aggregation world is getting informed consent for the aggregation of personal information.

What makes this area especially important for a book on audience ratings is that we are increasingly seeing these entities use their proprietorial databases to generate and market ratings-like information about the audiences for their services. Such knowledge aggregators are promising to fill an acknowledged gap in the media measurement of small audiences, and to provide more detailed profiles of the audiences for their services and their media consumption. They are also promoting themselves as providing more accurate information because it is built on registration systems somewhat analogous to Nielsen's Audimeter in the 1940s – measuring actual rather than self-reported behaviours. So at three distinct levels these aggregators are important: they represent another way of collecting and organizing the sample population to the side of the traditional ratings instruments; they represent potential competitors for ratings services; and in doing these they are fundamentally altering the compact audiences have with collecting and sampling agencies.

In many ways these aggregators have a much weaker relation to their audiences. With click-through contracts the order of the day there is a far weaker connection with audiences as volunteers and as a workforce for the ratings provider. Instead, the audience is forced into agreeing to participate in these services as a means of getting access to the services offered. This inevitably gives rise to a sense among audiences that knowledge aggregators are operating with, at best, only weak consent from them. In not being as centrally involved in the transaction they are likely to feel exploited in that someone else is making money out of them and their behaviour (so are increasingly likely to not respond to arguments of civic duty in other contexts); and they are likely to experience themselves as being treated as a commodity and a number more than as a representative population who is being respected by the process.

Knowledge aggregation takes many forms on the internet. User tracking is only one form. The term *news aggregator* describes websites or search engines that select, retrieve and link news from anywhere on the internet. Google News is an aggregator of news from thousands of sources. An RSS (Really Simple Syndication) is an aggregator as it pulls together threads relevant to the person who has subscribed to it. Knowledge aggregators like Google, as we know, are keen to be the ratings providers of the future. This is not surprising. The monetization of internet audiences is now well established. RSVP, an internet dating site, had 600,000 members in 2005 when Fairfax bought it for AUS$38.92 million. Fairfax group executive Alan Revell told the media that online dating had become a mainstream classifieds market (Australian Associated Press 2005). Jupiter Research estimated that in the United States alone, online dating will increase from US$900 million in 2007 to US$1.9 billion in 2012. This comes as no surprise, with internet advertising spending growing six-fold from 2004–9 (IBISWorld 2009). Advertisers and marketers have been quick to recognize that online sites have the potential to deliver rich data about audiences and the negative effects of this have also been recognized (Andrejevic 2002; Andrejevic 2003; Andrejevic 2005; Andrejevic 2006).

Audiences, though, have reacted negatively to attempts to retrieve their data from their sites (Fogel and Nehmad 2009). As discussed in Chapter 4, in 2009 Facebook planned to exploit the private information of its 150 million members (now 500 million) by creating one of the world's largest market research databases. Facebook would have allowed multinational companies to selectively target its members in order to research the appeal of new products (Musil 2009). Users were outraged and Facebook had to revert back to its old privacy policies (Walters 2009). The willingness of people to put intimate details about themselves on the internet is not the same as giving consent to have that data harvested and used by the service providers who store the data. Raynes-Goldie conducted a study to understand how Facebook users under 30 understood privacy by conducting a year-long ethnographic study starting in January 2008. The study was undertaken in Toronto, Canada, home to the second largest regional Facebook network. Raynes-Goldie concluded that:

> Contrary to much of the mainstream rhetoric, my participants *did* care about privacy. Specifically, my participants were more concerned with what I call their *social* privacy when using Facebook, rather their *institutional* privacy. In other words, they were more concerned about controlling access to personal information rather than how the company behind Facebook (which I will call Facebook Inc. for simplicity's sake) and its partners might use that information … The importance of social privacy was further demonstrated by the lengths to which some participants would go to maintain their social privacy, and in some cases, violate the privacy of others. (Raynes-Goldie 2010)

One of the main subversive ways that users were trying to protect their social privacy was through the use of an alias. The goal of these users, Raynes-Goldie found, was 'to make it difficult for people to find them via search, or to attribute their Facebook activities to their "real" identities'. But in using names in this fashion they were going against the Facebook 'Terms of Service', which stipulates that users must use their real names and identities when using the site. Indeed, Facebook will delete accounts using algorithms crawling the site to identify fake identities (Breyer and Zuckerberg 2005). The problem of identity is, of course, fundamental to social media, where people need to be able to trust that people are who they say they are, and, in any marketing research, lying about age and other demographics biases results. Facebook wants its online participants to be real people not only to protect other users but also to turn data into a revenue stream.

The ideal advertising situation for the advertiser is where an advertisement can be guaranteed to go to the right target person or group. A real person on Facebook with their real date of birth represents powerful data. The problem of how personal data is collected and how it might be safeguarded in digital contexts has not been missed by regulators. In 2009 a US House of Representatives subcommittee investigated whether Canoe Ventures, created by six cable TV operators, was going to use set-top boxes to monitor and store what people watch and then rollout targeted advertisements based on set-top data to viewers. If Canoe Ventures wanted to use set-top box data for targeted advertising, then it had to comply with existing cable laws protecting private consumer information. Using actual personal information to target advertisements is not allowed, except where an opt-in facility is provided (for example, clicking on a pizza advertisement to order a pizza on an interactive screen). The idea that privacy issues have been fully addressed, however, is far from the case.

> The biggest question in the industry, it seems, is not whether data from cable set-tops will be culled and analysed to give greater clarity on who is watching what – and when – but whether it turns into a new revenue stream for the cable operators, satellite companies and telcos who have control over the data. Mediapost is reporting that the advertiser and media company consortium CIMM (Coalition for Innovative Media Measurement) has sent out a questionnaire to the set-top box cabal pointedly asking the question of whether they plan to sell set-top box data, and whether they are setting up a unit that has the aim of eventually making viewership data a revenue stream. But, to me, asking about whether the data might be turned into a revenue stream is getting a bit ahead of itself. Before these companies start dispersing data, they need to focus on the issue of consumer privacy, which is the 800-lb. gorilla in the room, whether the industry is doing enough to safeguard privacy or not. The CIMM questionnaire also asks this: 'If privacy is currently a concern, how long do you think it will take for privacy issues to dissipate?' (Taylor 2010)

TiVo is a good example of a company that follows the privacy legislation but where even its subscribers wonder whether their data are protected. TiVo launched its StopllWatch ratings service in 2007, offering a sortable database of ratings for nationally run programmes and advertisements from cable and broadcast networks, with data going back to September 2006. The service tracks ratings for 93 networks from 5.00 a.m. to 11.30 p.m. In 2009 it launched StopllWatch for local markets, offering a sample of 25,000 TiVo subscribers in the top 20 markets down to 5,000 in the smallest local markets. Markets that are electronically measured by the current panels in comparison use less than 1,000 households. TiVo sporadically conducts random samplings of its subscribers.

TiVo found itself queried by its own audiences after one of its sporadic random samplings of 20,000 viewers, in this case of its Super Bowl broadcast:

> Janet Jackson's Super Bowl flash dance was shocking in more ways than one: some TiVo users say the event brought home the realization that their beloved digital video recorders are watching them, too. On Monday, TiVo said the exposure of Jackson's breast during her halftime performance was the most-watched moment to date on its device, which, when combined with the TiVo subscription service, lets viewers pause and 'rewind' live television broadcasts, among other features. TiVo said users had watched the skin-baring incident nearly three times more than any other moment during the Super Bowl broadcast, sparking headlines that dramatically publicized the power of the company's longstanding data-gathering practices. 'It's just sort of creepy,' longtime TiVo subscriber Sandra Munozshe wrote in an e-mail to CNET News.com. (Cnet News 2004)

TiVo has an opt-out number and publicly said that it has disclosed its data-gathering practices in user agreements, stripping out any information that could be traced back to individual viewers. TiVo could investigate an individual's viewing habits but it does not, according to TiVo. It does now and then take data from a random sampling of 20,000 homes viewing a particular programme. "'I can understand people's concerns," said spokesman Scott Sutherland. "But when weighted against reality, they are unfounded"' (Cnet News 2004).

> 'Make no mistake, I do clearly love the box,' engineer and longtime TiVo user Jerrell Wilson wrote in an e-mail to CNET News.com. 'I have been a tireless sales rep with all my friends. I should be on commission from TiVo. Thus arises the most severe form of anger: that deriving from a perceived betrayal of trust.' (Cnet News 2004)

What is occurring at present among audiences is the same phenomenon that occurred in Project Apollo. It is not that gathering extensive information from audiences is morally wrong or that companies like TiVo have breached regulations.

What is happening at present is the growing recognition among audiences about what is, indeed, happening with their data, identified or de-identified. The very act of them 'feeling watched' or that they feel they have to subvert the very services they join signal that these audiences are not in an audience-ratings convention that satisfies them – indeed, not in a ratings convention at all. The authors argue that the combination of increasing non-response rates and audience sensitivity about how data about them is collected and used through electronic means is a toxic mix. More than any other issue in the audience-ratings convention, it is this one that needs an agreement that guarantees audience participation in research in future.

Summary

Audiences are represented by statistics and those statistics are used as a representation of audience behaviour. The optimum delivery of an advertising message is one that goes exactly to the target group or individual concerned. In traditional media planning this would often mean there would be an element of waste in a media plan. Audience ratings statistics would give an indication when a particular target group was watching a particular programme. An advertisement placed at the same time, however, might or might not reach all of its audience. Repetition of an advertisement, therefore, guaranteed that a certain proportion of the target group would have at least seen the advertisement once. Set-top box and online audience data promise the tantalizing opportunity of placing an advertisement much more precisely with target individuals or groups.

The temptation to go what must seem a small step further and use the personal identity of the audience in media planning is enormous and should not be underestimated. The audience, however, remains one of the most important, if not the most important, player in the audience measurement. Its consent is still sought and needs to be sought. Its reactions to how it is represented are still important in decisions made about them. There have been several trends that are affecting the position that audience consent has in the audience-ratings convention.

Intimate publics: Audiences are now putting intimate details online and those data are of interest to knowledge aggregators. Just as there has become in the audience mind a blurring between telemarketing and real research, so has there become a blurring between big systems harvesting data from individuals and groups and the public interest side of audience ratings. The TiVo example is instructive here. TiVo might have covered all its privacy bases in drawing data from its 20,000 panel who watched the Super Bowl. But what is of interest for our purposes is the reaction of the audience, even those who had given consent. The idea that TiVo had broken trust reflected a deep seated feeling among the audience that something had gone wrong in the arrangement.

Non-response: The trends towards non-participation in survey research are likely to continue. This raises a broader societal concern about how data about individuals are going to be collected for the planning and delivery of services, let alone audience ratings. It is not within the compass of this book to go into detail about the problems of a survey-research-saturated public but there can be little doubt that audiences, where possible, are starting to use means to (i) distort their identity in order to protect their identity, and (ii) use technological tools to limit the access of researchers.

Limits to intrusion: The advantage of the earlier regimes of audience ratings was in their capacity to limit the intrusion of research into the lives of all individuals in society, by virtue of a representative sample. The amount of information sought was, likewise, limited. However, the demands for more information about individuals have escalated with no equivalent change to the audience-ratings convention and the role of audiences. Much of the literature focuses on how to collect more data, not on how to create new ways of enhancing audience consent. Project Apollo could have and should have foreseen what would happen with its audience. Audiences, as we have long known, put limits on intrusion, physical and mental.

10 The Critics

The whole business of audience measurement has to do with knowing the unknowable. The problem of modernity does not apply to previous societies where it is not necessary to know what a sovereign but dispersed and anonymous population thinks, either for political reasons or for campaigning commercial reasons. There has been since the last 200 or 300 years an increasing statisticalization, if that's the word, of the general population of modern societies in order to try and understand what it is that they know, what it is that they would like, and how they would behave. J. Hartley (Hartley 1992a)

Rather, as commodities themselves, the ratings were constructed in response to market pressures, including competition and monopolization as well as continuities and discontinuities in demand. The ratings producer was no scientist motivated by curiosity, but rather a company seeking its self-interest through the profitable manipulation of demand. E.R. Meehan (Meehan 1990: 201)

In Chapter 9, the authors introduced the audience as one of the most important parties to the audience-ratings convention. The audience is frequently missed as a party because it is often seen as a passive, not active, member of the ratings process (at least from outside the convention). We also saw that advertisers and marketers have been quick to recognize that online sites have the potential to deliver rich data about audiences and, indeed, are using aggressive methods to harvest those data. These 'intimate publics' online have reacted to harvesting, and audience research has come under real fire for being more like a surveillance tool than a democratic, non-intrusive, non-threatening form of research (Andrejevic 2002; Andrejevic 2003; Andrejevic 2005; Andrejevic 2006).

Hartley and Meehan's criticism that (i) audiences are 'unknowable', (ii) that statistical knowledge about them is a fiction, and (iii) that the motivations for their measurement are primarily commercial and a function of modern capitalist markets have all been made by industry actors including advertising strategists, sometimes many years previously. At the same time criticism of audience ratings as having negative effects as a force that leads media content to a common denominator is itself part of the promotions and strategy of different media providers such as HBO, which promotes its separation from this world under the slogan of being 'not television' while simultaneously using ratings data to build audiences! At the same time criticisms of the ratings as an adjunct to surveillance of modern society, intruding into people's privacy, are matched by proponents of ratings surveys that stress informed consent and the importance of the audience member as a respected respondent and informant, and often denounce new media audience development strategies that diminish the audience member and compromise the integrity of audience research.

While Hartley and Meehan might have provided a generation of media studies students with a criticism of the ratings, their criticism is only a small component of a now extensive critical vocabulary surrounding the ratings. In this chapter the authors provide an overview of the arguments of the critics of the ratings through the eyes of one of the most famous ratings intellectuals, Leo Bogart.

The Broader Context

Every opinion survey assumes that everyone can have an opinion; in other words, that producing an opinion is something available to all. At the risk of offending a naively democratic sentiment, I would contest this first premise. Secondly: it is assumed that all opinions are of equal value. I think it can be shown that this is untrue and that the accumulation of opinions do not all have the same strength leads to the production of meaningless artefacts. The third implicit postulate is this: putting the same question to everyone assumed that there is a consensus on what the problems are, in other words that there is agreement on the questions that are worth asking. These three postulates, it seems to me, entail a whole series of distortions that are found even when all the conditions of methodological rigour are fulfilled in collecting and analysing the data. Pierre Bourdieu (Bourdieu 1993: 149)

Pierre Bourdieu is saying that the methodology of public opinion research does not capture audience or public preferences. Public opinion research and audience ratings research are mirrors of each other in this regard. Bourdieu would no doubt have the same criticism of audience ratings; that summing the exposure of individuals to thousands of television or radio sets hides real differences in opinion or preference. Images of audiences – perceptions of what the audience or public *is* and what it *wants* – are in the heads of individual media professionals, whether television scriptwriters or journalists or programme selectors. Audience images are also in the strategies of organizations (Ettema and Whitney 1994: 9). Audiences in media organizations only have influence if they are recognized as being real and reflecting real preferences and choices by individuals. These institutionally effective audiences include *measured audiences* that are generated by research, sold by media channels and bought by advertisers; *specialized* or *segmented audiences* whose particular interests are anticipated – or created – and then met by content producers; and *hypothesized audiences* whose interest, convenience and necessity are, presumably, protected by regulators (Ettema and Whitney 1994: 5–6).

Bourdieu, in his reflection on public opinion research, appears to be talking primarily about snapshot research where individual and discrete surveys are undertaken on particular topics – not longitudinal surveys or indeed the more complex combination of methods deployed by those like Paul Lazarsfeld. Napoli (Napoli 2011) would probably disagree with Bourdieu on the argument that modern public opinion surveys do not measure what they say they measure. However, he would certainly argue that for the academic audience researcher that ratings data are not an adequate representation of audience media exposure. Napoli says that ratings analysis should be defined in terms of the source and purpose of the data being analysed. On this view, ratings analysis is defined as 'the analysis of the data, whatever its orientation, used by media industry stakeholders to assess performance and success in the audience marketplace' (Napoli 2011: 171). We are in an evolutionary stages where alternative criteria for monetization of audience have emerged, including recall, engagement and appreciation.

It would be reductive to propose a model that simply said that all measurement techniques do not yield genuine preferences of audiences. Napoli's idea of evolution (Napoli 2011) is instructive here as is Bourdon and Méadel's argument that measurements cannot be thought of independently of the audience:

> A complicated set of socio-technical conventions has to be agreed upon, which can change according to relations of the partners in the industry (public/private, big/small, advertisers/broadcasters ...), the different stages in television history, the technology available and developed at those different stages. The audience can never be considered independently of the instruments used to 'measure' it. (Bourdon and Méadel 2011: 9)

We have to be careful therefore not to make category errors in terms of where criticisms of audience ratings come from. Sometimes the criticisms will come from within the key stakeholders of the ratings, sometimes more broadly in society on how ratings are used and monopoly status, and from academic concerns of power and surveillance. The following typologies provide an insight into those criticisms.

The day-to-day operation of audience ratings attracts criticism from those who are directly involved in them, as media buyers, broadcasters, advertisers or as audiences expecting representation within the ratings itself. These criticisms are about the mechanics of audience ratings and focus on data collection (accuracy, representativeness, responsiveness, size of sample, questions of response rates). The ratings provider itself is often criticized over its power or its lack of oversight, separate from data collection issues. Academic criticism can cover all these areas, but most often you will find criticism under the following broad categories:

Criticisms from stakeholders

- from rival providers about the adequacy of the data collection method itself;
- from advertisers and media buyers on accuracy;
- from broadcasters sometimes representing minority constituencies and markets concerned about the makeup of the panel;
- from social advocacy groups concerned about inclusion of marginal groups;
- from politicians and non-governmental organizations on non-polling of rural constituencies.

Criticisms of ratings provider

- unresponsive monopoly provider;
- 'law unto itself';
- no check or audit (or weakly developed checks and audits);
- slow to innovate.

Criticisms from ratings provider

- many ratings users apply ratings beyond their design (without recognizing statistical tolerances and limits);
- ratings users often suffer from 'Ratingitis' – Archibald Crossley's term to describe an over-reliance on ratings;
- media buyers are often not educated in depth on the methodology and statistics of ratings.

Academic criticism

- audience ratings as surveillance;
- watching as a form of labour;

- ratings as a discursive construct that precludes actual social audiences (invented audiences, imagined collectivity);

- abstracted empiricism (contrived, artefactual, artificial endeavour, technicist);

- cultural democracy (ratings not the best way of expressing preferences in any description of culture and cultural needs).

Audience ratings are an enormously complex social structure and it is rare to see a comprehensive critique of ratings, inside and out. However, Leo Bogart is one of those rare figures that cross boundaries.

The Bogart Persona

For more than thirty years Leo Bogart was a trenchant and very public critic of the ratings as a technique of audience measurement and how they were being used by advertisers, advertising agencies, media planners and buyers, and the radio and television industries. Perhaps because his criticisms were always part of larger discussions, his sustained engagement with the ratings and the telling criticisms he made of its practice and uptake have not had close attention. Bogart had a wide-ranging agenda. He wrote about advertising strategy, the uses to be made of and possibilities for social and marketing research, the trajectories of the television industry and of commercial culture more generally, and developments in social and marketing research to which he contributed in no small measure. Bogart's criticisms mix practical experience and the theoretical knowledge of a methodologist, and are closely linked to who and what he was as an industry player and a virtuoso public commentator.

Bogart's insider reproach to the broadcast ratings is one of the field's most sustained and informed criticism of its shape and trajectory. Bogart devoted significant sections of a number of his books to a discussion of the ratings starting in the 1950s and extending right through to the mid-2000s. These criticisms document and criticize the transformation of the ratings and market research over the period to become the pre-eminent media research instrument in the United States and beyond. They cover the period in the United States when ratings provision was a contestable market and there were a number of rival ratings providers. They chart the beginning and maturing of auditing regimes for ratings provision out of the Congressional hearings, beginning in the late 1950s and moving into the 1960s, given pre-eminence through the quiz scandal. They cover the contemporary moment where ratings sit alongside an ensemble of other proprietary syndicated information sources increasingly constituting the horizon line of action for media planners and buyers, advertisers and media outlets.

While Bogart's criticisms provide one reason for scholarly attention, another is provided by the very thing which make his contributions difficult to assimilate to contemporary communication and media studies perspectives – the very public place from which he spoke. He was both a public intellectual and critic *and* an industry insider. As a social and marketing research methodologist he was responsible for major innovations in syndicated research. He was an important figure in a wide variety of research industry forums including the World Association for Public Opinion Research (WAPOR) and the American Association for Public Opinion Research (AAPOR). He was an AAPOR president, honoured with the association's highest award, and was closely linked with the association over his professional life. He may have been a trenchant critic but he contributed in no small measure to the very shape of the institutions and research enterprises that he criticized.

His criticisms therefore form an integral part of the *internal* intellectual and institutional history of the ratings and applied social research. He explicitly used his corporate and institutional location to prosecute a case for particular kinds of applied social research and particular approaches to this research. He did this in AAPOR meetings, in his publishing of books and articles of appeal to both specialist and non-specialist readers alike, and in his journal articles in specialist publications. He explicitly used his reputation as one of the foremost social and applied commercial research practitioners of his day to prosecute his case for the appropriate use of, disposition towards and flexible relation to social research. This combination of critical and practical attention made for a potent combination of ideas and public presentation. His criticisms were made with a combination of great intellect and rhetorical power. This speaking position is an important part of his story and provides his criticism of the ratings and ratings provision with contextual force. This combination of elements suggests that a close attention to the historical persona of Bogart as a ratings intellectual, critic and advocate for applied social research may provide a prism through which we can grasp aspects of a broader institutional history, including its transformation as an intellectual and professional field over Bogart's active professional life.

Bogart is perhaps best known today for the work of his later years – *Over the Edge* (Bogart 2005), *Commercial Culture* (Bogart 2000a) and *Finding Out – Personal Adventures in Social Research* (Bogart 2003). In this work he made very public criticism of the growing importance of media planning and buying, he was critical of the consolidation of applied social research into a handful of companies, he was appalled by the downsizing of television networks' research divisions and their increasing reliance upon syndicated data such as ratings in decision-making, he abhorred their increasing reliance upon 'mechanical' research tools such as peoplemeters and retail information derived from scanning technology and associated computing programs, and he argued for the baleful influence computers were having on the understanding of individual motivation and behaviour.

These trenchant criticisms when combined with his important earlier work on the social impact of television (Bogart 1958; Bogart 1972a), newspaper readership in the wake of television, opinion polling (Bogart 1972b) and advertising strategy (Bogart 1967; Bogart 1986a) not only provide us with a useful compendium of critical discussion of larger developments over the period but also, and more importantly for our purposes, point to larger institutional changes and changes in the kinds of practical knowledge, techniques and self-understandings of those practising, buying and using ratings research. These changes and realignments – changes which increasingly placed Bogart on the outside of an industry in which he had been an insider for so much of his professional life – can be usefully put into relief by a dual attention to both his ideas and thinking, and to the changing industry, institutional and intellectual formations within which this thought was exercised, valued and criticized.

Bogart's persona of an applied social researcher committed to innovations in social research method and practice across a wide variety of research areas is still alive today. But he himself recognized that the changes he was observing – larger corporate, institutional and research practice changes – were marking different configurations of research information and its application, and privileging the exercise of certain kinds of research knowledge over others. These new configurations were making the kind of thing he did, the positions he spoke from and the mix of institutional positions from which he spoke less in the mainstream than they once had been. It had become increasingly unlikely that his successors would have such a command of the territory or ability to exercise such a very public persona at the intersection of public debate, mediating the spaces among social research, marketing, advertisers, agencies and the like. As he himself recognized, research and researchers had become more specialized, and with this specialization and the growing routinization of the uses to be made of research outputs there was less space for mediating these knowledges. Bogart's successors could not and would not command the field in quite the same way as he once had.

By attending to what it means to be a ratings and social research methods intellectual – and the form and character of the comportments attendant to this role – we are able to investigate not simply an evidently extraordinary individual's career but also the kinds of mix of thought and action and self-presentation available to ratings intellectuals as they act and promulgate to inform and refine ratings instruments and industry uptake alike. The attention we are paying here to Bogart's persona is part of a larger attention we are paying to the history of the ratings, including the ratings as a form of intellectual, industrial and governmental thought.

To describe and do some justice to the knowledge work of these people the authors have called them ratings intellectuals. That designation helps us recognize the standing of these people as thinkers and methodologists dealing with – and thinking with – data and their limitations, and then communicating these limitations and possibilities to users and clients of the research. Bogart and his ilk brought their professional expertise to bear as advisors. They commonly produced information and data which was not always understood by those who used it and acted on its behalf. Bogart was also a methodologist responsible for innovations in syndicated research. He wanted to have discussions about methodology. Bogart was also a sceptic. And this sceptical persona was important to the role he played as enlightened critic and commentator on marketing, audience and broader trends in social research. Individuals such as Bogart need to be distinguished from those who use ratings and other forms of applied social research to construct a broadcast schedule, to analyse the reach and trajectory of a programme over a season and seasons, to identify appropriate 'slots' for broadcast messages and to report on the respective shares of broadcast networks.

Objections to Ratings

The authors are drawn to the idea of a persona as a means of thinking about this larger constellation of contextual issues around people like Bogart who were more than survey technicians but were also ratings intellectuals. While there is a variety of ways of thinking about persona as a kind of role-playing derived from the work of Erving Goffman and Marcel Mauss, which centre the triadic relation among inner self, role and society, our interest is in the uptake of persona 'as a manifestation and representative of an office' (Condren 2006: 66). For Condren, Hunter and Gaukroger, writing about the history of early modern philosophy and following R.G. Collingwood, they argue that in order 'to understand the answers philosophers have given, it is necessary to reveal the contingent and variable nature of their problems, even if history here is really the medium in which such problems are resolved' (Condren, Hunter and Gaukroger 2006: 3). For these writers this implied a shift of focus from 'philosophical problems to the institutional contexts in which they are delimited, and from the subject of consciousness to the persona of the philosopher that is cultivated in such contexts' (Condren et al. 2006: 7) The idea of an 'office' as in a 'public office' provides a way of exploring what in a former time we might have called a 'speaking position', which in being institutionally sanctioned was important to the carriage of the role. For Condren to be representative of an office means to be 'an embodiment of a moral economy' in the sense that a office entails 'a whole sphere of responsibilities, rights of action for their fulfilment, necessary attributes, skills and specific virtues, highlighted by concomitant vices and failures' (Condren 2006: 66).

These remarks suggest that we might usefully regard Bogart's writing and activism on behalf of himself and his profession as being informed by a sense of a sphere of responsibility to the profession, the industry, and to a larger public and social good. We can look to the kinds of actions that he took and deemed appropriate to take. We can look to the specific skills that were important to this exercise and ethical ways of acting and thinking that he advocated and practised. And we can open up an investigation of 'the vices and failures' of the professions he spoke to – how were these elaborated and denounced. Bogart provides a rich field for such inquiry. On the last matter alone there is Bogart's high-profile denouncement of both the concept of the spiral of silence and its proponent, Elizabeth Noelle-Neumann, for her Nazi propagandist past as providing one way of thinking about this. But such a larger inquiry must wait until another time. What we are interested in here is Bogart's specific criticism of the ratings and the institutional contexts in which these criticisms came alive.

Bogart's reproach came out of a particular standpoint and set of attentions in which the ratings and other syndicated data were fundamentally and primarily forms of social research. He sought often to make two related points: first, that the numbers that made up research always bore a particular relation to a social world made of individuals actions and activities; and, second, that research was a force in its own right and not 'just a means by which the media are attuned to the changing sentiments of the audience'. Both had specific practical and ethical entailments. As he put it in *Finding Out*:

> The seemingly abstract numbers are aggregated from many individual human consumption decisions and trace the commercial communications that affect them. Human actions, even at the trivial level of consumer choice, reflect values, beliefs, and judgements shaped by a dense web of social influences. Social science is dedicated to the systematic study of those influences, and its theory and insights are indispensable for the interpretation of data that represent what people do, think or say. (Bogart 2003: 281)

Ratings research was fundamentally social sciences research. This was so no matter how the ratings were put together or the diverse uses that surveys – and specifically ratings knowledge – could be put to by programme-makers, advertisers, media planners and buyers, public service broadcasters, free-to-air commercial stations and regulators. For Bogart the recognition of audience research as 'essentially a humanistic social science' (Bogart 2000a: 131) was important because it brought front of mind the relation between the aggregated numbers and the people, broader social arrangements, motivations and values these numbers always imperfectly addressed. It was therefore important for research and researchers that the 'human contact of the researcher with unique individuals' (Bogart 2000a: 284) not be diminished. For Bogart there was no incompatibility between qualitative and quantitative research as 'applied research' if both embodied a 'philosophy that research involves the human contact of the researcher with unique individuals'. What was important in this research whether undertaken through in depth interviews or through surveys was that it 'respect' the research subject's 'individuality' and that researchers listen 'carefully to what they say'. This, Bogart argued was 'the first step to finding out what they believe and why they do what they do' (Bogart 2000a: 284).

By foregrounding applied social research as a respectful encounter between the researcher and the researched he argued that it was possible to continue to have 'front of mind' the diverse social influences, actions, values and beliefs of respondents when one used survey research and the data tables it generated. This allowed users of research to always recognize the intrinsic limitations of all kinds of research including ratings when they handled research outputs and data. This was also a recognition that enabled the user of research such as the ratings to see that research only addressed this complex social environment in certain limited respects. He argued that this recognition was something of which sight could be lost as research instruments became more technological and mediated and less based on interviews, multi-faceted conversation and dialogue between the researcher and the researched. Here there was a risk that the numbers analysed by users of research became further removed and their data became disembodied 'from the original expression of human voices' (Bogart 2000a) – from their mixed circumstances of production, people's actual experience of media consumption and their diverse purposes and life ways. When the ratings were misrecognized in this way and the element of human contact removed, understanding and knowledge was the inevitable casualty and the research analyst was becoming little more than a 'collector and processor of data' (Bogart 2000a: 131). The other point that Bogart was making here was that research was so important that it required the close care and attention of all parts of the media spectrum and it needed to be recognized as an activity in its own right with its own priorities and its own integrity.

Bogart had three different related grounds for being concerned that this was not happening:

1   First – and this was a concern that he had throughout his life – how users
    of research took up and therefore understood the research enterprise,
    its opportunities and its limitations. This was never a critique of research

in the service of advertising decisions. Rather it was a critique based on the importance of research in providing 'a basic rationale for advertising decisions' and we might add here programming decisions. His criticism was that the users of this research 'commonly used [it] in disregard of its limitations, which deserve close scrutiny' (Bogart 2000a: 122). This criticism turned on the users of research not only choosing to remain ignorant of the nature and character of this research but the providers of this research – the ratings companies – aided and abetted this ignorance through their own practices which, at worst, pandered to this ignorance. The actions of the users of research made the research more than 'just a means by which media are attuned to the changing sentiments of the audience' but a 'powerful force in its own right' (Bogart 2000a: 126).

2 He was concerned about the contraction in the range and variety of research undertaken and utilised by those organizations – media companies and advertising agencies – which used audience research to make decisions. This meant that customized commercial research and a ready-to-hand research capability were no longer providing a counterbalance: whether to the data collected from syndicated data sources such as the ratings, or by providing an analytical competence in research methodologies to adequately understand the ratings as one among a number of forms of research. He saw this development as supported by how the media industry players had responded to changes in the buying and selling of advertising time, particularly on television, with the norm for advertising to be 'scattered around among programs' (Bogart 2000a: 105).

3 His third ground for concern was related to the changing circumstances in which the research was undertaken – by 'research analysts' in research firms, advertising agencies or in media companies – which was supporting both this contraction in the variety and range of research being undertaken and the related diminishing of the role, identity, and status of the research analyst. There were two distinct thrusts to this criticism. The first was organizational: a new generation of managers in all these organizations in the wake of media, advertiser and agency consolidation into fewer larger companies had come to see the research enterprise in a different and lesser light. It was a business input. This had the result of taking research 'out of the hands of the researchers'. He saw this as having a significant impact upon the conduct and orientation towards the research enterprise. It amounted to a deprofessionalization of the research enterprise.

Let us now deal with each of these criticisms in turn.

Bogart was all too aware of the gap – even gulf – separating the 'researcher' and the user of that research in the media industries. This was another version of the gap between expert and lay knowledge – except in this case the lay-knowledge workers were making significant corporate and even governmental decisions on the basis of the research (or rather on the basis of their limited understanding of the research and its intellectual bases). It was a gap his own work sought to bridge but it was also a gap that is the subject of much of his criticisms and deliberations. The gap partly turned on mistakes in uptake – the styles and character of the uptake – of research. It was as much about the sorts of things people did with this research and how this looped back to feed into the presentation and even frequency of the research itself.

Central to his criticism of the ratings and its uptake was the approach users took to the 'Audience Concept' itself. There was a basic misunderstanding of the kind and character of concepts developed in survey research which led users to endow the 'audience' with significance and reality it did not possess (something Ian Hacking takes up in his work *Taming Chance*) (Hacking 1990). So Bogart begins by calling into question its very validity as a concept. While noting that 'measurement of media audiences has absorbed vast effort and expense' (Bogart 1986a: 273) and that it is 'an indispensable component in every advertising plan,' there were 'reasons to be wary of the concept'. He outlines five problems with the concept. Upon closer inspection each turns less on problems with the underlying research method than upon the uptake of the research method and the inflated value given to the 'outputs' of these methods without attending to their inherent limitations by users of the data.

1   The first objection is that the word *audience* 'means something quite different from its original meaning and has been applied for quite different reasons to the consumers of broadcasting and print' (Bogart 1986a: 273). Bogart sees the construct of the audience in particular research methods being confused with 'real viewers and readers and listeners' and wants to insist that the reasons behind the development of measures of the audience in different media lead to differently organized kinds of information about audiences that make them not as commensurable as users would like. This was at heart a misunderstanding of the audience construct as an artefact of research for the purposes of research. It was a limited concept that was being generalized.

2   The second criticism was that 'audience measurements represent far-from-certain estimates that are in no sense comparable among media'.

Where the industry uptake suggests certainty in the figures and in the data Bogart wants to insist upon their uncertainty. The ratings results are never as certain as they appear to be and presented as being. Furthermore where the uptake suggests comparability Bogart wants to insist upon a modicum of incommensurability. Using data generated from different research instruments created unacknowledged problems for those seeking comparability across media.

3 A third objection was that 'audience data are intangibles and abstractions but are often dealt with by marketers as though they corresponded to real 'things' or physical objects'. This is a criticism that the users of the ratings outputs are dealing with the necessary 'intangibles' and 'abstractions' of any survey research in a way that makes him uncomfortable. There is a tendency observed in the first three objections to endow the audience with a reality and thereness it does not possess.

4 His fourth objection was that 'the preoccupation with audience size has led to erroneous decisions in the management of media content'. In this criticism those managing media content are not seeing the wood for the trees. They are concerned about the wrong things. They mistake size for value. They develop encouraged by reading of ratings data a 'conventional wisdom' about audiences. So awareness of how 'audience numbers vary between men and women and among various age and income groups' created stereotypical strategies for 'delivering' these different publics: 'college-educated men, with Sunday afternoon football games; high-school–educated women, with daytime talk shows'. The problem was not that these stereotypes were totally inaccurate but that they led to 'simplifications'. Here the obsession with audience size dovetailed with a dependency upon statistics which demonstrated misunderstanding of them.

5 His fifth objection was that 'the energy devoted to audience measurement has deflected concern from more useful research into the communication process'. This is criticism that a preoccupation with ratings data gets in the way of other kinds of research that might more usefully address the problems those making media decisions face. Much of his concern here is that the near exclusive attention paid to the ratings precludes – almost rules out of court – other kinds of research and research endeavour.

These objections all turned to a greater or lesser extent on the stances taken towards both surveys and statistics and the certainties they provided. The excessive and misplaced reliance upon statistics was brought about by a lack of understanding of what they could and could not tell the researcher. Bogart's criticism of statistics did not stem from any deep-seated animus towards them or conviction as to the intrinsic superiority of qualitative research. Rather his criticisms were always part of larger attentions to the research enterprise, its conduct and its proper integrity. It is therefore more a case of his insisting on their proper recognition and working with surveys and statistics. His was an educational insistence upon what can and cannot be said with them. A lot of Bogart's attention turned therefore on what we might call the proper orientation towards statistics. Bogart wanted, in the face of tendencies by users to invest them with especial significance, to insist that statistics is the science of uncertainty. In this his work bears some resemblance to books like *Statspotting* (Best 2008), which are designed in the language of the layperson to explain in a readily explicable way key misuses of statistical concepts and also to insist, where circumstances might otherwise push towards certainty, in recognizing the very uncertainty and the very tolerances in the research.

Setting Limits to Statistics

Bogart was in the business of setting limits to statistics. Some of what he wrote about ratings should be seen as nothing more or less than the 'statecraft' of statistics: letting people know what the discipline should be; emphasizing uncertainty where there was a tendency to impute certainty. Cultural studies people encountering this discussion of uncertainty seem to think that this is undercutting claims of ratings' truth. But this is not so: it was more asserting the kinds of truth claims that can be legitimately made. In his book *Strategy in Advertising*, Bogart says that the most interesting 'revelation' to come out of the Congressional hearings of the late 1950s and early 1960s on the ratings was 'the ratings services' major point of vulnerability: their stance of certainty' (Bogart 1986a: 297). As you saw in Chapter 4, 'The Audit', the hearings – drawing as they did upon the whizz-kid survey methodologists of the day – 'suggested that the illusion of exact accuracy was necessary to the ratings industry in order to heighten the confidence of their clients in the validity of the data they sell'. For Bogart this was partly an effect of presentation which created a sense of 'monolithic self-assurance' as 'the statistical uncertainties of survey data were transformed into beautiful, solid, clean-looking bar charts'. This illusion of exactness was further sustained 'by the practice of reporting audience ratings down to the decimal point, even when the sampling tolerances ranged over several percentage points'. If this criticism could be still held as ratings providers being hostage to demands of their client-users to report down to two decimal points and ignore the warnings of their providers, the next criticism was something else. For Bogart the illusion of certainty was further 'reinforced by keeping as a closely guarded secret the elaborate weighting procedures used to translate interviews into published projections of audience size.' This was a criticism that ratings providers were keeping closed to attention an important part of the black box of the ratings itself: a part which needed, he would contend, closer scrutiny because this move from data to projected audience was perhaps the most, not least, problematic step in the whole proceedings.

This was part of his wider criticism of Nielsen as the pre-eminent ratings provider. For Bogart the Nielsen company's origins in store auditing had created not only a path dependency within the company itself, disposing its agents to particular kinds of presentation of uncertain data as 'solid', but also in dispositions towards audience measurement as 'mechanical registration', which were arguably inappropriate. As Bogart put it:

Such practices were derived from the traditions of store auditing, a field in which the A.C. Nielsen Company first established its mark. When measurements are made of the actual movement of goods across the shelf in a store, the figures must be presented in a way that approximates the reality of goods shipped, stocked, inventoried, and sold. The figures have to look 'hard'. But this way of looking at the figures as 'hard' unfortunately has been carried over into the realm of survey research on audience behaviour. (Bogart 1986a: 297)

Bogart's criticism of the ratings turned on the reliance of the industry on a particular kind of research measure: regularly repeated, panel-based, longitudinal research constructed on 'scientific' principles of random sampling. But Bogart's reproach was not about its intrinsic unreliability. It was that it was being made to seem much more reliable than it was in reality. A number of times over a 30-year period he would tell the story of the wildly differing audience estimates from three differing ratings providers: 'radio station WAKY in Louisville at one time had a Nielsen share of 5, a Pulse share of 29, and a Hooper share of 42' (Bogart 2000a: 135). His prescription, after this telling, would always be the same. It was important to pay regard to these figures but not too much regard. It was important to rely on other kinds of information. This criticism of a systematic lack of methodological attention on the part of users took two forms. First there was a chronic lack of attention by users to what were seen as 'trivial technical matters' of methodology; second, there was the lack of institution-building attention to methodology – the auditing function had not been extended to the systemic comparison and evaluation of alternative research methodologies – existing and new.

Over his career Bogart saw significant problems stemming from users' chronic lack of attention to the details of the research instrument itself – the 'seemingly trivial technical matters'. He claimed that 'most of the people who deal with media research statistics' were 'not analysing them'. Rather they were 'quoting them, either to sell advertising or to justify their purchases of advertising to their clients or employers' (Bogart 1986a: 286). Thus:

Users of the numbers don't want to be bothered by what they regard as trivial technical matters, and so, for a quarter of a century, since the beginning of regular syndicated research, they have been sweeping the details under the rug. (Bogart 1986a: 286)

This lack of attention was leading to the 'routine acceptance of error' by users. They lacked the 'first hand feel for the fragility of survey data' that they would have had if they were alive to the technical matters. So it was quite typical when programme schedulers or advertising buyers compared one ratings report to the next that changes which might 'be the results of human mistakes and random probability' would become 'the subject of endless preoccupation and concern'. This made 'meaningless' and 'chance differences between percentages based on tiny subsamples' the basis for 'allocating millions of dollars of advertising investments' (Bogart 1986a: 286).

The problem then stemmed from how users worked with and understood ratings. Users were and remain typically impatient with 'statistical niceties'. For advertising and media people 'research methodology' was 'a big complicated bore' (Bogart 1986a: 296). Users were a major force behind presenting data in a way which rendered this research data in 'simple commonsense terms'. Even 'the elemental principles of sampling continue to remain a mystery to many intelligent laymen'. But this tolerance of 'inflated numbers' was not only due to the clients but the complicity of the ratings providers themselves: 'the tolerance of inflated numbers may in at least some cases coincide with self-interest and an unwillingness to rock the rather large boat' (Bogart 1986a: 296). The second criticism of a lack of an authoritative forum for the comparative evaluation of research methodologies was a significant institutional failure. A notable feature of the post-Congressional hearings landscape of the ratings was the institution of the Broadcast Rating Council in 1965 under the leadership of Hugh M. Beville – a figure of acknowledged standing within broadcasting research. Bogart was critical of this auditing regime – not because it was ineffective but because of how much more effective it could have been. He certainly acknowledged that the 1963 hearings had driven 'several minor ratings companies out of business by showing that they had merely produced reports without bothering to generate data first' (Bogart 1986a: 297).

However, he noted that the 'charges of interviewer cheating and improper or inadequate sampling' that got the headlines were easy to counter as the 'stock in trade' of the 'major ratings firms' was their 'integrity at the level of data collection and processing'. What the Broadcast Rating Council had done, including as it did 'advertiser and agency representatives as well as broadcasters', was to employ 'outside auditing firms to monitor the field work and data processing of all the ratings services and investigate occasional charges of impropriety'. All well and good. But for Bogart this missed a critical dimension which should have followed: 'the council's assignment of assuring the quality of execution does not extend to the comparative evaluation of the methods used by the individual services it oversees' (Bogart 1986a: 297). For Bogart, the methodologist, this was an important limitation further ensconcing particular pathways. In the period leading up to the Congressional hearings important public discussion of the ratings was inhibited by the practice of ratings providers to approach their operations with so many 'black boxes' protected from scrutiny by the commercial, in-confidence world of trade secrets and business strategies. In the period after the Congressional hearings the next black box to open in the interests of innovation and change was the ongoing comparative evaluation of methods and methodologies for ratings and other survey research of use to the media industries. For Bogart the Broadcast Rating Council could have become more of a force for innovation and change.

In an era of ratings sweeps, data was selectively available sometimes weeks later than the period being covered by the survey. Over time ratings sweeps not only became more regular but became available closer and closer to the time on which they reported. In a later era of fewer ratings sweeps available to decision-makers, there was some respite from the ratings. There would always be data and sets of expectations related to obtaining data from research customized to the particular problem at hand. In such circumstances the ratings data could become one more input and would, Bogart thought, be seen in a larger perspective. But with the move towards the more timely provision of ratings data and the rise of single-source ratings providers squeezing out competitors, there was no longer the ballast provided by alternative data source. There was not the evidence of differing results to provide for the opportunity of a conversation about the data, the methodologies being used to obtain the data and the like.

Problems with Increases in Scale

For Bogart the increase in the scale, regularity and timeliness of ratings data over the years was a decidedly mixed blessing. The increase in regularity implied a corresponding increase in scale and therefore budgets required to deliver the service. As the cost of the service went up for clients – whether advertising agencies or media companies or media planning and buying companies – there was a corresponding greater reliance upon it and a squeeze was put on the budgets available for other kinds of research. And as ratings data became more simultaneous, daily and repeatable, other customized research conducted on a different scale could look immediately dated. Buying-in the data from proprietary data sources had become more common and the researcher had become the research analyst. With this came a further lock in terms of the variety and kinds of research undertaken. Bogart thought that the bureaucrats who had increasingly taken over organizations in the media industry, from research companies to advertisers, from media planning and buying companies to media companies, in trying to operate 'scientifically' had 'become dependent on marketing statistics' (Bogart 2000a: 122).

The combination of cost and timeliness locked in the media system further into the ratings, with a greater reliance on its data and analysis. At the same time the arrival of ratings datasets made available on computer, instead of the paper-based ratings books, put the priority on their manipulation and not on seeing behind the database to the underlying survey data. With diverse research inputs into decision-making being reduced, the quality of media company, advertising agency and advertiser decision-making was declining as a consequence. The contraction in research budgets and size of research departments when coupled with the fashion against one's own customized research – a recommendation by now ensconced in market and strategy textbooks – ensured that there was the loss on the part of those making the decisions and analysing the research of a first-hand experience in research. There was no longer the opportunity to be able to develop in-depth understanding and to make competent, informed decisions. There was not the same scope for discussion generated by either different ratings results from different providers or different research results pointing in different directions about methodology. This meant users and research analysts alike were not able to develop the careful understandings of the limitations and possibilities of different research enterprises, particularly ratings research. Significantly, this was reducing the sources for innovation in applied social research and was locking the media industry further into ratings and associated syndicated data sources. We would now identify this as a particular sort of path dependency in ratings research which was making it increasingly difficult for alternative kinds of information, collected in different ways, to take root. Furthermore computing was making it much worse.

If Bogart naturally objected to the ratings being increasingly used as a substitute for research activities commissioned and overseen by agencies, media companies and media and planning agencies. His objection was that this removed the users of research from the experience of doing research and therefore appreciating the limitations and possibilities of such research. This absence removed a routine component of the armoury of the researcher in apprehending research. He worried that people not doing their own research, organized and constructed to address the specific issues that their business raised, would disempower decisions and decision-making. First, it would not equip them to understand the research provided by others, including the ratings, or to understand the limits – what could be said and what could not be said with the numbers. He also felt that there was no substitute for customized research – and therefore for doing your own research.

Impersonal Secondary Data

A related criticism was the trend towards the collection of what Bogart called impersonal secondary data. In this category he put ratings technology such as the peoplemeter. His criticism of the trend towards what he called the 'collection of impersonal secondary data' was a two-fold criticism. First, there was the problem associated with the loss of direct relation to people, and the second criticism turned on how this data was being understood:

> Research energies and budgets today are largely preoccupied with the collection of impersonal secondary data on markets and audiences. They rely increasingly on mechanical indicators, like scanner data and television tuning and Internet log-in records, rather than on direct reports obtained in interviews. Does this activity come under the heading of applied social research, in the spirit of my adolescent observations on the persuasive powers of Father Divine? It does, in a sense, because the seemingly abstract numbers are aggregated from many individual human consumption decisions and trace the commercial communications that affect them. (Bogart 2003: 281)

Changes in the political economy of broadcasting had encouraged this orientation. The rising costs of producing television shows had made it impractical for sponsors 'to maintain an exclusive identification with a show' (Bogart 2000a: 104). In the programme-sponsorship era advertisers had been concerned 'with their [programmes] qualitative aspects' as what was important to them was 'the rub-off from the excitement, good feeling, affection, or other sentiments evoked in the audience'. This made the numbers 'secondary'. But in television era dominated by advertising spots and their buying and selling a new 'ratings-dependent philosophy of media-buying put a premium on diversifying audiences'. Advertisers sought now to 'maximise their reach', spreading their commercials to 'different kinds of programs at different hours of the day' (Bogart 2000a: 104). For Bogart this meant that 'the purchase of commercial time had to be reduced to bureaucratic efficiency, with reliance on cost formulas, survey data of often dubious validity, computers, and armies of underpaid clerks' (Bogart 2000a: 105).

Changes in the political economy of research provision had likewise changed the equation. The demands for regularity and timeliness positively encouraged the development of single ratings providers. And it did so because the costs of providing this research had risen in tandem with expectations. Bogart was critical of the move towards single providers of research in particular areas. In this he would be left behind. But his thinking that it was necessary to have more than one research agency tilling the same ground had important resonance among his peers. He saw two or more entities as 'keeping each other honest' and as a source of innovation. Two different results ensured discussion and debate about methodology. Discrepancies in this context were not so much evidence of a flaw or a disadvantage compromising the standing of research – they were advantageous because it ensured that users of such numbers became more methodology-minded and therefore research-minded. It made them interested in how the numbers were constructed.

Bogart saw computers as having a particularly negative impact upon research. He acknowledged that this was counter-intuitive. The problem was that 'computer technology' demanded 'a constant input of fresh data, which become steadily less reliable and available from fewer sources' (Bogart 2000a: 122). His criticism here was that the presentation of ratings and other data in database form 'further disembodied' the research 'from the real phenomena they purport to represent':

> Universal access to computers and the opportunity to play off different types of numbers against each other should greatly enrich the amount of information available to decision makers. Instead databases are ever further disembodied from the real phenomena they purport to represent. Just as in the programmed trading of securities on Wall Street, formula programs for market planning or media buying take one number from Group A and one from Group B and put them together. The result is Gospel. (Bogart 2000a)

Bogart's criticism of the computer was not only related to a sense of the researcher-user and the researched being further removed from each other. It was also related to the adoption of routines and practices that relied more on habit and practice than logic or intent. If computer programs – database interfaces – stopped the user appreciating the nature of the underlying data and what it represented, a related criticism was the computer program was stopping the user from seeing the reality of consumption behind the figures. They were not stepping through to the data to see its complexity and its uncertainties. Instead, they were treating the numbers as 'gospel'.

The ready availability of computer-packaged statistical programs has facilitated complex analyses, but it has also spurred the disembodiment of data from the original expression of human voices. This tendency is heightened by the almost universally used procedure of weighting and adjusting results from flawed telephone or internet samples to make them conform to population characteristics known from the Census – itself an imperfect product. (Bogart 2000a)

Bogart's criticism here is that what was happening in the media research industry was a kind of 'epistemic drift', a phrase used by Fuller to describe approaches that change from ones of pushing back the frontiers of knowledge to ones that are likely to serve some socially desirable ends (Fuller 2002: xxi). The socially desirable ends here were the maintenance through tinkering of both survey research instruments and practices, and a resistance towards new practices and organization. As Fuller notes, the term 'epistemic drift' had been developed by Elzinga to highlight potential perversions of the research agenda that result from the existence of a state monopoly on research funding. The 'perversion' of the research agenda here, it could be argued, was the monopoly in research provision by particular companies such as Nielsen. However, for Fuller the legacy of epistemic drift was subtler, namely, the tendency for measures of *reliability* to be used as surrogates for measures of *validity* in the evaluation of knowledge claims. In other words, while scientists are officially concerned with whether their theories get closer to their target realities, they nevertheless measure success in terms of the regularity with which they can achieve more limited goals that are said to 'model' the target realities. And this is a point that Bogart would have appreciated.

Deprofessionalization of Media Research

Bogart concludes, overall, that the ratings are part and parcel of the deprofessionalization of media research. This is ironic given Arthur C. Nielsen's push for professionalization. The consequence of these moves was to take the 'analysis of information' in politics and business alike out of the hands of the researchers. In the stead of a media research professional straddling the different components of the information and analysis continuum there was a complex division of labour such that:

In 2002 scanner data are typically scrutinized by brand managers, audience data by media planners, political data by campaign consultants. These are not (necessarily) stupid people; some have taken a course or two in market research or statistics; all have absorbed social science terms and phrases that have passed into the common vocabulary of journalism. But their attention is typically confined within a narrow utilitarian spectrum. (Bogart 2003: 281)

This 'utilitarian' perspective meant that the inter-relation of these parts was no longer so possible. The data and their use had become increasingly one-dimensional and they had become so because of a narrowing of attention in research and research instruments brought on by particular cultures of management and corporate decision-making. This had seen an inflated attention being given to the ratings, which had been accompanied by a lack of attention to methodological and survey limitations of the ratings as a form of applied social research. Another, parallel, casualty of this narrowing of the research enterprise was in the narrowing of qualitative research, which had brought about analogous systematic misuses of qualitative research. Indeed, Bogart saw in the abuses of qualitative research a similar corporate logic. The 'counterpoise,' as he put it, of the 'abstraction and dehumanisation of survey findings' was the 'explosion of research using collective interviews with small groups of people'. No longer was this qualitative research interested in the 'why of opinion and tastes' but, rather, was interested in the 'what'. But such an attention, Bogart thought, only make sense 'if the findings are truly representative of the larger population' (Bogart 2000a: 283).

Writing about opinion polls in 1972, he could opine that, 'most survey research is devoted to the study of trivia; it is the study or minor preferences in the marketplace and in the media' (Bogart 1972b: 197). He went on to say that 'to a very large extent it is not a study of opinion at all but of purchasing and product usage'. This clear-minded view of a field with which he was so closely connected bears some comparison with the larger orientation towards and attitude to research embodied in the career trajectory of Paul Lazarsfeld and his collaborators. For Lazarsfeld the social research methodology was what was important, along with developing concepts for such research and getting someone to pay for it – it was not the actual research being undertaken that was as important as the prototype testing, the proof of concept being undertaken. Bogart shared this outlook. He certainly saw applied social research as a means of developing social research instruments which could become a means of solving and illuminating problems on a wider scale and canvas than mapping consumer decisions and preferences. He clearly believed that much of what was done in the space of marketing research was both narrow and limited, and on a broader scale and in the broader social context it might not amount to much.

Bogart's reproach to the ratings was, in a significant sense, a concern at the loss of office, of the standing and integrity of the applied social research intellectual. It was fundamentally a concern about the loss of a persona that went with it. This loss of room to move was tied into the narrowing of larger attentions to the research enterprise, its conduct and its proper integrity. Therefore, it is not surprising that his criticism of the ratings was accompanied by a parallel attention to what he perceived to be similar kinds of systematic misuses of qualitative research. Unlike some of the academic media researchers who followed him, Bogart's criticisms were not the 1980s criticism of 'positivism' that characterized some British sociology debates, leading notably to Catherine Marsh's defence of the survey as a social research tool (Marsh 1982). Neither was it a criticism of the general deployment of numbers. Anyone who has read Bogart's study of the press and its public (Bogart 1989) could not see his views in this light. His scepticism was not of a general kind related to the survey form and general deployment of numbers. It was a scepticism born from within numbers. Bogart's criticism of the ratings was part of a broader critique. As we have observed this was not a critique of research in the service of advertising decisions but rather a critique that, given that research 'provides the basic rationale for advertising decisions', this research and the forms it took, including but not limited to the ratings, were 'commonly used in disregard of its limitations, which deserve close scrutiny' (Bogart 2000a: 122). The disputes Bogart entered into become disputes over what is applied social research and what it is to be an applied social researcher. We could see these as 'protracted border conflict' over the scope of the field and the duties of researchers (Condren et al. 2006: 8). These disputes and arguments are best understood as 'formed by the moral habitus of overlapping institutional environments' (Condren et al. 2006: 8). Bogart saw himself fundamentally as a social researcher working in the commercial field. He was not, as increasingly became the case, a specific researcher working in a component of marketing and survey research.

Bogart was, the authors would argue, the last of the ratings intellectuals to be recognized as both an insider and outsider at once. Who replaced Bogart? The internal criticism of the ratings and ratings provision has remained but it is now an intra-mural rather than public conversation. It was increasingly undertaken in less public and more rarefied zones. While much of the work undertaken for CONTAM and by Gale Metzger from the late 1960s through to the early 1990s was available, these were technical reports written for a readership of methodologist specialists in market research firms, media companies and the ratings agencies themselves. They were forensic audits performed by a research methodologist auditor. Overall, these were not for a general readership.

Summary

There is a certain consistency to Bogart's criticism. His task was to be constructive. But this was not constructive in the sense of constructive for academic and generalist criticism but in an operational sense for those who used and abused the ratings as a longitudinally based panel-survey instrument. He provided in his criticism of the ratings, just as he had in his discussion of public-opinion polling, 'lessons' in how people in the industry were expected to use and read them. While there is a way of reading his criticisms to suggest that he had lost faith with the audience concept and in the numbers it provided, really that is mistaken. His was a plea for a more informed use of statistics and survey data; and a more open interrogation and discussion of what such longitudinally derived panel data was good for and what it was not good for. Judged from a holistic perspective, Bogart's fundamental reproach turned on too much being made of ratings data in some respects and not enough in other respects.

If audience ratings data are simply an ideological tool of capitalist masters in order to maintain hegemonic control over society, then the authors' analysis and Leo Bogart's analysis are empty and not worthwhile. However, Bogart provides an important insight into how the audience-ratings convention can fracture. In Chapters 5 and 8, we saw clear evidence that more and more computational tools are coming on to the market that claim to have the answer to predictive advantage in the world of audience research. Little is said on the foundations from which the data for these tools are collected, only that the results work. This is not to say that these packages are bogus, but it is a sign that the ratings provider in advanced industrial societies has lost part of its coordination role. The knowledge of the expert critic at the same time has become isolated as part of intra-mural debates within the industry rather than as *boundary spanners* influencing methodology and practice simultaneously. Art Nielsen is an excellent example of this – he could be competitive salesman, methodologist, engineer and critic at the same time. Metzger was a beneficiary of Nielsen's push for professionalism within media research.

Bogart's critiques are a bellwether for the future of the audience-ratings convention. They provide the answer to the current crisis in ratings. The ratings, as the authors have argued throughout this book, have a dual identity. This dual identity is lost at a cost.

11 The Future of Ratings

Our stations get a report card every morning from Nielsen. Those ratings determine the viability of our business.

- They determine the value of our advertising.

- This in turn determines how much money can be invested in new and better programming, and in new digital technology.

- And ratings also determine which programs remain on the air, and which ones will be taken off for apparent lack of viewer interest.

Today, all but one of Tribune's television stations have affiliated with the newer networks, the WB and Fox. We are eager to compete with our fellow broadcasters, and with the ever-increasing number of networks vying for viewers' attention over cable and satellite. But to do this we must have an honest report card. A trustworthy measurement of the size and composition of each competitor's audience. Mr Chairman, I regret to say that the measurement system we have today in the largest television markets is not worthy of public trust. It does not have the trust of our company or that of more than a dozen other responsible broadcasters.

Testimony of Patrick J. Mullen, President Tribune Broadcasting, before the US Senate Commerce Committee on the FAIR Act, 27 July 2005

The measurement of audiences is so contestable because, as Patrick Mullen's testimony makes clear, it is central to the organization and economic governance of the media. Ratings, as we have seen, fashion the broadcast schedule and a media firm's selling proposition to advertisers. They are a proxy for a media company's profit and loss. Investors and stockbrokers use the ratings as an important guide to stock performance. This makes the ratings agency for a broadcaster a cross between an auditor of its books and a seller of *its information* to third parties such as advertisers. Media proprietors are naturally vitally interested in a ratings convention that presents their *best case*. They are, by and large, not against the convention but want to reform it more in their favour. They typically want more control in setting the terms of the convention.

The Fairness, Accuracy, Inclusivity, and Responsiveness in Ratings (FAIR) Act did not go into legislation. In many ways, it did not need to. As we have shown in this book, the key parties to the audience-ratings convention in the United States have at some time or another put public pressure on one of the other parties to the convention, and not always the ratings provider. It was the broadcasting networks that put pressure on CAB and the advertisers to make its ratings results public in the 1930s. It was the ratings provider who put pressure on advertisers and the television networks to professionalize and, indeed, to standardize. Today, the audience is putting pressure on all parties to deal with the problems of intrusion or unreasonable expectations in the collection of private data. The convention has been shaped in the United States by this kind of continuing public competition for and posturing over the convention's formal constitution, its research, and its analytical and technological priorities by the different parties to the convention. In FAIR, a coalition of interests was seeking to reorganize the very terms under which the convention operates towards the kind of industry technical committee oversight and control model familiar in the UK and Australia. It argued this would secure greater transparency and accountability. While very few media markets see the different parties to the convention resort so readily and publicly to litigation, legislation and public disputation as in the United States, the very nature of the convention ensures there is the same competition to shape the convention albeit one conducted mostly behind closed doors and in technical committees, occasionally spilling over into wider public controversy.

However, the title of FAIR itself tells us something about audience ratings that is simply not found in other discussions of survey research, particularly in commercial contexts. Mullen's point was that there needed be 'public trust' in audience ratings, and this fits well the ethos of the audience-ratings convention that we have demonstrated in this book. There is no doubt that there is a range of complex sub-politics behind the creation of the FAIR Ratings hearings and its sometimes bitter exchanges. For our purposes here this does not matter as much as what this public controversy shows: the ratings convention unlike just about every other form of auditing and market research is publicly accountable and is routinely subject to robust debate and testing by the different parties to the convention. The audience-ratings convention and its key elements get tested in various ways, public and private, and the reasons for this can range from the good to the bad and the ugly. The overall outcome and target, however, is intended to be public trust. The FAIR hearings are but one instance in a long line of instances in every market in which ratings conventions operate where the ratings system itself is periodically called into question and identified as needing reform to retain its trustworthiness. This means that any public calling into question is always, at base, reformist. Proponents for change in the operation of a convention or in its technological base will always argue that they want the ratings to retain their currency as effective and appropriately managed research instruments. Defenders of existing arrangements will always point to the evidence of their effective management, transparency and responsiveness to market change.

The dual personality of audience ratings, as public and private at the same time, has been consistent across the history of ratings. In all new markets worldwide the problem of distortion always emerges, as it still does in established markets, and that distortion needs to be addressed. We saw that with China and Saatchi & Saatchi's push for a transparent system. The 'within-industry' discussions also, of course, use the same language. It is not artifice:

> There has been an interesting debate in India on the quality of Peoplemeters data. It all began when the identity of TV panel members in Mumbai was disclosed on a website by an unidentified person leading many to challenge the authenticity and quality of TV ratings provided by ORGMARG and TAM Media Research. The two companies however defended their position and attributed the entire episode to the mischief of some quarters whose interests were opposed to the availability of objective and independently measured ratings. *The controversy once again highlighted the strong need for an arm's length distance between TV audience measurement and those who either sell or buy airtime.* (TAM Pakistan 2001)

Because our media system is so saturated with ratings measurements and such measurements have become a gigantic enterprise dependent upon an infrastructure of precision engineering, a premium is necessarily placed upon the integrity of the system including the privacy of its informants and an arm's length distance between the measurement itself and the buyers and sellers of airtime. These are the very desiderata of the ratings. But controversies like the one in India where actors sought to actively compromise the integrity of the survey instrument have typically served to increase, not diminish, support for the ratings with attention and opprobrium typically shifting from the ratings provider towards the media outlets who were compromising the convention. And it is not hard to see why: in an advertiser-supported media system advertisers have an interest in regular and reliable data not subject to media outlet interference.

What audience ratings touch on is the intricacies of modern communicative spaces and how these are constructed, used and protected. Commercial and non-commercial media operate in those spaces. Audience ratings are a complex set of procedures, organizations and systems that deal with representation of the public. If there is perceived to be abuse of open communicative spaces, then we will often see a reaction to the abuse. The internet is perceived to be one such open space. The Net Neutrality debate is an example of the reaction of both industry and citizens when there is a perception that the communicative spaces will be distorted:

> In a Tuesday hearing held by the House Subcommittee on Telecommunications and the Internet over a proposed bill intended to ensure open access to the Web, 'Hannah Montana' exec producer Steve Peterman, speaking on behalf of the Writers Guild of America West, described the Internet as 'the new TV' and the best of the diminishing opportunities for independent artists to reach a large audience.
>
> Media consolidation over the last 15 years had reduced a once 'rich marketplace of ideas' into a tightly controlled environment ruled by seven congloms that determine 'nearly all of the information and content we see,' Peterman said. 'Because this small group now acts as producer, studio and network, there has been an inevitable stifling of creativity and diversity, and because they maintain a chokehold over distribution, there has been nowhere else for the creative community to go,' he declared. (Triplett 2008)

Triplett's article refers to debate on whether the internet requires legislation to protect its openness and the Federal Communications Commission (FCC) hearings which were held publicly to discuss the matter. An analogy with the audience-ratings convention is appropriate here because some of the debates about Net Neutrality have their parallel in the audience-ratings convention. One of the most important of these is the dual personality of audience ratings, as public vote and market mechanism at the same time. In the case of Net Neutrality it is argued that having a few big companies commercially restricting people's access to information or communication is unhealthy for democracy and unhealthy for business at the same time. The 'black box' of the internet, and its massive array of complex and often non-transparent algorithms run by companies that might selectively decide to limit a customer's access to traffic, has become part of the discussion about key communicative freedoms.

Audience ratings, likewise, have a complex technical and methodological substructure with political implications. The difference between algorithms in many systems on the internet and the inside of the technologies of audience ratings is in the gilt-edged, gold standard, auditing and overview that each step in the process has been exposed to over time in countries like the United States, Canada, Australia and the United Kingdom. This has made audience ratings an unusual phenomenon because they already have a complex set of parties involved in formal and semi-formal agreements over their structure and in their day-to-day operations. This is the ratings strength but it also helps explain how messy and controversial their operations can be.

Black boxes are those systems of operation or thought that are so complex most people do not have the time or the competence to work them out, sometimes even those, in fact, whose task it is to do so. At the time of the authors writing this book, the fallout from the interestingly although appropriately named 'global financial crisis' had involved the opening up to public view the operational financial mechanics of areas like 'collateralized debt obligations'. For example, General Re Securities, a derivatives dealer that Berkshire gained with its purchase of the insurer, General, had 14,384 contracts outstanding, involving 672 counterparties around the world, after winding down after 10 months (Pratley 2008). The 'mind boggling complexity' of these types of systems made valuations by auditors, let alone anyone else, difficult and often contradictory. Donald MacKenzie, in his *Material Markets: How Economic Agents are Constructed* (MacKenzie 2008), has teased out for his readers systems of technologies, cognitive frameworks, simplifying concepts and calculative mechanisms that have hidden or unforeseen effects. The difference between the audience-ratings convention and derivatives markets, however, is very instructive. For all intents and purposes the public of industrialized countries found out in financial markets that 'agreements' are not in place within the sector and do not lead to a reasonable set of rules for presenting value to the market. By contrast, in the audience-ratings convention, as the authors have shown, the operation of the currency is well understood, and the complex methodologies and technologies have been subject over time to rigorous test and debate at various levels, whether from the ratings intellectual, audit, legislature or audience. Distortions in the currency happen, as they do in other financial contexts, but that distortion is often picked up and corrected, as it was even in the early days of the audience-ratings convention.

The broadcast audience-ratings convention, or compact, on the authors' historical analysis, has had several important components. At base it:

1 has exposure as the key measurement;

2 must appeal to the inherent correctness of the measurement;

3 uses a probability, statistical, sample;

4 delivers a 'single number';

5 is syndicated to reduce costs to subscribers;

6 has generally been third-party;

7 is audited in an ongoing fashion by independent parties;

8 is expected to work in the public interest (that is, accurately represent the public audience).

We can see immediately the difference between the ratings as we have described them and the ratings-like data increasingly being provided by the internet and subscription TV and based on set-top box data. In these circumstances typically some, but not all, of these conditions are filled. There is often no structural separation between media provider and ratings provider, with the media provider also being the provider of ratings-like data on their service for use by advertisers and different channels. So, too, auditing is internal rather than the kind of ongoing external auditing familiar from the ratings.

At the heart of the current audience-ratings controversies are 'technical matters' of a longstanding character such as: survey issues related to the selection of a sampling frame and the overall sample size; worries over levels of non-response compromising the credibility of the random sampling frame; reservations about the robustness of the data as viewing levels get smaller; concerns over the biases intrinsic to both participation and inherent in the 'technology' for measuring the ratings; and concerns about the measurement of audiences with the increasing range of audio-visual devices connected with television viewing and radio listening. What marks out the contemporary period cannot be the nature of the problems encountered as all have been with us since the inception of the ratings: it must rather be that these problems have become more difficult and intractable. But have they? Over the history of the ratings we have encountered similar arguments at different times.

What we are encountering now is an intensification of familiar trends – old problems in new guises rather than new problems. Radio's increased mobility in cars, workshops and bedrooms led to a broader perspective on who was being covered and where in ratings collection. The proliferation of broadcasting, audio-visual recording and playback instruments in the home started making data collection more difficult and expensive in the early 1980s. First it was the VCR, timeshifting and a proliferation of channels with the advent of subscription TV and additional free-to-air channels; then it was DVD, fetch TV and YouTube, all of which needed to be factored into assessments of television viewing. Factoring in and keeping track of catch-up viewing has certainly become an increasingly complex task but not an insurmountable one.

The technical matters of the ratings range from appropriate sample sizes and mathematical models to new passive meter technologies. These are not mere details that safely can be set aside by communication scholars looking for the big picture. Yes, globalization and media fragmentation matter, but so too does the gamut of phenomena of the kind discussed by the authors, from the intuition of the advertising or media planner to the algorithm that generates data from the set box. What the authors have done in this book is to study the physicality, the corporeality and the technicality of the ratings. The evidence upon which the authors have drawn is predominantly interview and archival based, ideal for understanding the *actual intentions* of people involved in decisions and the organizational constraints within which they worked. The interviews are with those involved directly in the industry of audience ratings and the historical material is directly related to their construction or use.

This study complements what is perhaps the central tradition of recent 'material sociology'. Material and economic sociology, like that of Donald MacKenzie, draws on actor-network theory and argues that inanimate objects-procedures-systems are real *intentional* actors, that they can make decisions and act on them. The authors have not bought into this overarching approach of actor-network theory but they do embrace the idea that complex systems in modern society that are beyond the generalized competence of the citizen need to be brought into their understanding in straightforward and explanatory ways. The authors have to this end investigated actual parties to a real convention and the tangible *agreements* between those parties, formal and informal, that shape what happens next. We have also seen how the relative dispositions of those parties may change over time:

- *The disposition of broadcasters and broadcasting.* The relative power of broadcasting networks has changed over time, not least in the United States when audience share shifted to other channels in a deregulated market. The television networks in the United States, however, helped in their historical trajectory to standardize the whole process of forecasting and planning based on audience ratings.

- *The disposition of advertisers and national, regional and local advertising.* Advertisers have the capacity to shift money away from one medium towards another, or away from media advertising altogether. Their role in the audience-ratings convention has been to force exposure of methods for counting audiences to evaluation for the purposes of deciding on the future of currency. This has taken its most dramatic form in the contemporary push for engagement as the formal metric. Motivational research, of which engagement is a part, has always been an important part of advertising research, but interest in the measurement of attention and involvement has expanded both within the advertising industry and, indeed, among clients themselves who are funding neuroscience or biometrics laboratories.

- *The disposition of knowledge intermediaries.* Ratings providers have had to deal with competing demands and powerful players in the market. In the contemporary moment, companies like Nielsen are trying to incorporate diverse interests into an expanded audience ratings regime. These tensions exist in competitive and joint industry markets.

- *The disposition of the regulation or governance environments.* There have been historical government or regulatory interventions in the operation of audience ratings, not least on issues associated with transparency and accreditation.

As the authors' analysis proceeded we found that the dispositions of the different players in the audience convention are also influenced by overarching elements of the convention. Table 11.1 provides a summary of those elements.

All of these overarching elements, in one way or another, are under pressure in the current media-saturated environment in advanced industrial countries. If we look at the voracious appetite of modern citizens for media we can again see why these pressures are there. US citizens, for example, are voracious consumers of media services and US companies have a voracious appetite for media ownership. In the September 2004–September 2005 television season, the average household tuned into television for 8 hours, 11 minutes a day, over 12 per cent higher than 10 years previously, and the highest level recorded since television viewing was first measured by Nielsen Media Research in the 1950s.

By June 2005 in the United States there were 109.6 million TV households, compared to 108.4 million in June the previous year; 86 per cent, or 94.2 million, TV households subscribed to a Multichannel Video Programming Distributor (MVPD) service. Cable serves the largest percentage of MVPD subscribers, but its share of the MVPD market continued to decline, with 69.4 per cent of MVPD subscribers receiving video programming from a franchised cable operator, compared to 71.6 per cent in June 2004. Direct Broadcast Satellite (DBS) subscribers comprise the second largest group of MVPD households, representing 27.7 per cent of total MVPD subscribers as of June 2005, compared to 25.1 per cent in June 2004, an increase of over 10 per cent. As of June 2005, approximately 26.1 million US households subscribed to DBS

Table 11.1 Essential elements of the audience-ratings convention

Element	Description
Dual identity	Audience ratings represent the public, are a public vote and a market measure at the same time
Transparent	Audience ratings methodology must be transparent and the results not distortable by vested interests
Audited	Audience ratings require a formal, independent audit
Syndicated	Audience ratings costs should be borne by all parties to the convention (historically this has not been equal)
Limits on trade-offs	Audience ratings measures and the corresponding methods to be currency should appeal to appropriate trade-offs in Case Rich and Data Rich designs and cost efficiency
Limits on intrusion	Audience ratings requires limited intrusion into the lives of the audience and its privacy
Limits of statistical knowledge	Audience ratings styles of reasoning should not substitute computation for judgement

service. This represents an increase of 12.8 per cent over the approximately 23.2 million DBS subscribers we reported last year. DBS operators continue to add local-into-local broadcast television service. In 167 of 210 television markets (designated market areas, or DMAs), covering 96 per cent of all US TV households, at least one DBS provider offers the signals of local broadcast stations (local-into-local service). As of June 2005, there were 206,358 households authorized to receive High Speed Data (HSD) services, a decrease of 38.5 per cent from the 335,766 reported in 2004.

In this context, we can see why regulators come to the fore in terms of ownership of media. When it thought that Section 612(g) of the US Communications Act might have been breached, the FCC called for a review. The Act provides that when cable systems with 36 or more activated channels are available to 70 per cent of households within the US, and when 70 per cent of those households subscribe to them, the FCC can introduce additional rules to increase diversity of media. While this is not an audience-ratings convention issue per se, it does serve to highlight the overwhelming dominance of media in everyday life.

In this book we have investigated some of the major concerns that have emerged in a media-saturated environment:

1 From the advertisers' view, there is massive 'clutter' in the modern media environment and there are genuine problems with how to convey an advertising message to an audience in a cost-efficient way, the same problem advertisers have always had. Even if an advertiser/client can afford the Super Bowl advertising costs, for example, there would still be the question of ROI: 'I'm spending $2.7 million on a 30-second Super Bowl commercial. How do I know I'm getting full ROI? Equally important, am I doing everything necessary across the entire marketing and media mix to increase ROI?' Capturing information on the fate of an advertising message with online and broadcast audiences becomes a major concern. Online debate about a product that was going to be advertised at the Super Bowl or online discussion about an advertising message after the Super Bowl become useful data. The very idea of capturing the conversation of an audience over time also raises for the advertiser the possibility that there are different ways of presenting a message to audiences and indeed different ways of measuring the engagement of audiences with those messages. This is why engagement as a metric has captured the imaginations of advertisers. If an audience is fully engaged and involved with a message, no matter where or when they receive it, or how many times, then the cost efficiencies of delivery are significant. In the advertising-industry discussion there has been continuous flagging of the possibility of the GRP. Brain scans, neuroscience, biometrics, galvanic skin response, heart rate, reptilian brain – there is a long list of suggestions and

actual research that tries to obtain the secret answer to optimal delivery of the advertisement. But the gold standard of the ratings systems – a convention where there is agreement on currency – remains the *overarching aim*.

2   From the ratings-provider point of view it is, indeed, possible to cover all the many small audiences, but the cost of increasing the size of the ratings panel would not be economic and the advertiser is not willing to bear the cost of this. Project Apollo is a good example where advertisers, ratings providers and others got together to try to develop a single-source solution but intensified the demands on the audience to provide information. Touchpoints and Touchpoints 2 following Project Apollo and other attempts to provide a buyer-graphics analysis do not solve the problem raised by multiple channels and their measurement for a single currency. However, ratings providers are working with data aggregators like Google and cable and pay-TV media providers to experiment with alternative ways of gathering data that are compatible with the ratings convention.

3   From the media providers view, there is a demonstrated hunger to try to set up alternative measurement platforms which often present themselves as competitors to ratings providers, whether in monopoly-provider ratings environments like the United States or joint industry ratings provision like the United Kingdom. This has been done by proclaiming a census-like approach to audience data collection, using set-top box data, for instance, as a signal that detailed and robust audience information can be collected in a way that the traditional audience-ratings convention could not provide. As we have seen, however, such forays are sometimes stalking-horse attempts by companies to get ratings providers to become more responsive to their individual needs or complementary data to assist the companies in their own understanding of their audiences. However, proprietary-based, hidden, audience data in thousands of different media content-provider locations is in many ways like derivatives – not visible and easily inflated. The small channel and small audience needs, though, are real and much like the explosion of radio channels in the 1940s in the United States, the current environment appears to be one of exploration of ways to include the diversity within the audience-ratings convention.

4   From the audience point of view, its voice is being missed in the overwhelming push for more information about it. Much of the civic ethos that underpinned early audience research design in obtaining consent has gone with only the ratings holding on to this civil convention of securing the informed consent of participants. The role of audience panels and samples was, ironically, to minimize intrusion. A small sample could yield significant information about a

whole society without having to intrude on all of them each day and every day of the week. It is not surprising, perhaps, that the advertiser, media content provider and, indeed, the ratings provider have been caught up in the desire for more from the audience-as-consumer when their own research is telling them that the audience-as-citizen has reached its limits and its willingness either to participate in research or to accept additional privacy intrusions. It is, in fact, the audience that will, the authors argue, represent the greatest threat to the audience-ratings convention as its consent is, in the end, the most important of all the audience measurement needs. Telemarketing, push-polling and other means of persuading modern audiences have merged in the audience mind with market-research-in-the-general. In addition, as we saw in Chapter 2, audiences also have expensive media technologies they do not want to have intruded upon, by anyone. This is a toxic mix for the future of survey research, let alone the audience-ratings convention. At first glance, you might say that it is the multiplication of media channels, the growth of the internet and the massive amount of information available to the consumer that has eroded the possibility of appealing to civic duty. The rhetoric of the 'the new digital world', 'the new mediascape', argues that the audience is 'in control', compared with the old media world where they were not. This is, of course, not so. Citizens are not going to give up their privacy and their intimate details without a corresponding trade-off. This trade-off is not going to be achieved as it is at the moment by click-through contracts obligating audiences to accept data disclosure to third parties as a condition of accessing services, or by offers of more money or more gifts or subtle coercion to participate in market research, including the ratings. In a world of click-through contracts, the audience-ratings convention's traditional reliance upon direct and ethical dealings with its public, its long experience in organizing and maintaining systems of agreement with a culturally diverse general public, and its hard won public credibility, may prove invaluable in restoring the audience's trust in the integrity of market research and its instruments. The dual personality of the ratings as public and private which seems to so disadvantage it against the 'total universe' offered by web-trawling tools and click-through contracts on set-top boxes has the advantage of respectful audience-assent. It alone provides the kinds of assurance of the independence of market research and its integrity and trust.

The future of the audience-ratings convention, and by extension the measurements themselves, will depend on the same established processes and debates that countries like the United States, Australia and the United Kingdom have been involved in from the beginning of their respective systems. Table 11.2 provides a selective summary of the evolution of some of the major organizations that were involved in measurement. The authors have not included in Table 11.2 the rise of the internet measurement companies and a range of other organizations dealing with contemporary measurement. This is because the authors argue that the pattern of decision-making and the dynamism of formal and semi-formal agreements within the convention are now so well established and tested that any internet measurements will by necessity have to fulfil the same standards set up under traditional audience-ratings agreements. There are differences internationally in the nature of governance of ratings. The Joint Industry Committee for Television Advertising Research (JICTAR) in the United Kingdom, for example, is a very different type of organization compared with the Media Rating Council (MRC) in the United States. The same elements of the audience-ratings convention, however, would apply to both jurisdictions.

Table 11.2 Selective summary of early evolution audience ratings measurement in the United States, Australia and the United Kingdom

	United States	**Australia**	**United Kingdom**
1930s	Archibald Crossley, Cooperative Analysis of Broadcasting (CAB), owned by advertisers and ratings available to broadcasters in 1936. Same day telephone recall measured national network programmes, changing to telephone coincidental in 1940s 1934 C.E. Hooper and Montgomery Clark began with magazine publisher support and then independent radio ratings. Hooper bought out CAB after the war. Telephone coincidental		Robert Silvey, head of BBC audience research 1936–60. No audience ratings research
1940s		Bill McNair, independent radio ratings. Personal interview	1946 Reopening of BBC TV, TV questions added to 24-hour aided recall to measure radio audiences

		George Anderson, independent radio ratings. Diary	
	1941 Sydney Roslow, The Pulse of New York. Interviews – roster recall measured local radio stations, out of business 1978		
	Arthur C. Nielsen, Audimeter.		
	Launched 'radio index' in 1942. Acquired Hooper's national business in 1950. Ended radio measurement in 1964 to focus on TV		
1950s	1949 James Seiler, American Research Bureau, later Arbitron conducts first survey. Merged with Tele-Que in 1951 and took over Hooper's local business in 1955. Left TV in 1993 to focus on local radio		1952 BBC begins continuous TV measurement
			1955 Nielsen operating Nielsen Television Index using Audimeters and audilog diaries. TAM report on panel of 100 homes using Tammeters and Tamlogs. Pulse using aided recall
	Tom Birch, Birch Radio. Telephone recall, provided competitive service to Arbitron until 1992		1957 TV Audience Advisory Committee (TARAC) created
			1957 National Readership survey began reporting ITV viewing data
			1958–9 experiments with Instantaneous Ratings (TAM/ Nielsen)
			1958 London Viewing Surveys 1 and 2 (Pulse)
			1959 Nielsen Television Index ceased; TAM jointly owned by Nielsen-Attwood companies

Continued

Table 11.2 Continued

	United States	Australia	United Kingdom
1960s			1960 Investigation into TAM technique, Professor M.G. Kendal for TARAC
			1961 Joint Industry Committee for Television Advertising Research (JICTAR) formed, owned by Independent Television Companies Association (ITCA), the Incorporated Society of British Advertisers (ISBA) and Institute of Practitioners in Advertising (IPA)
			1964 TAM awarded JICTAR contract for further 3 years
			1968 JICTAR transfers contract to Audits of Great Britain (AGB). JICTAR replaced TARAC
			1962–4 JICTAR seven-day aided recall studies used quarter-hour records to produce data on more demographic groups than meter diary
			1962 'Television in a Family Setting' study
			1963 'A Study of Housewives who are Light ITV Viewers' by TAM
			1964 An investigation in Audience Measurement Techniques, ASKE Research for JICTAR
			October 1966 Tony Twyman appointed technical adviser to JICTAR
			1967 Ehrenberg & Twyman, 'Measuring television audiences', published in *Journal of the Royal Statistical Society*
			'Television in Family Setting Attention Research' (JWT)

1970s–2000s	Gale Metzger and Gerald Glasser, Statistical Research Inc (SRI) create RADAR in 1969. Telephone recall for network radio listening and meter for SMART for wireless recording of programme viewing	1973 McNair and Anderson merge, becoming McNair Anderson 1980s McNair Anderson sold to AGB to become AGB McNair and later ACNielsen 2001 Nielsen Media Research Australia loses peoplemeter contract to OzTAM/ATR	

The broadcast ratings measurement system is unusual because of the extent of the checks and balances that are intrinsic to its operations. It is also unusual for the diverse purposes to which this measurement is routinely put. The authors have been at pains throughout this book to emphasize the dual character of the ratings as simultaneously public and private, and to demonstrate that there is a particular public politics to the ratings. This political aspect to the operation of the convention, far from compromising the ratings, is intrinsic to it continuing to innovate and change, and to its very trustworthiness. Not only do the ratings actively solicit public trust through the very form of their notably respectful dealings with the public, whereas much contemporary market research is disrespectful, but they also solicit trust through the robust cut-and-thrust of dealing with the diverse interests of those who are party to the ratings convention in shaping its future.

The authors trust that you will come to the conclusion from this book that audience ratings history touches on some of the most important problems facing modern society – how to represent people in their behaviour in ways that are acceptable to the people themselves, those who need audience data for commercial purposes, and the management of contemporary media content in a complex media environment. There are today calls for 'zero ratings' and for different measures other than exposure, such as engagement, as ways of understanding modern audiences and for the economics of audience markets. However, as the authors have attempted to demonstrate, any attempt to change the audience ratings apparatus is not just an attempt to change a 'measure'; it is an attempt to recast the audience-ratings convention. This book has been one step towards theorizing the audience-ratings conventions and their impact.

Bibliography

Adams, W.J. (1994), 'Changes in ratings patterns for prime time before, during, and after the introduction of the people meter', *Journal of Media Economics*, 7: 15–28.

Advertising Research Foundation (2009), 'On the road to a new effectiveness model: Measuring emotional responses to television advertising', Advertising Research Foundation, http://www.thearf.org [accessed 5 July 2011].

Andrejevic, M. (2002), 'The work of being watched: Interactive media and the exploitation of self-disclosure', *Critical Studies in Media Communication*, 19(2): 230–48.

Andrejevic, M. (2003), 'Tracing space: Monitored mobility in the era of mass customization', *Space and Culture*, 6(2): 132–50.

Andrejevic, M. (2005), 'The work of watching one another: Lateral surveillance, risk, and governance', *Surveillance and Society*, 2(4): 479–97.

Andrejevic, M. (2006), 'The discipline of watching: Detection, risk, and lateral surveillance', *Critical Studies in Media Communication*, 23(5): 392–407.

Andrejevic, M. (2007), *iSpy: Surveillance and Power in the Interactive Era*, Lawrence, KS: University Press of Kansas.

Andrews, K. and Napoli, P.M. (2006), 'Changing market information regimes: a case study of the transition to the BookScan audience measurement system in the US book publishing industry', *Journal of Media Economics*, 19(1): 33–54.

Ang, I. (1991), *Desperately Seeking the Audience*, London: Routledge.

Ang, I. (1996), *Living Room Wars: Rethinking Media Audiences for a Postmodern World*, London and New York, NY: Routledge.

Arbitron (2008), 'Planning and buying radio advertising in a PPM world', Abitron, http://www.arbitron.com/downloads/arbitron2008mediaplan.pdf.

Arlen, M.J. (1980), *Thirty Seconds*, New York, NY: Farrar, Straus & Giroux.

Atkinson, C. (2009), 'Nielsen rival – real or ruse?', *Broadcasting and Cable*, 20 August.

Austin, B.A. (1989), *Immediate Seating: A Look at Movie Audiences*, Belmont, CA: Wadsworth.

Australian Associated Press (2005), 'Fairfax buys online dating service', *Sydney Morning Herald*, 11 July.

Bakker, G. (2003), 'Building knowledge about the consumer: the emergence of market research in the motion picture industry', *Business History*, 45(1): 101–127.

Balnaves, M. (2010), 'Media measurement and using media research', in P.J. Kitchen (ed.), *Integrated Marketing Communications: Addressing the Challenges and How to Measure ROI*, London: Palgrave Macmillan.

Balnaves, M. and Caputi, P. (2001), *Introduction to Quantitative Research Methods*, London: Sage.

Balnaves, M. and O'Regan, T. (2002), 'The ratings in transition: the politics and technologies of counting', in M. Balnaves, T. O'Regan and J. Sternberg (eds), *Mobilising the Audience*, St Lucia, Queensland: University of Queensland Press, 29–64.

Balnaves, M. and O' Regan, T. (2008), 'Constructing an audience ratings convention', Paper presented at the ANZCA 08 Conference, Power and Place, Wellington, New Zealand.

Balnaves, M. and Varan, D. (2002), 'Beyond exposure: Interactive television and the new media currency', *Media International Australia*, 105: 95–104.

Balnaves, M., O'Regan, T. and Sternberg, J. (eds), *Mobilising the Audience*, St Lucia, Queensland: University of Queensland Press, 29–64.

Banks, M.J. (1981), 'A history of broadcast audience research in the United States, 1920–1980, with an emphasis on the rating services', Unpublished doctoral dissertation, University of Tennessee, Knoxville, TN.

Barker, M. (1998), 'Film audience research: making a virtue out of a necessity', *Iris*, 26: 131–47.

Barnathan, J. (1964), 'The business of research', in Yale Roe (ed.), *Television Station Management: The Business of Broadcasting*, New York, NY: Hastings House, 171–80.

Barnes, B.E. and Thomson, L.M. (1988), 'The impact of audience information sources on media evolution', *Journal of Advertising Research*, 28(5): RC9–RC14.

Barnes, B.E. and Thomson, L.M. (1994), 'Power to the people (meter): Audience measurement technology and media specialization', in J.S. Ettema and D.C. Whitney (eds), *Audiencemaking: How the Media Create the Audience*, Thousand Oaks, CA: Sage, 75–94.

Barnouw, E. (1978), *The Sponsor: Notes on a Modern Potentate*, New York, NY: Oxford University Press.

Barwise, P. and Ehrenberg, A. (1988), *Television and its Audience*, London: Sage.

Beam, R. (1995), 'How newspapers use readership research', *Newspaper Research Journal*, 16(2): 28–38.

Berkowitz, D. and Allen, C. (1996), 'Exploring newsroom views about consultants in local TV: the effect of work roles and socialization', *Journal of Broadcasting and Electronic Media*, 40(4): 447–59.

Bermejo, F. (2007), *The Internet audience: Constitution and measurement*, New York, NY: Peter Lang.

Bernt, J.P., Fee, F.E., Gifford, J. and Stempel III, G.H. (2000), 'How well can editors predict reader interest in news?', *Newspaper Research Journal*, 21(2): 2–10.

Beville Jr, H.M., (1940), 'The ABCDs of radio audiences', *Public Opinion Quarterly*, 4(2): 195–206.

Beville Jr, H.M. (1988), *Audience Ratings: Radio, Television, Cable*, Hillsdale, NJ: Lawrence Erlbaum Associates.

Bielby, W.T. and Bielby, D.D. (1994), '"All hits are flukes": Institutionalized decision making and the rhetoric of network prime-time program development', *American Journal of Sociology*, 99(5): 1287–313.

Bodey, M. (2008), 'Ratings system for the future', *Australian*, 20 March.

Bogart, L. (1956), 'Media research: A tool for effective advertising', *Journal of Marketing*, 20(4): 347–55.

Bogart, L. (1957), 'Opinion research and marketing', *Public Opinion Quarterly*, 27(1): 129–40.

Bogart, L. (1958), *The Age of Television: A Study of Viewing Habits and the Impact of Television on American Life*, 2nd edition, London: Crosby Lockwood & Son.

Bogart, L. (1966), 'Is it time to discard the audience concept?', *Journal of Marketing*, 30: 47–54.

Bogart, L. (1967), *Strategy in Advertising*, New York, NY: Harcourt, Brace & World.

Bogart, L. (1969), 'Where does advertising research go from here?' *Journal of Advertising Research*, 9(1): 3–12.

Bogart, L. (1972a), *The Age Of Television: A Study Of Viewing Habits And The Impact Of Television On American Life*, 3rd edition, New York, NY: F. Ungar.

Bogart, L. (1972b), *Silent Politics: Polls and the Awareness of Public Opinion*, New York, NY: Wiley-Interscience.

Bogart, L. (1976), 'Mass advertising: The message, not the measure', *Harvard Business Review*, September/October: 107–116.

Bogart, L. (1986a), *Strategy in Advertising: Matching Media and Messages to Markets and Motivations*, 2nd edition, Lincolnwood, IL: NTC Business Books.

Bogart, L. (1986b), 'What forces shape the future of advertising research?', *Journal of Advertising Research*, 26(1): 99–104.

Bogart, L. (1986c), 'Progress in advertising research?', *Journal of Advertising Research*, 26(3): 11–15.

Bogart, L. (1989), *Press and Public: Who Reads What, When, Where, and Why in American Newspapers*, 2nd edition, Hillsdale, NJ: Lawrence Erlbaum.

Bogart, L. (2000a), *Commercial Culture: The Media System and the Public Interest*, New Brunswick, NJ, and London: Transaction.

Bogart, L. (2000b), 'Buying services and the media marketplace', *Journal of Advertising Research*, September–October: 37–41.

Bogart, L. (2003), *Finding Out: Personal Adventures in Social Research – Discovering What People Think, Say, and Do*, Chicago, IL: Ivan R. Dee.

Bogart, L. (2005), *Over the Edge: How the Pursuit of Youth by Marketers and the Media Has Changed American Culture*, Chicago, IL: Ivan R. Dee.

Bonner, F. (2003), *Ordinary Television: Analyzing Popular TV*, London: Sage.

Born, G. (2002), 'Reflexivity and ambivalence: Culture, creativity and government in the BBC', *Cultural Values*, 6(1): 65–90.

Borneman, E. (1947), 'The public opinion myth', *Harper's*, July: 30–40.

Bortner, B. (2008), 'Professional survey takers: Still a threat! How to reduce corruption risk from voracious online survey takers, Forrester Research, http://www.forrester.com/rb/Research/professional_survey_takers_still_threat!/q/id/44514/t/2 [accessed 6 July 2011].

Bourdieu, P. (1993), 'Public opinion does not exist', in P. Bourdieu (ed.), *Sociology in Question*, London: Sage.

Bourdon, J. and Méadel, C. (2011), 'Inside television audience measurement: Deconstructing the ratings machine', *Media, Culture & Society*, July.

Braverman, H. (1974), *Labour and Monopoly Capital*, New York, NY: Monthly Review Press, 144–5.

Breyer, J. and Zuckerberg, M. (2005), 'From Harvard to the Facebook', Stanford, CA: Stanford Technology Ventures Program, http://itunes.apple.com/us/itunes-u/entrepreneurial-thought-leaders/id384233886 [accessed 7 July 2011].

Briggs, A. (1995), *A History of Broadcasting in the United Kingdom*, vols I–V, Oxford: Oxford University Press.

Broadbent, S.R. (1966), 'Media planning and computers by 1970', *Applied Statistics*, 15: 234–56.

Brooks, T., Gray, S. and Dennison, J. (2010), 'The state of set-top box viewing data as of December 2009', Report to the Set-Top Box Committee of the Council for Research Excellence, 24 February.

Brubaker (1984), *The Limits of Rationality*, London: Allen and Unwin.

Buck, S. (1987), 'Television audience measurement research – yesterday, today and tomorrow', *Journal of the Market Research Society*, 29(3), 265–78.

Businessweek (2006), 'Web numbers: What's real? Competing methods of measuring traffic online leave advertisers, investors, and even net companies almost flying blind', *Businessweek*, 23 October, http://www.businessweek.com/magazine/content/06_43/b4006095.htm [accessed 30 November 2010].

Butsch, R. (2000), *The Making of American Audiences: From Stage to Television, 1750–1990*, New York, NY: Cambridge University Press.

Butsch, R. (2008), *The Citizen Audience: Crowds, Publics, and Individuals.* New York, NY: Routledge.

Buxton, W.J. (1994), 'The political economy of communications research', in R.E. Babe (ed.), *Information and Communication in Economics*, Norwell, MA: Kluwer, 147–75.

Buzzard, K.S. (1990), *Chains of Gold: Marketing the Ratings and Rating the Markets*, Metuchen, NJ: Scarecrow Press.

Buzzard, K.S. (2002), 'The peoplemeter wars: A case study of technological innovation and diffusion in the ratings industry', *Journal of Media Economics*, 15(4): 273–91.

Buzzard, K.S. (2003), 'James W. Seiler of the American Research Bureau', *Journal of Radio Studies*, 10(2): 186–201.

Caemmerer, B. (2009), 'The planning and implementation of integrated marketing', *Communications Marketing Intelligence & Planning*, 27(4): 524–38.

Canning, S. (2007), 'Turmoil as ratings split looms', *Australian*, 12 April: 15.

Carey, J.W. (1980), 'Changing communications technology and the nature of the audience', *Journal of Advertising*, 9(2): 3–43.

Carlson, M. (2006), 'Tapping into TiVo: Digital video recorders and the transition from schedules to surveillance in television', *New Media and Society*, 8(1): 97–115.

Chaffee, S.H. (2000), 'George Gallup and Ralph Nafziger: Pioneers of audience research', *Mass Communication and Society*, 3(2/3): 317–27.

Chambers, R.W. (1947), 'Need for statistical research', *Annals of the American Academy of Political and Social Science*, 254: 169–72.

Chappell, M.N. and Hooper, C.E. (1944), *Radio Audience Measurement*, New York, NY: Stephen Daye.

Chozick, A. (2010), 'NBC rallies for the count', *Wall Street Journal*, 16 February.

Cirlin, B.D. and Peterman, J.N. (1947), 'Pre-testing a motion picture: a case history', *Journal of Social Issues*, 3(3): 39–41.

Clancey, M. (1993), 'To be or not to be (counted)?', *Journal of Advertising Research*, 33(3): RC3–RC5.

Clark, N. (2009), 'Online advertising overtakes TV sales for first time ever. Paid-for search, led by Google, is proving "recession-friendly"', *Independent*, 30 September, http://www.independent.co.uk/news/media/advertising/online-advertising-overtakes-tv-sales-for-first-time-ever-1795274.html [accessed 30 November 2010].

Cliff, N. (1996), 'Ordinal methods for behavioral data analysis', Mahwah, NJ: Lawrence Erlbaum.

Cnet News (2004), 'TiVo watchers uneasy after post-Super Bowl reports', *Cnet News*, 5 February.

Coffey, S. (2001), 'Internet audience measurement: a practitioner's view', *Journal of Interactive Advertising*, 1(2).

Coleman, P. (1969), 'The coming war in advertising', *Observer*, 31: 677–80.

Collings, O. (2008), 'Putting TV under the microscope', *B and T Weekly*, 13 June.

Commercial Radio Australia (2007), 'Commercial Radio Australia: an overview', Commercial Radio Australia, http://www.commercialradio.com.au [accessed 5 July 2011].

Committee on Nationwide Television Audience Measurement (1991), *How People Use Television I*, Westfield, NJ: Statistical Research Inc.

Committee on Nationwide Television Audience Measurement (1992), *How People Use Television II*, Westfield, NJ: Statistical Research Inc.

Coutant, F.R. (1939), 'Determining the appeal of special features of a radio program', *Journal of Applied Psychology*, 23(1): 54–7.

Cover, R. (2006), 'Audience inter/active: Interactive media, narrative control and reconceiving audience history', *New Media and Society*, 8(1): 139–58.

Cowan, A.S. (1962), 'General Manager, address to advertising students', Speech, Federation of Australian Commercial Television Stations (FACTS), 10 May.

Creamer, J. (1942), 'A study of FM listening', New York, NY: Bamberger Broadcasting Service.

Crossley, A.M. (1957), 'Early days of public opinion research', *Public Opinion Quarterly*, 21(1).

Crossley, H. (2008), Personal communication.

Curtin, R., Presser, S. and Singer, E. (2005), 'Changes in telephone survey nonresponse over the past quarter century', *Public Opinion Quarterly*, 69(1), 87–98.

Dale, D. (2007), 'Making viewers as thin as the models', *Sydney Morning Herald*, 17 April: 18.

Davidson, B. (1954), 'Who knows who's on top', *Collier's*, 29 October: 23–7.

De Vany, A. (2004), *Hollywood Economics: How Extreme Uncertainty Shapes the Film Industry*, New York, NY: Routledge.

DeWerth-Pallmeyer, D. (1997), *The Audience in the News*, Mahwah, NJ: Lawrence Erlbaum.

DiMaggio, P. and Useem, M. (1979), 'Decentralized applied research: factors affecting the use of audience research by arts organizations', *Journal of Applied Behavioral Science*, 15(1): 79–94.

Dimling, J. (1985), 'Measuring future electronic media audiences', *Journal of Advertising Research*, 25: RC3–RC7.

Dooley, R. (2009), 'Five videos: Your brain on Superbowl ads', *Neurosciencemarketing*, blog, 27 February.

Doscher, L. (1947), 'The significance of audience measurement in motion pictures', *Journal of Social Issues*, 33(3): 51–7.

Douglas, Jeanne-Vida (2005), 'New channels not a major selling point for set-top boxes', *Australian Reseller News*, 24 November.

Downing, J.D.H. (2003), 'Audiences and readers of alternative media: The absent lure of the virtually unknown', *Media, Culture and Society*, 25: 625–45.

Durant, H. (1955), 'ITA audiences – who is wrong? A simple answer', ITA Archive, Audience Research – Gallup Poll 301/4, 14 December.

Dygert, W.B. (1939), *Radio as an Advertising Medium*, New York, NY: McGraw.

Eaman, R. (1994), *Channels of Influence: CBC Audience Research and the Canadian Public*, Toronto: University of Toronto Press.

Eastman, S.T. (1998), 'Programming theory under stress: The active industry and the active audience', *Communication Yearbook*, 21: 323–78.

Ehrenberg, A. (1964), 'A comparison of TV audience measures', *Journal of Advertising Research*, 4(4), 11–16.

Ehrenberg, A. (1996), 'Measuring TV audiences: reinventing the wheel again', *Journal of the Market Research Society*, 38(4): 549–51.

Ehrenberg, A. and Twyman, W.A. (1967), 'On measuring television audiences', *Journal of the Royal Statistical Society Series A (General)*, 130(1): 1–59.

Elms, S. (1966), '"Initiative Media", reports on the ARF/ESOMAR conference on broadcast research, held in San Francisco in April', *Admap*, June.

Emmett, B.P. (1968), 'A new role for research in broadcasting', *Public Opinion Quarterly*, 32(4), 654–65.

Ettema, J.S. and Whitney, D.C. (1994), 'The money arrow: An introduction to audiencemaking', in J.S. Ettema and D.C. Whitney (eds), *Audiencemaking: How the Media Create the Audience*, Thousand Oaks, CA: Sage, 1–18.

Feldman, M.S. and March, J.G. (1981), 'Information in organizations as signal and symbol', *Administrative Science Quarterly*, 26: 171–86.

Fiske, M. and Handel, L. (1946), 'Motion picture research: Content and audience analysis', *Journal of Marketing*, 11(2): 129–34.

Fiske, M. and Handel, L. (1947a), 'Motion picture research: Response analysis', *Journal of Marketing*, 11(3): 273–80.

Fiske, M. and Handel, L. (1947b), 'New techniques for studying the effectiveness', *Journal of Marketing*, 11(4): 390–93.

Fogel, J. and Nehmad, B. (2009), 'Internet social network communities: Risk taking, trust and privacy concerns', *Computers in Human Behavior*, 25: 153–60.

Foster, D. (2000), Personal communication.

Foster, R., Daymon, C. and Tewungwa, S. (2002), *Future Reflections: Four Scenarios for Television in 2012. A Scenario Analysis Study of the Television Industry*, Bournemouth: Bournemouth University, Independent Television Commission and British Screen Advisory Council.

Fuller, S. (2002), *Social Epistemology*, 2nd edition, Bloomington, IN: Indiana University Press.

Furchtgott-Roth, H., Hahn, R.W. and Layne-Farrar, A. (2006), 'Regulating the raters: The law and economics of ratings firms', Working Paper, AEI-Brookings Joint Center for Regulatory Studies, New Haven, CT: Yale.

Gallup, G. (1928), 'A new technique for objective methods for measuring reader interest in newspapers', Unpublished doctoral dissertation, Iowa City, IA: University of Iowa.

Gandy Jr, O.H. (2002), 'The real digital divide: Citizens v. consumers', in L. Lievrow and S. Livingstone (eds), *The Handbook of New Media*, Thousand Oaks, CA: Sage, 448–60.

Gans, H.J. (2005), *Study of CBS Evening News, NBC Nightly News, Newsweek, and Time (Medill Visions of the American Press)*, Chicago, IL: Northwestern University Press.

Garland, I. (2008), Personal communication.

Garrison, L.C. (1972), 'The needs of motion picture audiences', *California Management Review*, 15(2): 144–52.

Gitlin, T. (2000), *Inside Prime Time*, Berkeley, CA: University of California Press. Glickman, L.B. (2006), 'The consumer and the citizen in personal influence', *Annals of the American Academy of Political and Social Science*, 608: 205–212.

Gluck, A. and Pellegrini, P. (2008), 'Using RFID technology to passively measure print readership: an analysis of Arbitron's lab and field tests. Polls for the public good', *American Association for Public Opinion Research, 63rd Annual Conference, May 15–18*, New Orleans, LA: *American Association for Public Opinion Research*.

Goldman, W. (1983), *Adventures in the Screen Trade*, New York, NY: Warner.

Goldsmith, B., Gibson, R., James, A.L., Chandler, D., Pattinson, H.A. and Bell, P. (2010), 'Outside the box', *Media Education Research Journal*, 1(1).

Goodhardt, G.J. (1966), 'Constant in duplicated television viewing', *Nature*, 212: 1616.

Goodhardt, G.J., Ehrenberg, A.S.C. and Collins, M.A. (1975), *The Television Audience: Patterns of Viewing*, London and Lexington, MA: D.C. Heath.

Goss, J. (1995), '"We know who you are and we know where you live": The instrumental rationality of geodemographic systems', *Economic Geography*, 71(2): 171–98.

Green, A. (1996), 'Television in China: The story of the ratings. How a new joint venture could bring China into the front line of TV audience measurement', London: Saatchi & Saatchi.

Green, K. (2002), 'Mobilising readers: Newspapers, copy-tasters and readerships', in M. Balnaves, T. O'Regan and J. Sternberg (eds.), *Mobilising the Audience*, St Lucia, Queensland: University of Queensland Press, 213–34.

Gunter, B. and Wober, M. (1992), *The Reactive Viewer: Review of Research on Audience Reaction Measurement*, Cornwall: John Libbey and Company.

Hacking, I. (1990), *The Taming of Chance*, Toronto: University of Toronto.

Hagen, I. (1999), 'Slaves of the ratings tyranny: Media images of the audience', in P. Alasuutari (ed.), *Rethinking the Media Audience: The New Agenda*, London: Sage, 130–50.

Handel, L. (1950), *Hollywood Looks at its Audience: A Report of Film Audience Research*, Urbana, IL: University of Illinois Press.

Handel, L. (1953), 'Hollywood market research', *Quarterly Journal of Film, Radio and Television*, 7(3): 304–310.

Harris Interactive and MTV Networks (2008), 'The next wave in media measurement and engagement: Multi-screen engagement study finds greatest advertising value among audiences that cross platforms and are the most engaged', Press release, 25 June.

Harris, R. and Seldon, A. (1954), *Advertising in a Free Society*, London: Institute of Economic Affairs.

Hartley, J. (1992a). *The Politics of Pictures: The Creation of the Public in the Age of Popular Media*, London: Routledge.

Hartley, J. (1992b), *Tele-ology: Studies in Television*, London: Routledge.

Hartley, J. (2005). '"Read Thy Self." Text, audience and method in cultural studies', in M. White and J. Schwoch (eds), *The Question of Method in Cultural Studies*, Oxford: Blackwell.

Hayes, D. and Bing, J. (2006), *Open Wide: How Hollywood Box Office Became a National Obsession*, New York, NY: Miramax.

Heath, R. (2007), 'How do we predict attention and engagement?', Paper presented at Advertising Research Foundation Convention.

Heath, R., Brandt, D. and Nairn, A. (2006), 'Brand relationships: Strengthened by emotion, weakened by attention', *Journal of Advertising Research*, 46(4): 410–19.

Herbst, S. and Beniger, J.R. (1994), 'The changing infrastructure of public opinion', in J.G. Ettema and D.C. Whitney (eds.), *Audiencemaking: How the Media Create the Audience*, Thousand Oaks, CA: Sage, 95–114.

Hesmondhalgh, D. (2007), *The Cultural Industries*, 2nd edition, Los Angeles: Sage.

Hirsch, P.M. (1972), 'Processing fads and fashions: An organization-set analysis of cultural industry systems', *American Journal of Sociology*, 77(4): 639–59.

Hoffman, D.L. and Batra, R. (1991), 'Viewer response to programs: Dimensionality and concurrent behavior', *Journal of Advertising Research*, 31(4): 46–56.

Hujanen, J. (2008), 'RISC Monitor audience rating and its implications for journalistic practice', *Journalism*, 9(2): 182–99.

Hurwitz, D. (1983), 'Broadcast "ratings": The rise and development of commercial audience research and measurement in American broadcasting', Unpublished doctoral dissertation, Urbana, IL: University of Illinois.

Hurwitz, D. (1984), 'Broadcasting ratings: The missing dimension', *Critical Studies in Mass Communication*, 1(2): 205–215.

Hurwitz, D. (1988), 'Market research and the study of the US radio audience', *Communication*, 10: 223–41.

IBISWorld (2009), *Advertising Services in Australia*, Melbourne: IBISWorld.

Ivie, G. (2005), 'Statement of George Ivie, Executive Director/CEO, The Media Rating Council, Inc', *Hearing before the Committee on Commerce, Science, and Transportation, United States Senate, July 25, 2005*, Washington, DC: US Government Printing Office, http://www.gpo.gov/fdsys/pkg/CHRG-109shrg65216/pdf/CHRG-109shrg65216.pdf [accessed 6 July 2011].

James, E.P.H. (1937), 'The development of research in broadcast advertising', *Journal of Marketing*, 2(2): 141–5.

Jeffrey, L. (1994), 'Rethinking audiences for cultural industries: Implications for Canadian research', *Canadian Journal of Communication*, 19(3), http://www.cjconline.ca/viewarticle.php?id=253 [accessed 19 January 2008].

Jones, C. and Bednall, D. (1980). *Television in Australia: Its History through the Ratings*, An Australian Broadcasting Tribunal Research Report, Canberra: Australian Broadcasting Tribunal.

Joseph, A. (2008), 'Call to smash the quintile class system', *B and T Weekly*, 11 July: 17.

Kang, S. (2008), 'TNS aims to take bite out of Nielsen: Boxes from DirecTV to mine new data on viewing patterns', *Wall Street Journal*, 31 January: B8.

Kang, S. and Vranica, S. (2008), 'US marketers look beyond surveys to get clearer picture of target audience', *Wall Street Journal*, 13 May: B6.

Karol, J.J. (1938), 'Analysing the radio market', *Journal of Marketing*, 2(4): 309–313.

Keane, J. (2008), 'Monitory democracy: A new idea of democratic practice in the age of new media', *Open Times*.

Keegan, C.A.V. (1980), 'Qualitative audience research in public television', *Journal of Communication*, 30(3): 164–72.

Keller, P. (1966), 'Patterns of media-audience accumulation', *Journal of Marketing*, 30(2): 32–7.

Kent, R. (ed.) (1994), *Measuring Media Audiences*, London: Routledge.

Kingson, W.K. (1953), 'Measuring the broadcast audience', *Quarterly Journal of Film, Radio and Television*, 7(3): 291–303.

Klopfenstein, B. (1990), 'Audience measurement in the VCR environment: An examination of ratings methodologies', in J. Dobrow (Ed.), *Social and Cultural Aspects of VCR Use*, Hillsdale, NJ: Lawrence Erlbaum, 45–72.

Korda, M. (2001), *Making the List: A Cultural History of the American Bestseller, 1900–1999*, New York, NY: Barnes and Noble.

Kover, A.J. (1967). 'Models of man as defined by marketing research', *Journal of Marketing Research*, IV(May): 129–32.

Kreshel, P.J. (1990), 'John B. Watson at J. Walter Thompson: The legitimation of "science" in advertising', *Journal of Advertising*, 19(2): 45–59.

Kreshel, P.J. (1993), 'Advertising research in the pre-depression years: A cultural history', *Journal of Current Issues and Research in Advertising*, 15(1): 59–75.

Krugman, D.M. (1985), 'Evaluating the audiences of the new media', *Journal of Advertising*, 14(4): 21–7.

Laird, P.W. (1998), *Advertising Progress: American Business and the Rise of Consumer Marketing*, Baltimore, MD: Johns Hopkins University Press.

Lancet Neurology (2004), 'Neuromarketing: Beyond Branding', *Lancet Neurology*, 3(2): 71, http://www.neurosciencemarketing.com/blog/articles/neuromarketing-videos.htm#more-428 [accessed 15 March 2010].

Lavidge, R.J. and Steiner, G.A. (1961), 'A model for predictive measurements of advertising effectiveness', *Journal of Marketing*, 25: 59–62.

Lazarsfeld, P.F. (1939), 'Radio research and applied psychology: Introduction by the guest editor', *Journal of Applied Psychology*, 23(1): 1–7.

Lazarsfeld, P.F. (1947), 'Audience research in the movie field', *Annals of the American Academy of Political and Social Science*, 254: 160–68.

Lazarsfeld, P.F. and Field, H. (1946), *The People Look at Radio*, Chapel Hill, NC: University of North Carolina Press.

Lazarsfeld, P.F., Berelson, B. and Gaudet, H. (1944), *The People's Choice*, New York, NY: Duell, Sloan and Pearce.

Lee, J. (2005), 'No more rubbery figures as media advertisers nut out who watches what and when', *Sydney Morning Herald*, 3 February, 28.

Lee, N., Broderick, A.J. and Chamberlain, L. (2006), 'What is neuromarketing? A discussion and agenda for future research', *International Journal of Psychophysiology*, 63(2).

Lenthall, B. (2007), *Radio's America: The Great Depression and the Rise of Modern Mass Culture*, Chicago, IL: University of Chicago Press.

Levy, M.R. (1982), 'The Lazarsfeld-Stanton Program Analyser: An historical note, *Journal of Communication*, 32(4): 30–38.

Likert, R. (1936), 'A method for measuring the sales influence of a radio program', *Journal of Applied Psychology*, 20(2): 175–82.

Livingstone, S. (2003), 'The changing nature of audiences: From the mass audience to the interactive media user', in A. Valdivia (ed.), *Companion to Media Studies*, Oxford: Blackwell, 337–59.

Livingstone, S., Lunt, P. and Miller, L. (2007), 'Citizens and consumers: Discursive debates during and after the Communications Act of 2003', *Media, Culture and Society*, 29(4): 613–38.

Longstaff, H.P. (1939), 'A method for determining the entertainment value of radio programs', *Journal of Applied Psychology*, 23(1): 46–54.

Luscombe, K., (1966), 'Marketing Controls and Advertising Measurement – US', Australian Association of National Advertisers 1966 Convention: 'Method' Advertising, 10–12 October, Perth.

McChesney, R. (1993), *Telecommunications, Mass Media, and Democracy: The Battle for the Control of US Broadcasting, 1928–1935*, New York, NY: Oxford University Press.

McCourt, T. and Rothenbuhler, E. (1997), 'SoundScan and the consolidation of control in the popular music industry', *Media, Culture and Society*, 19: 201–218.

McCutcheon, M. (2006), 'Is pay TV meeting its promise?', Unpublished PhD thesis, Perth: Faculty of Arts, School of Media, Communication and Culture, Murdoch University.

McIntyre, P. (2007), 'Barbie viewers don't rate a mention', *Sydney Morning Herald*, 12 April: 24.

McKenna, W.J. (1988), 'The future of electronic measurement technology in US media research', *Journal of Advertising Research*, 28(3): RC3–RC7.

MacKenzie, D. (2006), *An Engine, Not a Camera*, New York, NY: MIT.

MacKenzie, D. (2009), *Material Markets: How Economic Agents Are Constructed*, London: Oxford University Press.

McManus, J.H. (1994), *Market-driven Journalism: Let the Citizen Beware?*, Thousand Oaks, CA: Sage.

McNair, I. (2000), Personal communication.

McNair, W.A. (1937), *Radio Advertising in Australia*, Sydney: Angus and Robertson.

McQuail, D. (1969), 'Uncertainty about the audience and the organization of mass communications', *Sociological Review Monograph*, 13: 75–84.

Marsh, C. (1984), *The Survey Method. The Contribution of Surveys to Sociological Explanation*, London: George, Allen and Unwin.

Mattelart, A. (1991), *Advertising International: The Privatization of Public Space*, London: Routledge.

Mayer, M. (1991), *Whatever Happened to Madison Avenue? Advertising in the '90s*, New York, NY: Little, Brown, 157

Maxwell, R. (2000), 'Picturing the audience', *Television and New Media*, 1(2): 135–57.

Meehan, E.R. (1984), 'Ratings and the institutional approach: A third answer to the commodity question', *Critical Studies in Mass Communication*, 1(2): 216–25.

Meehan, E.R. (1990), 'Why we don't count: The commodity audience', in P. Mellencamp (ed.), *The Logics of Television: Essays in Cultural Criticism*, London and Bloomington, IN: Indiana University Press/BFI, 117–37.

Meehan, E.R. (1993), 'Heads of household and ladies of the house: Gender, genre, and broadcast ratings, 1929–1990', in W.S. Solomon and R.W. McChesney (eds), *Ruthless Criticism: New*

Perspectives in US Communication History, Minneapolis, MI: University of Minnesota Press, 204–21.

Metzger, G. (2008), Personal communication.

Miller, P.V. (1994), 'Made-to-order and standardized audiences: Forms of reality in audience measurement', in J.S. Ettema and D.C. Whitney (eds), *Audiencemaking: How the Media Create the Audience*, London: Sage, 57–74.

Miller, P.V. (2009), 'US electronic media audience ratings: A view from the inside', Ratings Seminar, Centre for Critical and Cultural Studies, University of Queensland, 16 July.

Milman, O. (2008), 'Where next in TV tracking wars?', *B and T Weekly*, 4 April, 7.

Morrison, D.E. (1978), 'Kultur and culture: The case of Theodor W. Adorno and Paul F. Lazarsfeld', *Social Research*, 45(2): 331–55.

Mullarkey, G.W. (2004), 'Internet measurement data – practical and technical issues', *Marketing Intelligence and Planning*, 22(1): 42–58.

Musil, S. (2009), 'Facebook opens up vote on new terms of service', Cnet News, 16 April, http://news.cnet.com/8301-1023_3-10221676-93.html [accessed 21 April 2009].

Mytton, G. (2007), *Handbook on Radio and Television Audience Research*, Paris: UNICEF/UNESCO.

Napoli, P.M. (2003), *Audience Economics: Media Institutions and the Audience Marketplace*, New York, NY: Columbia University Press.

Napoli, P.M. (2005), 'Audience measurement and media policy: Audience economics, the diversity principle, and the local people meter', *Communication Law and Policy*, 10(4): 349–82.

Napoli, P.M. (2008), *The Rationalization of Audience Understanding*, New York, NY: The Donald McGannon Communication Research Center, Fordham University.

Napoli, P.M. (2009), *Audience Measurement, the Diversity Principle, and the First Amendment Right to Construct the Audience*, New York, NY: The Donald McGannon Communication Research Center, Fordham University.

Napoli, P.M. (2011), *Audience Evolution: New Technologies and the Transformation of Media Audiences*, New York, NY: Columbia University Press.

Nature Neuroscience (2004), 'Brain Scam?', *Nature Neuroscience*, 7: 683.

Hollywood Reporter (2007), 'NBC refunds advertisers as ratings plunge', 11 December.

Neely, M. (2000), Personal communication.

Negus, K. (1999), *Music Genres and Corporate Cultures*, London: Routledge.

Nelson, G. (2000), Personal communication.

Neuman, W.R. (1991), *The Future of the Mass Audience*, New York, NY: Cambridge University Press.

Newman, K.M. (2004), *Radio Active: Advertising and Consumer Activism, 1935–1947*, Berkeley, CA: University of California Press.

Nicholas, S. (2006), 'The good servant: The origins and development of BBC Listener Research 1936–1950', *BBC Audience Research Reports. Part 1: BBC Listener Research 1937–c.1950*, Wakefield: Microform Academic.

Nielsen (2007), 'Nielsen Launches Commercial Minute Ratings in Standardized File', Nielsen Media Research press release, 31 May, http://www.nielsenmedia.com/nc/portal/site/Public/menuitem.55dc65b4a7d5adff3f65936147a062a0/?vgnextoid=7f3a957da42e2110VgnVCM100000ac0a260aRCRD.

Nightingale, V. (2003), *Media and Audiences: New Perspectives*, Maidenhead: Open University Press.

Ohmer, S. (1999), 'The science of pleasure: George Gallup and audience research in Hollywood', in M. Stokes and R. Maltby (eds), *Identifying Hollywood Audiences: Cultural Identity and the Movies*, London: British Film Institute, 61–80.

Ohmer, S. (2006), *George Gallup in Hollywood*, New York, NY: Columbia University Press.

O'Regan, T. (2002), 'Arts audiences: Becoming audience-minded', in M. Balnaves, T. O'Regan and J. Sternberg (eds), *Mobilising the Audience*, St Lucia, Queensland: University of Queensland Press, 104–30.

Owen, B.M. and Wildman, S.S. (1992), *Video Economics*, Cambridge, MA: Harvard University Press.

Peterson, R.A. (1994), 'Measured markets and unknown audiences: Case studies from the production and consumption of music', in J.S. Ettema and D.C. Whitney (eds), *Audiencemaking: How the Media Create the Audience*, Thousand Oaks, CA: Sage, 171–85.

Phelps, S. (1989), 'A reconsideration of the ARF model', *Marketing and Media Decisions*, November: 98.

Philport, J.C. (1993), 'New insights into reader quality measures', *Journal of Advertising Research*, 35(5): RC5–RC12.

Plunkett, J. (2009), 'TV ratings system to reflect change in viewing habits', *Guardian*, 16 March.

Politz, A. (1943), 'Family versus individual in measurement of audiences', *Journal of the American Statistical Association*, 38(222): 233–7.

Pontin, J. (2009), 'But who's counting?', *Technology Review*, 112(2), 64–9.

Potter, D. (1967), 'The historical perspective', in S. Donner (ed.), *The Meaning of Commercial Television*, Austin, TX: University of Texas Press, 51–68.

Powell, W.W. (1978), 'Publishers' decision-making: What criteria do they use in deciding which books to publish?', *Social Research*, 45(2): 227–52.

Pratley, N. (2008), 'Wall Street crisis: Is this the death knell for derivatives?', Guardian, 15 September.

Raboy, M., Abramson, B.D., Proulx, S. and Welters, R. (2001), 'Media policy, audiences, and social demand: Research at the interface of policy studies and audience studies', *Television and New Media*, 2(2): 95–115.

Raynes-Goldie, K. (2010), 'Aliases, creeping, and wall cleaning: Understanding privacy in the age of Facebook', *First Monday*, 15(1).

Razlogova, E. (1995), 'The voice of the listener: Americans and the radio industry, 1920–1950', Unpublished doctoral dissertation, Fairfax, VI: George Mason University.

Robichaux, M. (2002), *Cable Cowboy: John Malone and the Rise of the Modern Cable Business*, Hoboken, NJ: John Wiley.

Robinson, L. (2000), 'Radio research in transition', *International Journal of Market Research*, 42(4): 381–94.

Robinson, W.S. (1947), 'Radio audience measurement: and its limitations', *Journal of Social Issues*, 3(3): 42–50.

Rogers, E.M. (1994), *A History of Communication Study*, New York, NY, Free Press.

Rogers, N. (1969), *Puck's Promise – A Short History of Television*, London: British Bureau of Television Advertising (BBTA).

Rohle, T. (2007), 'Desperately seeking the consumer: Personalized search engines and the commercial exploitation of user data', *First Monday*, 12(9).

Roscoe, T. (1999), 'The construction of the World Wide Web audience', *Media, Culture and Society*, 21: 673–84.

Rossman, G. (2008), 'By the numbers: Lessons from radio', in S.J. Tepper and B. Ivey (eds), *Engaging Art: The Next Great Transformation of America's Cultural Life*, New York, NY: Routledge, 257–70.

Rubens, W.S. (1984), 'High-tech audience measurement for new-tech audiences', *Critical Studies in Mass Communication*, 1(2): 195–205.

Sautet, F.E. (2002), *An Entrepreneurial Theory of the Firm*, London: Routledge.

Savage, P. (2006), 'The audience massage: audience research and Canadian public broadcasting', Paper presented at the RIPE@2006 conference, Amsterdam.

Schiavone, N.P. (1988), 'Lessons from the radio research experience for all electronic media', *Journal of Advertising Research*, 28(3): RC11–RC15.

Schoemaker, P. and van der Heijden, K. (1992), 'Integrating scenarios into strategic planning at Royal Dutch/Shell', *Planning Review*, 20(3): 41–6.

Schudson, M. (1984), *Advertising, the Uneasy Persuasion: Its Dubious Impact on American Society*, New York, NY: Basic Books.

Schudson, M. (2006), 'The troubling equivalence of citizen and consumer', *Annals of the American Academy of Political and Social Science*, 608: 193–204.

Schultz, D.E. (1979), 'Media research users want', *Journal of Advertising Research*, 19(6): 13–17.

Schulze, J. (2006), 'Pay-TV to split from free-to-air over ratings system', *Australian*, 28 July: 21.

Schwartz, P. (1991), *The Art of the Long View*, New York, NY: Doubleday Currency.

Schwoch, J. (1990), 'Selling the sight/site of sound Broadcast advertising and the transition from radio to television', *Cinema Journal*, 30(1): 55–66.

Seldes, G.V. (1950), *The Great Audience*, New York, NY: Viking.

Seles, S. (2009), 'Audience Measurement 4.0', Futures of Entertainment, 24 July, http://www.convergenceculture.org/weblog/2009/07/audience_measurement_40.php.

Shoebridge, N. (2009), 'Web usage system gets an audience', *Australian Financial Review*, 16 February: 41.

Sills, D.L. (1987), *Paul F. Lazarsfeld 1901–1976. A Biographical Memoir*, Washington, DC: National Academy of Sciences, 251–82.

Silvey, R. (1944), 'Methods of listener research employed by the British Broadcasting Corporation', *Journal of the Royal Statistical Society*, 107(3/4), 190–230.

Silvey, R. (1951), 'Methods of viewer research employed by the British Broadcasting Corporation', *Public Opinion Quarterly*, 15(1): 89–94.

Silvey, R. (1974), *Who's Listening? The Story of BBC Audience Research*, London: George Allen and Unwin.

Simmat, R. (1933). *The Principles and Practices of Marketing*, London: Pitman.

Sinclair, L. (2004), 'Pay-TV audience figures disputed, *Australian*, 11 November: 19.

Sinclair, L. (2005), 'Method in madness of pay ratings', *Australian*, 17 February: 21.

Sinclair, L. (2007), 'Ratings figures on taped TV by 2010', *Australian*, 6 December: 33.

Sinclair, L. (2008), 'Pay-TV ad-skip meter hits free-to-airs', *Australian*, 24 March: 29.

Singleton, J. (1979), *True Confessions*. Sydney: Cassell Australia.

Smythe, T.C. (1986), 'The advertisers' war to verify newspaper circulation, 1870–1914', *American Journalism*, 3(3): 167–80.

Socolow, M. (2004), 'Psyche and society: Radio advertising and social psychology in America, 1923–1936', *Historical Journal of Film, Radio and Television*, 24(4): 517–34.

Starr, P. and Corson, R. (1987), 'Who will have the numbers? The rise of the statistical services industry and the politics of public data', in W. Alonso and P. Starr (eds), *The Politics of Numbers*, New York, NY: Russell Sage Foundation, 415–47.

Stavitsky, A.G. (1993), 'Listening for listeners: Educational radio and audience research', *Journalism History*, 19(1): 11–18.

Stavitsky, A.G. (1995), '"Guys in suits with charts": Audience research in US public radio', *Journal of Broadcasting and Electronic Media*, 39(2): 177–89.

Stavitsky, A.G. (1998), 'Counting the house in public television: A history of ratings use, 1953–1980', *Journal of Broadcasting and Electronic Media*, 42(4): 520–34.

Steiner, G.A. (1963), *The People Look at Television: A Study of Audience Attitudes*, New York, NY: Alfred A. Knopf.

Stewart, D.W. and Pavlou, P.A. (2002), 'From consumer response to active consumer: Measuring the effectiveness of interactive media', *Academy of Marketing Science Journal*, 30(4): 376–96.

Stigler, S.M. (1999), *Statistics on the Table: The History of Statistical Concepts and Methods*, Cambridge, MA: Harvard University Press.

Stone, D. (2001), *Policy Paradox: The Art of Political Decision-making*, 3rd edition, New York, NY: W.W. Norton.

Story, L. (2008), 'Nielsen looks beyond TV, and hits roadblocks', *New York Times*, 26 February.

Strasser, S. (1989), *Satisfaction Guaranteed: The Making of the American Mass Market*, Washington, DC: Smithsonian Books.

Sumpter, R.S. (2000), 'Daily newspaper editors' audience construction routines: A case study', *Critical Studies in Media Communication*, 17(3): 334–46.

Syvertsen, T. (2004), 'Citizens, audiences, customers and players: A conceptual discussion of the relationship between broadcasters and their publics', *European Journal of Cultural Studies*, 7(3): 363–80.

Taylor, C.P. (2010), 'Before selling data, set-top box providers have to protect privacy', CBS Business Interactive Network, http://www.bnet.com/blog/new-media/before-selling-data-set-top-box-providers-have-to-protect-privacy/5808 [accessed 6 July 2011].

Time (1946), 'Exit Crossley', *Time*, 30 September.

Time (1941), 'Radio: Statistics to the wars', *Time*, 3 February.

Townely, B., Cooper, D.J. and Oakes, L. (1999), 'Performance measures and the dialectic of rationalization', Paper presented at the Critical Management Studies Conference, Manchester.

Triplett, W. (2008), 'Congress addresses net neutrality', *Variety*, 6 May.

Turow, J. (1997), *Breaking up America: Advertisers and the new Media World*, Chicago, IL: University of Chicago Press.

Twitchell, J.B. (1996), *Adcult USA: The Triumph of Advertising in American Culture*, New York, NY: Columbia University Press.

Val Morgan Cinema Network (2010), 'Campaign reach and frequency', Val Morgan Cinema Network, http://www.valmorgan.com.au/effectiveness/accountability/reach-and-frequency/

van der Heijden, K. (1996), *Scenarios: The Art of Strategic Conversation*, Chichester: John Wiley and Sons.

Vogel, H.L. (1986), *Entertainment Industry Economics: A Guide for Financial Analysis*, New York, NY: Cambridge University Press.

Wack, P. (1985a), 'Scenarios, uncharted waters ahead', *Harvard Business Review*, September–October: 73–90.

Wack, P. (1985b), 'Scenarios, shooting the rapids'. *Harvard Business Review*, November–December: 131–42.

Walker, R.R. (1967), *Communicators: People, Practices, Philosophies in Australian Advertising, Media, Marketing*, Melbourne, Lansdowne Press.

Walters, C. (2009). 'Facebook's new terms of service: "We can do anything we want with your content. Forever"', Message posted to www.consumerist.com, Industry blog, 15 February [accessed 21 April 2009].

Webster, J.G. and Phalen, P.F. (1994), 'Victim, consumer, or commodity? Audience models in communication policy', in J.S. Ettema and D.C. Whitney (eds), *Audiencemaking: How the Media Create the Audience*, Thousand Oaks, CA: Sage, 19–37.

Webster, J.G., Phalen, P.F. and Lichty, L.W. (2005), *Ratings Analysis: The Theory and Practice of Audience Research*, Mahwah, NJ: Lawrence Erlbaum.

Wehner, P. (2002), 'No place like home? Media audience research and its social imaginaries', Working paper for the Emory Center for Myth and Ritual in American Life, http://www.marial.emory.edu/pdfs/wp015_02.pdf.

Whiting, S. (2004), 'Testimony of Susan D. Whiting, President and CEO of Nielsen Media Research, before the Senate Committee on Commerce, Science, and Transportation Communication Subcommittee', Nielsen Media Research, http://www.nielsenmedia.com/forclients/SDW-Testimony_7-15-04.pdf [accessed 5 July 2011].

Wiebe, G.D. (1939), 'A comparison of various rating scales used in judging the merits of popular songs', *Journal of Applied Psychology*, 23(1): 18–22.

Wilcox, S. (2000), 'Sampling and controlling a TV audience measurement panel', *International Journal of Market Research*, 42(4): 413–30.

Wilmoth, P. (2001), 'Just when you thought it safe to rely on the ratings ...', *Age*, 24 May.

Wood, J.P. (1962), 'George Gallup', *Journal of Marketing*, 26(4): 78–80.

Wurtzel, A. (2009), 'Now. Or never. An urgent call to action for consensus on new media metrics', *Journal of Advertising Research*, 49: 263–5.

Zeisel, H., *Say it with Figures*, 5th edition, New York, NY: Harper and Row, 1968.

Index